Top Brass and No Brass

The inside story of the alliance of Britain and America

Winston S. Churchill

Imperial War Museum

President
Franklin D. Roosevelt

Imperial War Museum

TOP BRASS AND NO BRASS

The inside story of the alliance of Britain and America

Ralph Kilner Brown

The Book Guild Ltd.
Sussex, England

The Book Guild Ltd.
25 High Street,
Lewes, Sussex.

First published 1991

Set in Baskerville
Typesetting by Ashford Setting & Design,
Ashford, Middlesex.
Printed in Great Britain by
Antony Rowe Ltd.,
Chippenham, Wiltshire.

British Library Cataloguing in Publication Data
Brown, Ralph Kilner 1909-
Top brass and no brass
1. Great Britain. Foreign relations with United States, history.
2. United States, foreign relations with Great Britain, history.
I. Title
327.41073

ISBN 0 86332 603 X

CONTENTS

LIST OF ILLUSTRATIONS

To

Rosemary, soldier's wife, soldier's daughter, soldier's granddaughter and a soldier herself.

ACKNOWLEDGEMENT

The Author and Publisher wish to thank Her Majesty's Stationery Office for permission to reproduce the Sketch Plans used in the Eisenhower Report to the Combined Chiefs of Staff, and also extend their thanks to the United States Government Printing Office and the US Embassy in London.

The Author is grateful for the advice of a war time colleague, Colonel W.H. Jackson, C.B.E., D.L., late the Royal Warwickshire Regiment, to tone down some of his severely critical observations.

PREFACE

From the time that I was at university and throughout all the years that followed, I have been happily privileged to enjoy the friendship of many Americans, some directly, some because of marriage to friends and colleagues. Individually they have been and are quite delightful — attractive, charming and generous-minded — the very salt of the earth. In the aggregate, the American people can be most capricious; for the most part as a nation they are kindly, helpful and understanding; on occasion, probably because they have never been taught the truth, they can be somewhat narrow-minded and totally lacking in appreciation of what other countries have achieved, often in the face of great difficulty and adversity.

These conflicting characteristics were both on display during the years of the Second World War, and whereas at the level at which I served my experience was always of the happiest, the same unfortunately could not be said of all of 'the top brass'. True, the insensitive and imperious behaviour at times of some of the British and my own Commander-in-Chief, Field Marshal Montgomery in particular, provided plenty of material for criticism of the 'Limeys'. In all the vast number of books produced on both sides of the Atlantic since the end of the war, there has been a marked imbalance in favour of the American contribution with inadequate recognition of the part beleaguered Britain played in the Alliance which finally broke the Nazi tryanny. Ambassador Bullitt of the United States wrote a book entitled *How We Won the War and Lost the Peace*. He was quite right to acknowledge that it was American policy which lost the peace and substantially led to the 'cold war', but he was very wrong to claim that it was his nation which won the war. The United States never won the war any more than Russia or

Britain and the Empire did. Without the participation of all three in a common cause there would have been no victory.

Because I was the only one involved with the planning for the invasion of Europe even before the Americans arrived in the United Kingdom, who then worked with them and lived with the preparations for this colossal enterprise throughout, and finally served in its execution with the British Headquarters of 21 Army Group until after the war was over, I was uniquely in a position to judge and evaluate the strengths and weaknesses of individuals and the strains and stresses of the alliance of Britain and the United States. This book does not attempt to go over the same ground which has been covered in excess already, but set in the context of the actual historical background, seeks to demonstrate, with personal knowledge of incidents which occurred and contact with practically all those at the top level of affairs, that in many fields the British were superior — something which may well surprise the vast majority of the American public and the Hollywood film makers in particular!

It would be presumptuous to imagine that the events and incidents recorded in this book will result in any alteration to official histories or top commanders' accounts of what they did and what happened in the war. Nevertheless it is personally satisfying to demonstrate from actual knowledge that so much of official records and purported reminiscence is inaccurate and distorted, and that, although all history may not be 'bunk' as Henry Ford I described it, it frequently represents what people would like it to be and not what it actually was. At times and in certain places I have been able to say to myself with a degree of pleasure — 'That is "bunk". I know it is, for I was there!'

London, England, 1991

1

BACKGROUND TO WAR

In the years between the Peace Treaty of 1919 which marked the end of the Great War and the outbreak of the Second World War in 1939, Britain slipped into inertia and the United States fell back into its policy of isolationism. The withdrawal of the United States from the League of Nations, the adopted brainchild of their own President Woodrow Wilson, was a tragedy for the world and also for the American people who were denied the opportunity to halt the rise of the European dictators or to take any steps to be prepared for war. They were compelled partly by circumstances and partly by government to concentrate their efforts on the economic front, and to cope with the financial disasters flowing from the Wall Street crash of 1929 and the introduction of the various measures put forward by President Roosevelt, known generally as the New Deal. There was no sign of any alliance with Britain and precious little evidence of any special relationship between the two countries. The friendly relations between Americans and British were entirely in terms of person to person friendship. In the event, the British Government was ultimately forced into recognition that war was probably inevitable, and made belated preparations. When war broke out, the British had to learn the hard way, and gradually developed a Navy, an Army and an Air Force welded into an efficient war machine under the control of commanders and senior staff officers of excellence and experience. From June 1940 until June 1941, when the Germans invaded Russia, Britain and the Empire stood alone against the all-conquering might of Germany and her allies and satellites. The entry of the Japanese on the side of the Germans and the cowardly attack on the American Naval base at Pearl Harbor in December 1941 brought the United States into a war for which they were unprepared and direct involvement in which they had tried persistently to avoid. The Americans were therefore pitched into active participation without the opportunity to learn the harsh reality of actual warfare.

To judge from their performance in the war years between 1942 and 1945 and actual personal experience, the American senior staff officers and top commanding generals were not as good as their British counterparts. The relative performance at lower levels quickly reached equal comparison once initial inexperience was overcome. Those with 'no brass on their hats' were more modest, more eager to learn and more anxious than their seniors to make the alliance of Britain and the United States a success.

There were of course exceptions to this sweeping observation. General Eisenhower was dedicated to the Allied cause. Although in the direction of war his strategical and tactical skills were indifferent, his contribution to the successful alliance was unsurpassed because he was determined to make it work, and insisted on complete co-operation between the officers of the two nations. His Chief of Staff, Lieutenant-General W. Bedell Smith, was a more able soldier than his master and earned the confidence and respect of those British with whom he came into contact. General Omar N. Bradley was a consistently successful and totally professional commander, respected by his troops, who was not interested in nor deflected by mere nationalist or political considerations. Nevertheless, partly because of a personal dislike for Field Marshal Montgomery, and partly because the Americans, and General Patton in particular, believed in constant thrust forward regardless of the risk of disaster, Bradley never really agreed with Montgomery's application of the basic principle of war, which was that a commander should never get caught off balance, should if necessary stand or even withdraw to absorb an enemy attack, and then use reserve forces to go on to the offensive against an exhausted foe. In Normandy in 1944 the Americans got away with their policy once the British and Canadian Armies had performed the absorbing role. One of the best of all the United States commanders was Lieutenant-General J. Lawton (Lightnin' Joe) Collins. He earned his spurs as a Divisional

Commander in Guadalcanal in 1943. In Normandy in 1944 and again in the Ardennes he never put a foot wrong. Most importantly, the troops under his command had complete faith and trust in his ability and leadership.

For six or seven months in the year 1942 I was privileged in a fairly lowly capacity to walk the corridors of power and to meet many of the great men at the helm of the Allied war effort. This spell of duty as a 'Whitehall Warrior' was an intensely interesting interlude in a military career which, as a lawyer in civilian life, began as a private in a Territorial infantry battalion in the year 1938 and ended with transfer to the Territorial Army Reserve of Officers in 1952. A commission in March 1939 led to a call to the colours two months before war was declared, followed by a period of two years as a regimental soldier and a course at the Staff College, and thereafter a variety of staff appointments in operational headquarters. Much of this later time involved co-operation with officers of the United States Army, which resulted in a deeper mutual understanding of the practical problems which arise in a wartime alliance of different nations. A genuine and friendly relationship was much more evident amongst the respective staff officers than appeared to be the case at top commanding officer level.

Most of the American top commanders were loyal to the alliance because, fortunately, the Supreme Allied Commander was American, and whatever dislike they may have felt for Field Marshal Montgomery when he behaved badly, they did what they were told by General Eisenhower. On the other hand, some top American Commanders like Generals Douglas MacArthur, a brilliant strategist, and George Patton, a dashing thruster, were so convinced of their own excellence that they were a menace to a harmonious alliance; and even though the American public were understandably led to regard them as heroes, many of their equals from their own country found them an acute embarrassment.

Looking back at the five or six years before war was declared on 3 September 1939, it is clear now that although they were wasted years in so far as my chosen profession of the law was concerned, they provided an experience and maturity which many of my contemporaries lacked. I was just thirty years old at the start of the war. My practice as a barrister was developing in promising fashion; in politics I was one of the leaders of the Young Liberals and was already a prospective Parliamentary candidate. As an international athlete, participation in athletics meetings on the Continent had made me aware of the compelling and at times hysterical attraction of Fascism and Nazism for the young people of Italy and Germany.

Anyone who heard and witnessed Mussolini and Hitler screaming defiance at the League of Nations and the rest of the world could only fear the worst unless other peoples could join together to present a firm and united opposition to the aggressive conduct of the dictators. Unhappily, the United States of America had declined to join the League of Nations and was not prepared to get involved in the affairs of Europe. Nor were the people of this country or the Dominions of the British Empire sufficiently alerted to the dangers which lay ahead. It is no doubt true that the leaders of a country based on a democracy would have to carry with them an understanding and supportive population in order to challenge and oppose the actions of a dictator. Britain was gripped by inertia, France by timidity, and neither country enjoyed the bold and courageous leadership which was imperative.

It was and still is fashionable in some circles to put on Neville Chamberlain a major share of the blame for the Munich Pact of 1938. But in truth he reaped the harvest of a pusillanimous policy of appeasing the dictators which went back in time to December 1935, when the notorious Hoare-Laval pact was signed on behalf of Britain and France, an agreement endorsed by Baldwin and his Cabinet which recognized much of Mussolini's conquest of Ethiopia and Abyssinia. The pernicious and disastrous doctrine of appeasement was based on the fundamental fallacy that, if the alleged wrongs suffered by Germany under the Peace Treaty of 1919 were recognized and corrected, both Germany and Italy would re-enter the League of Nations from which they had broken away, and then co-operate with the rest of the world in pursuit of peace and stability. Mussolini had decided in the autumn of 1934 to ignore the League of Nations, and prepared for war against Abyssinia, which he began a year later without prior declaration and with overwhelming force. The reaction of the League of Nations was to impose on Italy a series of economic sanctions which were incomplete, half-hearted and given up after seven or eight months. The disastrous abandonment by Baldwin and the British Government of his 1935 General Election pledges to support the League of Nations and Laval's acquiescence on the part of France in Mussolini's conquest of Abyssinia gave heart to Hitler.

Britain was faced with the irreconcilable attitudes of France and Germany. France wanted security for herself at any cost: this included pandering to Mussolini in order to keep him away from an alliance with Hitler. Germany wanted equality, the removal of restraints which were felt to be intolerable, and the restoration of territory which was regarded as rightfully hers. The first priority was considered by Hitler to be the ending of the demilitarization of the Rhineland and of the embargo on the stationing of any armed forces in that part of Germany. The second was the recovery of the Sudetenland, the Austro-German element of the state of Czecho-Slovakia. Both of these were the result of the Peace Treaty of 1919. Undoubtedly Germany had a legitimate argument for pursuing these aims, but Hitler, encouraged by the failure of the League of Nations and of Britain and France in particular to deal with Mussolini, judged that he too could disregard the League of Nations and abrogate by force some of the terms of the Peace Treaty. In March 1936, using as a pretext that the Franco-Soviet Pact was in breach of the Locarno Agreement, Hitler ordered the march of German troops into the Rhineland. Rightly, as it turned out, he judged that Britain and France would do nothing. It was appeasement yet again. In fact, as later recourse to contemporary documents has disclosed, if France and Britain had agreed to send in French troops to drive the German soldiers out, the generals and leading industrialists in Germany would have backed down and disowned Hitler, and possibly even have caused his overthrow. Hitler's reliance on force paid off, and, led by the head of the Air Force General Goering, the German military leaders were only too ready for Germany to join with Mussolini and to exercise their new weapons of war by assisting General Franco to crush the left-wing Republicans in Spain. There was now an Axis of Germany, Italy and Spain, and the worst fears of the French, with which they had so supinely dealt, were now realized. But appeasement once begun could not be reversed. Perhaps the lowest depths of degradation were reached when Neville Chamberlain, who had succeeded Baldwin as Prime Minister in 1937, gave way in February 1938 to an arrogant

Mussolini who fulminated against the Nyon Agreement, which sought to prohibit the piratical threat to use Italian submarines to sink any British ship approaching Spanish ports. Anthony Eden, the British Foreign Secretary who had brought about this agreement, felt himself compelled to resign his office when Chamberlain yielded. Not content with this, Chamberlain concluded a treaty which gave Mussolini effective control of the Mediterranean. In retrospect it can be said that that this was a more shameful episode than the making of the Munich Pact some seven months later.

Hitler was now further encouraged. In March 1938 he marched his troops into Austria, deposed and imprisoned its leader Chancellor Von Schuschnigg, and annexed the country. In May the same year, Hitler encouraged the Sudeten Germans in Czecho-Slovakia to agitate by public demonstrations in favour of their return to the Fatherland. In face of a threat of armed intervention, President Beneš ordered full mobilization of the country's armed forces and Hitler backed down. The independence of Czecho-Slovakia was guaranteed by France. Britain was linked by treaty in support of France. True, the actual use of force by France, even if backed by Britain, may not have been a feasible proposition because the people of neither country were sufficiently interested in the troubles of a far-off land to wish to be involved. Nevertheless, if France had been prepared to do what Beneš had done, and backed verbal protests with even a partial mobilization of troops, the mere possibility of a clash of armed forces may well have driven Hitler to acquiesce in negotiation for the return of Sudetenland.

However, France abandoned her treaty obligations, and resorted once more to an act of appeasement in which Britain joined. Neither country was prepared openly to protest and to call upon the rest of the world and America in particular to condemn the use of further force and to threaten Germany with united opposition. Instead secret discussions took place, and France and Britain agreed that the Sudetenland must be transferred. Inevitably the same pattern followed. Hitler continued to rant and rave against the Czechs. At the beginning of September 1938 he proclaimed that the Sudetenland was part of Germany, and by mobilizing troops on the borders of the disputed territory implied that he would resort to armed force if Beneš swould not agree to his demands.

Trapped as both Britain and France were in a situation resulting from the policy of appeasement over the years, the only course now open to Chamberlain was to try and compel Beneš to accept the inevitable and to recognize a cession of the Sudetenland, and for Hitler to hold his hand and to avoid recourse to force. On 1 September Chamberlain went to Berchtesgaden to tell Hitler that Britain and France had accepted Germany's case. At a second visit a week later at Godesborg, Hitler, true to the form expected of a determined dictator, produced an ultimatum that all Czech officials and soldiers should evacuate the Sudetenland and allow German soldiers to move in. This was intolerable, even to a dedicated peacemaker like Chamberlain. In a desperate attempt in the cause of peace, he humbled himself and went off yet again, this time to Munich, in order to plead with Hitler not to resort to armed force against the Czechs. On 30 September 1938 the notorious agreement was signed.

The Munich Pact contained a declaration which applied Hitler's assertion that he had no territorial demands other than the Sudetenland, and was to the effect that none of the signatories would resort to military action. Waving the piece of paper on his return to England, Chamberlain rashly and brashly boasted that it meant 'peace in our time'. How worthless the agreement was became clear when Hitler invaded and conquered first Czecho-Slovakia in March 1939 and then Poland in September 1939. Quite apart from Chamberlain's genuine and sincere desire to have peace at almost any cost, no doubt the British and French Governments may well have been afraid that too vigorous a reaction to the threats and the rape of Czecho-Slovakia would have resulted in warlike action by Germany against them. In reality this was an improbable option at that time, as a study of contemporaneous German records has revealed. The German armed forces were then quite insufficient and inadequately equipped to launch any major offensive action against France and Britain, and remained so until May 1940. Moreover, Hitler genuinely had no desire to embroil himself with Britain, whom he believed could be persuaded to let him push his empire towards Eastern Europe. For France, with some justification, he felt little more than contempt and rightly judged that, in relying on the static defences of the Maginot line, there was no risk of her troops being ordered out beyond that line in pursuance of her treaty obligations. If ever it came to warlike action against France, Hitler understood, and France lamentably forgot, the elementary principle of war that any static defence line can be bypassed and turned, which is precisely the method adopted by the German armies in the offensive of May 1940. In the event, the occupation of Czecho-Slovakia provided a huge increase in Germany's capacity for the manufacture of arms and weapons, and the capitulation of Poland brought an enormous reserve of forced labour and conscripted troops.

Topham

David Lloyd George

The Munich Pact was widely acclaimed, not only in Britain, but throughout the world. President Roosevelt of the United States, Mackenzie King, Prime Minister of Canada, and General Smuts of South Africa all joined in expressions of appreciation and congratulation. In the debate in the House of Commons which followed Chamberlain's return, the only opposition to a Motion of Approval consisted of the whole of the Labour Party, Anthony Eden, David Lloyd George and Winston Churchill, who made a powerful speech of criticism. The attitude of the Labour Party was quite disgraceful, since they had regularly over the years voted against any proposal, however meagre and inadequate, to increase the power and number of the armed forces. One would have expected a pacifist party to have welcomed a pacifist pact. David Lloyd George, on the other had, had watched with increasing dismay the dismantling of the Peace Treaty he had worked so hard to bring about, and had led the van in condemning the policy of appeasement from 1935 onwards. He had furthermore made the wholly feasible suggestion of using the British Navy to blockade Mussolini's ships from the use of the Suez Canal at the time of the attack on Abyssinia. When Baldwin abandoned sanctions against Italy, before any other country, Lloyd George's condemnation in the House of Commons was said by those who heard it to have been the most devastating exposure of a cowardly retreat at a time when firm support of collective action against aggression was the only sensible and honourable course.

Anthony Eden had consistently advocated support for the League of Nations, and urged collective resistance to the deeds of both Mussolini and Hitler. He had resigned from Chamberlain's Cabinet rather than yield to Mussolini's arrogant conduct in the Mediterranean. It was however Winston Churchill who, after years of isolation from the heart of affairs, now took over the leadership of those who thought that the only course open to Britain was to oppose Hitler at every step, and called for immediate and massive rearmament. He was also later to pay tribute to the efforts of the small band of Liberals in the House of Commons led by Sir Archibald Sinclair, who abandoned their previous opposition to rearmament and came in behind Winston Churchill in the recognition that Hitler would have to be met by the threat of force, and that vigorous steps were necessary to increase the strength of Britain's armed forces. At long last the British people were being made to awake from a lengthy period of torpor and laziness.

In reality the only justification for the Munich Pact was that the great mass of the British people realized that it was a last desperate attempt to avoid war, and if Hitler were to ignore the pact and break his word, as he did, then the country would be united in the will to fight. It is not fair to criticize Chamberlain for the signing of the pact merely because of its failure and its rejection by Hitler. The real criticism should be directed at the policy of appeasement, adopted first by Baldwin in conjunction with Laval, and then carried to its lowest depths by Chamberlain well before the events of September 1938. In the end, the making of the Munich Pact was the only option available to a man with a genuine love of peace. Then, after Hitler cynically and brutally marched into Czecho-Slovakia, the people of Britain, like Chamberlain himself, understood that if Hitler attacked Poland it would be inevitable that war must be declared against him.

Neville Chamberlain

Imperial War Museum

Although lugubrious in manner and appearance, Neville Chamberlain personally was a sincere and kindly old gentleman. He lived in Edgbaston, Birmingham, just round the corner from the house where we as a family made our home in the years immediately after the war was over. His old gardener used to tell how Chamberlain would come down from London on a Friday evening, and the next day find his relaxation in lighting and standing over a bonfire which had previously been laid for him. Bonfires he may have enjoyed, but he was totally lacking 'fire in the belly', which was so marked a characteristic of those great war leaders David Lloyd George and Winston Churchill. He must also have been devoid of judgement, otherwise he would never have rashly and optimistically said of the Munich Pact that it meant 'peace in our time', or that during the 'phoney' war of the winter of 1939 to 1940 that Hitler's failure to take the offensive meant that Hitler had 'missed the bus'. He should not however be blamed for the most serious and devastating consequence which flowed from the making of the Munich Pact. Stalin himself later admitted, after Hitler once more broke his word and attacked the Russians, that the 1939 Russo-German treaty of non-aggression was the response to Munich in order, vainly as it turned out, to preserve Russia from being included in German expansion eastwards, and which deliberately left Poland open to German invasion, which in turn led to the outbreak of war.

Many of those who seek to justify the Munich Pact instead of fastening on its uniting effect, in so far as the British people were concerned, tend grossly to overstate their case. It has been and still is said that it gave this country a year's 'breathing space' which was put to good use, and as an example reliance is placed on the fact that in 1939 the Royal Air Force had a large number of eight-gunned Spitfire fighter aircraft and a chain of radar defence which it did not have in 1938. This is factually correct. But to argue that because of this the Munich Pact was justifiable is little short of nonsense. Contemporary German records give the lie to the assumption that without the pact there would have been war in 1938. Indeed the Germans needed the breathing space as much as, if not more than the British, and they used the year far more effectively in the build up of their armed forces. Whereas the RAF was much better equipped, the Army was not. True, the War Office took steps to increase hugely the number of men in the Territorial Army and the new Militia, but, to the dismay of those who were thus enrolled, there were scarcely any arms or equipment for them to use. Such effort as was made was concentrated on the purely defensive and passive role of protecting the civilian population against enemy air raids by the making of air raid shelters, provision of silly little gas masks in cardboard boxes, and mercifully some anti-aircraft artillery. The inadequate use of the so-called 'breathing space' can be illustrated by two examples. When war was declared a Machine Gun Battalion was given the task of defending the East Coast from Harwich to Newcastle. Its weapon strength was fifty-six guns, that is, one for every eight miles of coast. How much louder the laughter in enemy circles if it had been known that twenty-eight of the fifty-six were wooden dummies. Even in the Blitzkreg of May 1940, our only Armoured Division went to war with its command vehicles made not of armour plating but of plywood!

There were those who, like myself, made fiery speeches against the dictators, and who began to appreciate that words must be matched by deeds. In my case, this realization was in the first place brought about by a participation in a minor capacity in a large public meeting at which Anthony Eden and Harold Macmillan were the main speakers. Both of them had fought bravely and with distinction in the First World War. Their credentials for urging a stand against the dictators were impeccable. Incidentally, it is interesting to recall that Macmillan, both on the platform and in private, made an impression of being the stronger and more impressive personality of the two, even though Eden was the more publicized and popular figure at the time.

Thus it was that at the beginning of 1938 I sought a commission in the Territorial Army. It never occurred to me that this would be a difficult exercise. There were many and varied units of all arms in and around Birmingham where my law practice was based, and several of the commanding officers were known to me personally. One after the other they said the same thing. I was too old at the age of twenty-nine, and had achieved too much to come in as a junior officer underneath those who were much younger and with less achievement to their credit. It would create embarrassment if I were to take a commission as a subaltern and rank beneath them. I did not agree, but had to accept it, just as two years later I had to accept the rejection of an application to transfer to the RAF for pilot training, which was given on the basis that a lawyer aged thirty-one was too old and too intelligent, presumably a polite way of indicating that in the heat of battle there is no time for logical analysis. Finally the realization came that, with the doubling up of the Territorial Army and the creation of the Militia, there would be an increased need for officers in the long run, and that it would be better to get in quick and join the ranks. So I did, and became a private in the South Staffordshire Regiment. It was now nearing the end of 1938.

In the winter of that year there was a growing concentration on the Air Defence of Great Britain. The first line infantry battalions of the Territorial Army remained as such, but the second line battalions were converted into all sorts of units for Anti-Aircraft Command. Most were turned into Heavy

Anti-Aircraft Regiments of Royal Artillery; some became Light Anti-Aircraft units; others were converted into Searchlight Battalions of the Royal Engineers. Support units such as Royal Signals and Supply and Transport units of the Royal Army Service Corps were also required. Whatever the original wishes of the volunteer recruits may have been, this desire could no longer be recognized, and the choice of regiment or unit was decided for them. They had to be what they were told to be or join whatever unit was available to them.

The headquarters of the South Staffordshire Regiment Territorial Army Battalion was at Walsall, and at the beginning of 1939 a new independent unit was hived off to become an RASC Transport Company in Anti-Aircraft Command. I was transferred to this and was offered and accepted a commission as Second Lieutenant. We were provided with one army lorry, four revolvers for the use of officers, and three rifles. There was absolutely nothing for us to do except basic infantry training and drill. I had already brushed up my school cadet experience, and as the Officer Commanding was a Major with a gallant Great War record in the Lancashire Fusiliers, we became in effect an infantry training unit. Indeed we remained much the same, with the addition of lorry driver instruction after the outbreak of war in September 1939.

As a temporary break from this routine there was a posting to France in May 1940, but this was cancelled the day before the evacuation from Dunkirk began, and there then followed a few days assisting to man the cliffs and beaches of Southern England against a possible German invasion! I finished with the Second AA Division as officer commanding another independent transport company, which again had little to do except to train raw recruits.

After the nomination for the Staff College, the War Office did their best to provide a thorough preparation for someone who had spent two years messing about in a form of regimental soldiering. Attendance at a very tough infantry commanders' battle school and commando assault exercises at Combined Operations training centre was followed by a secondment to the 6th Battalion of the Gordon Highlanders, which included an introduction to the off-duty wearing of a kilt, and finally a posting as a Staff Learner to the 2nd Infantry Brigade Headquarters, during which Exercise 'Bumper' took place. This was a mammoth affair controlled by General Sir Alan Brooke, the Commander in Chief Home Forces, and one of the Force Commanders was Lieutenant-General Alexander, while Lieutenant-General Montgomery was the Chief Umpire. No individual could have been better prepared for a Staff College course. The Directing Staff must have been surprised to find that an officer wearing the badges of the RASC was in fact a fully trained infantry company commander with an experience which led them to recommend an important Grade 2 Staff Officer appointment. In that way my entrance to the corridors of power was brought about.

2

THE FORGING OF THE ALLIANCE

In the winter months of 1939 to 1940, whilst thousands and thousands of troops at home were enduring harsh weather with increasing boredom, and the British Expeditionary Force was slowly getting fit for war, complacency ruled in high places. Nothing was to be done to aggravate Hitler. Britain's bomber aircraft were forbidden to drop bombs on the building up of the German fortifications of the Siegfried Line, but were used to drop pamphlets over enemy territory for the edification of the German people. Far from 'missing the bus' as Chamberlain had bragged, Hitler was busily preparing to launch his forces in a step by step domination of Western Europe. On 9 April 1940 Denmark and Norway were invaded. A feeble and futile expedition to Norway by the British ended in a humiliating withdrawal at the beginning of May. This was too much, even for a large number of Chamberlain's own supporters, who openly opposed him in Parliament. He resigned and was succeeded as Prime Minster by Winston Churchill on 10 May.

On the day that Churchill took over the leadership of the British people, Hitler launched a massive offensive directed against the French Armies and the British Expeditionary Force. First he overran Holland, and three days later the Dutch capitulated and the government went into exile. The main thrust was then made against the French and the 9th Army on the Allies' right flank soon collapsed against the weight of the German armour. The BEF first moved into Belgium in an attempt to hold up the advance. The Belgian Army crumpled, and the French yielded on the right leaving the British forces in danger of being cut off and isolated. On 16 May the BEF began its fighting withdrawal. The story of the gallant retreat and the miracle of the evacuation through Dunkirk is an epic in the annals of war. When the operation was finished on 4 June, a quarter of a million British troops were saved and returned to England together with well over 100,000 of other nationalities. General Sir John Dill who had been one of the Corps Commanders in France now succeeded General Ironside as Chief of the Imperial General Staff (CIGS), having been withdrawn from the BEF a week or so earlier. The Corps Commander who bore the brunt of the bitterly contested withdrawal was on his safe return honoured with a Knighthood and became General Sir Alan Brooke. Within days, he was ordered by Dill at the behest of the War Cabinet to return to France with fresh British troops in a hopeless attempt to shore up the remains of the French Armies, and to prevent the Germans from overrunning and controlling the whole of the Pas de Calais and Normandy sea board. Failure was inevitable, but he was finally able to rescue 150,000 British and another 47,000 Allied troops who were successfully evacuated through Cherbourg and St Malo.

General Sir Alan Brooke

Imperial War Museum

Britain now faced the imminent threat of an invasion across the Channel. The command of the tattered and disorganized troops in beleaguered England was entrusted to General Sir Alan

Brooke. Marshal Petain assumed the headship of the defeated French nation and capitulated to the victorious German Armies. In the meantime, Mussolini, like a jackal scavenging a corpse, had responded to the Axis agreement of 1936 and joined the war on Germany's side on 10 June 1940, while Japan, the third member of the Axis, announced its participation on 27 September. Petain was prepared to let the Germans occupy and take over complete control of half of France, and except for some brave but few members of the Resistance there was no impediment in the way of the country being used as a base for operations against Britain.

Britain and the Empire stood alone against such overwhelming forces. This was the time when Winston Churchill reached the peak of his greatness, rallying the people with his stirring broadcasts. Putting on the appearance of a bulldog with firmly clamped jaw, growling with ferocity, he was the epitome of John Bull defiant. This was indeed 'Britain's finest hour'. While Churchill declaimed defiance, Brooke was gearing up the forces of defence, and the fighter planes of the Royal Air Force were poised to defend the skies against the might of the German Luftwaffe.

With hindsight, it is clear that Hitler and the German General Staff considerably overestimated the strength of the British forces available to resist the contemplated invasion, and if 'Operation Sea Lion' had gone ahead at the beginning of September as the British Chiefs of Staff expected, heaven knows what would have happened. From the German point of view, the most cautious approach was that of Admiral Raeder, the Naval Commander-in-Chief, who was of the opinion that the German invasion barges and surface naval craft would not be able to get across the Channel without crippling losses. They knew that the Royal Air Force had not been completely knocked out in beating off the German daytime bombers, but even more importantly, they were aware that the Royal Navy had built up a formidable quantity of destroyers, frigates, motor gun boats and motor torpedo boats which were patrolling off the places where landings might be expected.

The explanation for the almost incredible strengthening of the British naval forces was the step by step release from Atlantic convoy duty of escort ships, which were being gradually replaced by the fifty First World War destroyers from the United States, which President Roosevelt agreed to trade for the lease of naval and air bases in the Atlantic colonies. Although it is natural that the British people should regard Winston Churchill as the one really great and inspiring war leader to whom the greatest credit of all should be given, the debt which this country owes to President Roosevelt was incalculable. Whereas Churchill led a nation which, with its back to the wall, responded to the call to fight for survival, the majority of the American people were not interested in nor troubled by a Nazi threat to Britain, and a sizeable minority were actively supportive of the Germans and intensely anti-British. Roosevelt had to contend with a campaign against Britain led by Charles Lindbergh who, by virtue of his solo flight across the Atlantic, was regarded as a national hero, and the task could not have been made easier by the insidious and insistent denigration of Britain by Joseph Kennedy, the United States ambassador in London. Fortunately for Europe and the Western World, Roosevelt understood the threat to a democratic way of life which a victory for Hitler would have entailed. Gradually there was an impact from the messages sent across the Atlantic by those American friends of ours who shared with us the horrors of the nightly bombing raids, and particularly from journalists and broadcasters like Ed Murrow, who were able to give a day by day account of the way that British people were standing firm.

The provision of the fifty mothballed destroyers was understood by even the most isolationist American as a fair trading exchange for the acquisition of naval and air bases in the Western Atlantic. These bases were to the direct advantage of the defensive needs of the United States, whose navy was sufficiently powerful without the destroyers. On the other hand, the sale to Britain of thousands and thousands of rifles, machine guns and 75 mm field guns and ammunition to go with them was strongly, but mercifully unsuccessfully resisted by American Service Chiefs. Almost to a man, they wrote off Britain's chances of survival. A certain Major Walter Bedell Smith, the Assistant Secretary to the General Staff, went so far as to suggest that the transfer of nine hundred field guns was an act of treason. Somewhere along the line he must either have changed his mind or conveniently forgotten what he had written, because he later turned up as Major-General, Chief of Staff to General Eisenhower in the United Kingdom, and remained with him for both the North African and the European campaigns.

It took several months of cultivation of American public opinion in favour of Britain before Roosevelt felt himself able to demonstrate publicly his support. But the tide was turning. A Gallup Poll conducted in January 1941 indicated that nearly seventy per cent of the American public had come to believe that the defeat of the Axis Powers was important for the future of the United States. It was not merely the courageous stand of the British people which impressed them, but with remarkable foresight they perceived that the addition of Japan to the Axis Powers posed a potential threat to the whole of the western seaboard of North America. But the pro-German and anti-British faction now openly resisted any tendency to be involved in a European war, and there followed a long and bitter argument in Congress which lasted for two months before the Lend Lease Act was passed through both the House of Representatives and the Senate on 11 March, 1941. This in general terms made the United States the 'arsenal of democracy' and provided for the immediate transfer of existing war supplies to Britain. One of the factors which led to this decision was a typical stirring speech by Churchill in February, who was able to use the fact that his mother was American, and called on his hearers to 'give us the tools and we will finish the job'.

We in Britain had already been provided with tremendous moral support by the appointment of Harry Hopkins as the personal representative of President Roosevelt in London, and then further when Wendell Wilkie, the former Republican candidate for the Presidency, agreed with Roosevelt's attitude after he had made a fact-finding visit to this country. Henry Stimson was the US Secretary for War and General George Marshall was Chief of Army Staff. Both of them as Colonels in France in 1918 realized that the ultimate defeat of the Germans lay in Europe, and were prepared to support President Roosevelt, provided that his actions in helping Britain were ultimately for the benefit of the United States. For a long time however, General Marshall remained sceptical of Britain's ability to match the Germans, and regarded the British commanders as inferior. He once observed that we were always six months behind the opposition with our military planning. In this he was less than fair. As a result of the lamentable failure of the governments of Stanley Baldwin and Neville Chamberlain to

General George Marshall

Imperial War Museum

press on with a military build up and the crippling losses we had suffered in France in 1940, we were always forced to operate with inadequate forces in various theatres of war all over the world at the same time. Initially the American Service Chiefs were unable to appreciate that we had learnt the hard way to make the best use of our limited resources, and never to indulge in a large scale operation until we were properly prepared. That was the lesson, incidentally, which General Montgomery applied at the Battle of Alamein in the desert war. Nor could the Americans ever rid themselves of an unfair belief that our interest in the Mediterranean was governed by the desire to preserve the British Empire.

The respective British and American Chiefs of Staff, General Sir Alan Brooke and General George Marshall, did not hit it off together to begin with, and were never fully confident of the other's ability. Brooke found Marshall to be attractive in personality but lacking in strategic competence. Marshall thought that Brooke was too pessimistic and difficult.

Nevertheless each was a great man. As a measure of General Marshall's greatness there was his ultimate recognition that the British reluctance to open up a Second Front in Europe with inadequate forces was justifiable, and he became a firm though at times a critical supporter of the Allied cause. For this change of heart perhaps the greatest credit should go to Field Marshal Sir John Dill, who, after handing over to Alan Brooke as Chief of the Imperial General Staff, became the British representative with the American Chiefs of Staff at the Pentagon in Washington. Marshall and Dill worked together in close harmony, and Dill was perhaps the only man whose quiet, courteous persistence could ultimately persuade the Americans that the British had a point and were probably right. Of course, a further measure of Marshall's greatness was his recognition that, whereas Britain had bankrupted herself and spent all her reserves to win the war, the United States emerged commercially very well off indeed; and after the war was over he earned for himself a permanent place in history as the man in charge of the programme for the aid of devastated Europe to which he gave his name.

Field Marshal Sir John Dill

Imperial War Museum

The American Naval Chiefs, although in no way pro-British, were the first to move over to Roosevelt's way of thought, but it was always the President who set the pace and called the tune. As early as the end of March 1941 the United States began to take a line openly hostile to the Axis. A lot of Italian, German and Danish shipping was impounded in American ports. Step by step the Americans were becoming more closely involved in the struggle to preserve the Western way of life and to prevent an Axis victory. Following a secret series of meetings between British and American Staff officers in Washington which lasted from January 1941 to March of that year, a group of American officers visited Britain to discuss the question of bases for their troops if there should be a direct involvement in the war in Europe. The American Staff advised the President that the principal United States military effort should be in Europe.

The next open step was the announcement in June 1941 that the German and Italian consulates in the United States were to be closed down by the middle of July. Following that announcement, American troops were landed in Iceland in 7 July, and Iceland and Greenland were declared to be under the protection of the United States. Charles Lindbergh and the Irish-Americans who sided with him against the British were now completely disregarded. Moreover, as early as the beginning of July, America as well as Britain had begun the delivery of vast quantities of military supplies to Russia which had been invaded by the Germans on 22 June 1941.

The German campaign against Russia was the clearest indication that Hitler had, for the time being at least, abandoned an invasion of the British Isles, but the necessity to supply Russia with arms by sea to Vladivostock across the Pacific and to Murmansk across the Atlantic and the North Sea required a much closer co-operation between the United States and Great Britain. Roosevelt and Churchill had an even wider vision. In August 1941 they met aboard an American cruiser off the coast of Newfoundland and drew up the famous 'Atlantic Charter'. In Churchill's mind, the Charter with its endorsement of the 'Four Freedoms' was a statement of the principles under which the democracies would fight to overcome military dictatorship and establish peace in Europe. Roosevelt intended that Britain should pay a price for any success which might result from American assistance. In common with most Americans he held the belief which stemmed from the creation of the United States in 1776 after colonial revolt, that any Colonial Empire, however much it produced benefit to the natives, was inconsistent with the 'Four Freedoms', and was not to be tolerated. Roosevelt and his Chiefs of Staff throughout the whole of the war, once they became allies of Britain, were coloured in all their strategic thinking by a suspicion that any military proposal other than a direct assault in Europe was based on the preference by the British for a course of action which would prevent the break-up of the British Empire. This political narrow-mindedness reached its nadir at the Yalta conference in February 1945, when the British viewpoint was disregarded by the Americans and preference given to Stalin's ideas, an attitude which in all the forty-five years after the end of the war the more sensible American people have never ceased to regret.

However during the summer of 1941 events were gradually bringing the United States closer to active participation in war against Germany. In September, a German U-boat fired a torpedo at an American destroyer which, although it missed, so enraged Roosevelt that, in his capacity as Commander in Chief of all the United States forces, he ordered all warships to shoot first at any German or Italian surface or underwater craft which might be found in Atlantic waters.

It is often believed, particularly by the American people, that Pearl Harbor marked the entry of the United States into the war, but effectively war had already been joined with the German/Italian Axis, partly because of reaction to attacks by U-boats, but also because of the supply of arms and ships to Britain and of military supplies to Russia. The attack on Pearl Harbor in December 1941 marked the active entry of Japan as a member of the Axis. Simultaneously the Japanese began their drive against the British Empire in Malaya and Singapore, and a month later against Burma. Thus by January 1942 it was truly a World War, with Britain and the Empire, the United States and Russia the chief protagonists on one side and Germany, Japan and Italy on the other. The American people had been dealt a savage blow to their navy and their pride by the Japanese, and it is understandable that there were strongly held opinions that the war against Japan should take precedence over any ventures in Europe. Nevertheless, attack against Germany was the view of a strong section of military opinion headed by General George Marshall himself. Indeed, he and those who thought the same were all for rushing into immediate action on the continent of Europe, and could not understand the reluctance of the British to be equally aggressive.

In fact, although the threat of invasion had receded, we in the British Isles had plenty of troubles of our own. Losses of merchant shipping to attacks by German U-boats were reaching staggering proportions. Night after night the big cities and London in particular were devastated by aerial bombing. Some 23,000 civilians had already been killed in these raids, and over 30,000 seriously injured. In the Western Desert, after an initial brilliantly successful campaign against the Italians, the advent of the Afrika Korps under General Erwin Rommel and the attacks by German bombers operating in the Mediterranean in a to and fro campaign had led us perilously close to defeat.

Winston Churchill was constantly demanding offensive action, and in his capacity as Minister of Defence as well as being Prime Minister, had taken over control of the Joint Planning Staff which was intended to be a joint services team to advise and prepare papers for the Chiefs of Staff Committee and thence to the War Cabinet. Churchill at times expressed extreme annoyance with 'those damned planners' because they seemed to him invariably to produce reasons why this operation or that operation was not possible. He became increasingly irritated with General Sir John Dill, who as Chief of the Imperial General Staff was the Army member of the Chiefs of Staff Committee, but whose courteous and reasonable arguments led Churchill to think that he lacked courage and vision whenever he pointed out the difficulties involved in any proposed plan. The Chairman of the COS was Admiral Sir Dudley Pound, whose ability to control the differing views of the chiefs of the three arms of the Services and to present a coherent view to the War Cabinet was sadly lacking. The reason, as it later emerged, was that he was showing the signs of a fatal illness which led to his resignation and death a couple years later. In fact, because in the early months of 1941 the threat of invasion had not been lifted as it was by the attack on Russia in June, the first priority after the Navy's preoccupation with the war against the German U-boats was still the creation of a strong and well equipped Army in Britain. Consequently Churchill saw more and more of General Sir Alan Brooke, and came to admire and respect his vigour and tireless activity and his forthright expression of opinion. He would listen more to Brooke's objections that the Home Forces must not be weakened by transferring units and formations to the Western Desert or to Greece or to Syria or wherever than he would to the views of the CIGS or the Joint Planning Staff as to a proper balance of strategic activity.

The headquarters of Home Forces was at St Paul's School in Hammersmith, and Churchill himself, when he was not in the comparative seclusion of Chequers in the country, was exposed to considerable risk to his own safety if he operated from Downing Street and the Houses of Parliament. So in February 1941 the Prime Minister and Mrs Churchill moved into a flat deep down underground in a large Government building at the corner of Great George Street and Horseguards Parade which was known as Storey's Gate, although strictly speaking it was across the road. General Sir Alan Brooke's Battle Headquarters were moved there from St Paul's School as well. The War Cabinet Room and the Chiefs of Staff Committee rooms were all close together in the same heavily protected basement. Some of these rooms are now, nearly fifty years later, open for the public to see them as they were in the year 1941 — the nerve centre of the Government and the Armed Forces, safe from any damage by bombing.

As I learnt from my own experience a year later, this close physical proximity made it easier for Churchill to interfere directly with the professional judgement and work of his Service advisers and to initiate schemes of his own, which he expected them to act upon within a matter of hours. Many of his ideas were quite madcap, but at least it can be said that without his boundless energy and vigorous imagination the professionals would probably have proceeded with an excess of caution which might well have been disastrous. Churchill's great gift was his ability to make his Service chiefs put effort before hesitancy. All of the Service Chiefs said the same — that they had to be clear and firm if they did not agree with his ideas. He could be furiously angry if he was thwarted, but, time after time, when he cooled down he would yield to the advice which he had been given.

Although the year 1941 marked the end of our fear of invasion, it was otherwise a year of unmitigated disaster. The initial relief which was felt when Hitler turned east against the Russians gave way to grim foreboding as it seemed that the Germans were going to overrun most of that vast country and capture the oil wells and the wheat fields of the Ukraine. True, the Americans were gradually moving towards an alliance with us, but would they be able to join in before it was too late? If Russia was overwhelmed the Axis powers would be unbeatable, even if the United States ultimately became fully involved. General Sir Alan Brooke clearly foresaw that, whatever the future might hold, it was nevertheless necessary to go ahead with the building of a strong, well-equipped army at home. If the threat of invasion was to return we must be well prepared to resist; if the tide turned and we were to go over to the offensive, we must be equally prepared in that situation.

From bases in the British Isles the Royal Navy and the Royal Air Force were fully extended. In the summer the Royal Air Force was pounding away night after night at military targets in Germany. The Royal Navy was waging war against the U-boats and the occasional breakout of German surface raiders and battle cruisers. The Army had failed to prevent the Greeks from being overrun, and had lost Crete. In the Western Desert the pendulum swung to and fro, but it was all that we could do to hang on and safeguard Egypt and the Suez Canal. At the end of the year, even worse disaster struck when the Japanese overran Malaya and Singapore, and the Navy lost the battle cruiser *Repulse* and the battleship *Prince of Wales* at the hands of the Japanese bombers.

Before these final disasters which brought the year to a close, there had been one or two significant moves at home. One was the development of Combined Operations as a separate arm of the Services. In the autumn of 1940 Churchill had appointed Admiral of the Fleet Lord Keyes to be Director of Combined Operations. As Vice Admiral Roger Keyes he had commanded the naval forces which in April 1918 had first landed a small raiding party and then blocked the harbour of Zeebrugge by blowing up several ships. Inevitably this idea of combined operations was a Navy-dominated one. The original concept of the marine commando was based on the historical use of small landing parties composed of sailors and marines put ashore from ships anchored off the coast. The name commando was however first used with reference to bands of Boer soldiers in the South African War. It began to be recognized that the specialist skills of a landed raiding party were more appropriately undertaken by soldiers and marines, and a Combined Operations Training Centre was set up in the Western Highlands. The training schools for the use of landing craft were at Ayr, Troon and Largs on the western coast of Scotland.

General Sir Alan Brooke always maintained that commando training should have been an Army function and that commando units should have been part of an Army formation. Undoubtedly a separate organization which, after Lord Louis Mountbatten took over from Lord Keyes, was upgraded to equivalent status with the Navy, Army and Air Force, was regarded with suspicion and considered to be unnecessary by the top commanders of the three established Arms of the Services. Even a year later, when I became closely involved with joint planning, the domination of the Navy way of thinking was very obvious. The staff at Combined Operations Headquarters always put the capture of a port as first priority, and Lord Louis Mountbatten was no exception. The idea of a massed landing over beaches hardly entered into their thinking. Indeed there was a ribald saying current among the Army planners that the Navy's idea of an assault landing was to 'let the brown jobs out on the beach for a quick pee'. When Mountbatten was first appointed he was Churchill's own special choice, for he was a man after his own heart — dashing, courageous, but not much given to thinking a problem right through in all its aspects. He was at a later stage put on to the Chiefs of Staff Committee, but mercifully was sufficiently sensitive and sensible to realize that it would be folly to get too closely involved with Churchill as an individual, and that as a member of the Chiefs of Staff he must never go behind a joint services consideration. General Sir Alan Brooke's original resentment at Mountbatten's membership of the Chiefs of Staff Committee quickly faded as he realized that his fears were groundless.

Thwarted as he continuously was by Sir John Dill, who could always convincingly demonstrate that a particular scheme was mad or impossible, Churchill turned to Combined Operations Headquarters as a means of embarking upon some offensive action. At Churchill's insistence they undertook small seaborne raids upon fringe territory in occupied Europe or upon offshore islands like the Lofoten Islands. What good they did except to keep Churchill quiet is anybody's guess. Presumably their real value was as a propaganda exercise, for they were widely publicized and their effect blown up out of all proportion to reality.

Churchill continued to press for some kind of operation against the Germans on the Continent, in order to compel the enemy to use some of his reserves and take some of the pressure off the Russians, who were being overrun and in danger of being overwhelmed. He had instructed the Joint Planning Staff, who were now under his direct orders, to prepare a scheme, and in September 1941 they came up with a plan to attack Cherbourg and the Cotentin peninsula. Of course, as soon as Alan Brooke got to hear of it he was able to support Sir John Dill and the Chiefs of Staff Committee in a withering criticism of the absurdity of such a plan. Even Churchill must have been persuaded that it was pointless, because the idea was quietly dropped. But a month later he came up with another idea. This time it was to have a seaborne attack upon Trondheim on the Norwegian coast. As Commander-in-Chief Home Forces, General Sir Alan Brooke was instructed to appoint a Force Commander, which he did in the person of General Sir Bernard Paget, of whom he had a high opinion. Alan Brooke was further instructed to mount an expeditionary force and to plan the operation in detail. When the Chiefs of Staff examined the project in outline they were unanimously opposed to it. Alan Brooke started to carry out his orders to prepare a plan in detail, and in the course of so doing in conjunction with Navy and Air Force chiefs he soon became convinced that the operation was a dangerous and hopeless one.

Fortunately Churchill had already become impressed with Alan Brooke's vigour and determination, and in consequence he was prepared to listen to the arguments which were advanced, even though he was furiously angry with his generals for putting forward reasons against the scheme instead of producing a plan for how it should be carried out. In the end Churchill gave way because Alan Brooke said that he would only agree if the First Sea Lord would support the Army by sailing the Fleet in to Trondheim fjord. This he refused to do; so that was that.

Although Churchill did not hold it against Alan Brooke, the abandonment of his cherished design merely added more fuel to the smouldering fire of dissatisfaction with the unfortunate Sir John Dill, the military member of the Chiefs of Staff

Vice-Admiral
Lord Mountbatten
'NOT A CLUE'

Imperial War Museum

Committee. In the middle of November 1941, Churchill decided that Dill should be promoted to the rank of Field Marshal and retired to some appointment such as the Governorship of one of the Indian Provinces. His plan was for Alan Brooke to succeed Dill on the Chiefs of Staff Committee, that is, to be Chief of the Imperial General Staff, as the office was then called. This in fact took place on 1 December. Lord Louis Mountbatten, now promoted to the rank of Vice-Admiral, had already taken over as Director of Combined Operations, but was not at this time a member of the Chiefs of Staff Committee even in a limited advisory capacity. He was, however, in direct and frequent contact with Churchill, which caused the Chiefs of Staff Committee some anxiety lest the two of them should embark upon some harebrained scheme behind their backs. Mercifully Dill was not relegated to oblivion. When Alan Brooke succeeded him he was able to persuade Churchill not to retire Dill, but to use his great talent and experience as Head of the British Military Mission in Washington, and later to be the British link with the American members of the Combined Chiefs of Staff Committee. This proved to be a masterstroke because Field Marshal Sir John Dill and General George Marshall got on together famously. Each respected the other, and Dill was able to put over the difficulties in the way of an early assault against the Germans on the Continent in a manner which was more acceptable than from any other British military figure. Alan Brooke was not at all receptive to George Marshall's opinions and, reciprocally, Marshall did not respond to Alan Brooke.

Churchill took Dill with him along with the Naval and Air Force members of the Chiefs of Staff Committee when he visited the United States to talk with President Roosevelt in December 1941. He left behind Clement Attlee, the Leader of the Labour Party and Deputy Prime Minister to run the Government and War Cabinet, and Alan Brooke to be in charge of the Chiefs of Staff Committee. Each rose to the occasion and coped manfully with all the disasters flowing from the onslaught of the Japanese. The only comforting feature was the news of the Russian success in stemming the German invasion. It began to look as if Hitler's Russian venture would turn out to be, as it was in the end, an horrendous mistake.

In the United States Churchill and Roosevelt got on remarkably well together, for their political views, except on the British Empire, were identical. But each created great anxieties for their respective military and naval advisers, because together they were regularly tending jointly to favour some strategy or some operation which their Staffs had not discussed with each other. Although in the end the British and American General Staffs combined well together and produced a tolerably harmonious joint organization, at this time they were poles apart. Thus the American Staff paper of March 1941 at the time of the secret discussions with the British planners made the point that, by themselves, naval and air forces seldom win a war and that a war can only finally be won by armies on land. Moreover they were of the opinion that British military thinking was conditioned by a desire to preserve the commercial interests of Britain and the Empire, This was hardly fair. The British planners, it is true, did not envisage the use of large forces of infantry, but pinned their faith on a naval blockade, massive aerial bombing and widespread use of resistance activity to sabotage the movement of enemy troops and supplies by rail and road. This approach was conditioned not so much by a desire to preserve commercial interests as a desire to avoid the wholesale slaughter of young men such as had occurred in the

First World War. In this they had an overwhelming case which the Americans failed to appreciate. Although the people of the United States were led to believe that they had won that war, the casualties suffered by them were quite puny compared with those countries which had been slugging it out for over three years before the Americans joined in. The United States lost no more than 126,000 men. The British Empire mobilized nine million men, of whom one million lost their lives, that is, nearly ten times the losses sustained by the United States. Added to the British figures were those of the French, who suffered even more grievously than the British. One out of every six men called to the colours lost his life. Indeed the remembrance of these dreadful losses was largely responsible for the defensive and defeatist attitude of the French commanders in 1939 and 1940.

The fundamental difference of approach between the British and American strategists was, however, that whereas the Americans favoured a concentrated attack upon the heart of the enemy, that is, a direct and massive assault in Western Europe, the British preferred constant pressure upon the periphery of the enemy-held territories. Thus, in the immediate aftermath of the fall of France, the major concentration of offensive British military force was in the Mediterranean, East Africa and the Middle East against the Germans and their Italian and French collaborators. Churchill himself favoured ventures such as attacks upon Norway and North Africa, but his military advisers were constantly asking to be allowed to concentrate their resources in the Western Desert and East Africa, and later in Burma. They were anxious that when Churchill and Roosevelt got together they might commit the British and the Americans to some operation which would be to the detriment of the first priorities, as they saw them.

As early as November 1941, the British Joint Planning Staff had produced a study of the various offensive possibilities which might supplement the operations in the Mediterranean and East Africa. A proposed invasion of northern Norway, which was Churchill's own preference but which was rejected by the Chiefs of Staff, was given the code name 'Jupiter'. A plan to occupy the Atlantic seaboard of French North Africa and to make use of this as a base for a later operation against southern Europe was known by the title 'Gymnast'. A limited attack upon a part of occupied France in order to meet Stalin's insistence upon military action by opening a Second Front in support of Russia was called 'Sledgehammer', and a full scale invasion of North West Europe was given the name 'Round Up'. It has to be remembered that all these various plans were produced by the Joint Planning Staff at the persistent prodding of Churchill. They were all objected to by Alan Brooke. 'Round Up' was recognized to be a real possibility in the long run, but it would need a year of two of preparation before it could be contemplated, and in the meantime British forces were fully committed elsewhere. Even before the December and January meetings these various plans were made known to the American planners, who, as has already been observed, did not believe that the British Service Chiefs had their heart in any one of them. Thus it was that the American Service Planners who wanted immediate action in Europe had to persuade General Marshall first, and then to get him to persuade President Roosevelt in turn to get the British to move. In fact General Marshall needed no persuading, because the staff papers merely mirrored his own thinking.

At this time there was a rapidly rising star amongst the American senior staff officers. Dwight Eisenhower, although commissioned before the United States entered the First World War in 1917, did not go to France on active service. In the years following he held various junior commands with training units, and also a number of staff appointments. He had earned favourable attention, no doubt more because of his clear mind and charm of manner and attractive personality than his skill in military high command, of which he had no experience. He was fortunate to have impressed General George Marshall, and when his name came up before Roosevelt, the President knew all about him because his brother, Milt Eisenhower, was one of the Presidential civil advisers. Eisenhower had served in the Philippines as Staff Officer to General MacArthur, of whom he had a low opinion, and whose lobbying for priority to be given to the Pacific and Far East he persistently resisted, fortunately for the British. A Lieutenant-Colonel in 1941, he went on to Brigadier-General (one star), to Major-General (two stars), to Lieutenant-General (three stars) in less than a year. As Head of the War Plans Division in the Pentagon he had shared Marshall's belief that immediate offensive action in Europe was essential, and in the middle of March 1942 produced a paper to this effect, which was adopted by Marshall and by

Stimson the Secretary for War. It became known as the Marshall Memorandum, was accepted by Roosevelt, and grudgingly acknowledged by Churchill as the official American strategy to which he would have to give serious consideration.

Although the British Chiefs of Staff had been forewarned by Dill as early as January 1942 that this plan and this policy was likely to be adopted, and took steps to set up an organization to cope with the situation in advance, they were none the less dismayed to see how far their strategic position had been undermined. General Sir Alan Brooke considered that the plans were the work of armchair strategists with no practical experience of military command and no perception of practical possibilities. The plan advocated a large scale invasion of Europe with joint British and American forces along the lines of 'Round Up' and this to take place in the Spring of 1943 and to be launched across the Channel, in the area between Boulogne and Le Havre. What was worse, it contemplated the possibility of an emergency limited attack in 1942. This was operation 'Sledgehammer'. It was an operation which could only be carried out by British forces and would entail enormous and sacrificial losses, but it was hoped by the Americans, but not the British, that it would enable a small bridgehead to be established from which 'Round Up' could be launched the following year. Alan Brooke knew that these schemes were something he had to live with and that detailed examination of practical possibilities was essential. It was necessary to provide a British Command structure in case some sort of offensive action in Europe was forced upon him and the Chiefs of Staff. Furthermore, the planning of any such action would be better done by a small staff answerable directly to the prospective force Commander. They could take over from the Joint Planning Staff all the detailed planning involved in either a 'Sledgehammer' or a 'Round Up' situation.

3

THE EARLY PLANNING FOR INVASION

In January 1942 General Sir Alan Brooke, informed by Sir John Dill of the way things had been going in Washington during December 1941, had moved in anticipation and set up an embryo command structure and a small planning staff for detailed planning of cross-Channel operations. He based this upon GHQ Home Forces. General Sir Bernard Paget, the Commander-in-Chief, was designated as Force Commander, but this additional appointment was not an active operational command, but advisory and supervisory. Under him there was a small planning staff which was to take over the planning of a European invasion from the Joint Planning Staff at the War Office, who were concerned with the overall strategic planning for all the various theatres of war. This small group was headed by Brigadier Colin McNab, a Seaforth Highlander. Under him a few officers were being selected to join the team. Brigadier McNab had already had appointed under him two majors to be General Staff Officers, grade 2 (GSO2), to be responsible for the operational and tactical details within the authorized strategical plan. Denys Buckle, an experienced RASC officer, had been taken away from instructing at the Staff College, promoted to acting Brigadier and was to head the sub-section dealing with questions of build up, supply and maintenance which the Americans called logistics, but which we referred to as administration. In this section, known as Q Plans, I was one of two majors, the other being George Hodnett, a year of two older than me and a former Territorial Army officer who in peace time had been a solicitor practising in Newcastle-upon-Tyne. As it was obvious that transportation by sea was a basic factor, we had as advisors Captain Norris of the Royal Navy and Brigadier MacKillop, a Movements and Transportation specialist from the Royal Engineers. On the Air Force side we had Group Captain Victor Groom. As neither Alan Brooke nor Bernard Paget wished Combined Operations HQ to be any more than specialist advisors in the techniques of assault landings, whereas Mountbatten and his staff considered that they should be planners for the whole operation, there was a lot of petty jealousy and bickering between us and them, and a great deal of overlapping and unco-ordinated planning going on at the same time. Fortunately for the three of us who were designated the Q Plans Staff, there was no one at Combined Operations HQ who was required to deal with the actual logistic problems, and so we went our own way without any of these embarrassments. It was the unfortunate Brigadier MacKillop who had to shoulder the burden of dealing with Mountbatten's team, and who had constantly to put them in their place and to limit their excessive enthusiasm for encroaching upon the prerogative of the designated Army Force Commander and his military staff. He was highly strung in temperament and quite unsuited to this sort of petty in-fighting. It was in the end too much for him, and the strains and stresses and the overwork which resulted led some months later to a complete mental breakdown, and sadly he took his own life.

So I became an original member of the planning team which laid the foundation for the ultimate 'Overlord' invasion of Europe. Moreover, I think I can claim to be the only officer who lived with the planning all the way through, and who was privileged to be a part of its execution as a member of General Montgomery's Headquarters still to be there at its final successful outcome on 8 May, 1945. I was never more than a backroom boy, toiling away at dull detail, but the initial introduction gave me an opportunity to see the manner in which Allied high strategy developed and the way the great men at the top behaved and operated.

The task which was given to us was to examine in detail the two strategic plans tentatively outlined by the British Joint Planning Staff and given the code names of 'Sledgehammer' and 'Round Up'. At this stage the Marshall Memorandum based on Eisenhower's Staff Paper had not yet officially seen the light of day, and we were therefore, to begin with, a British team dealing with the problems in a purely British context. Although a month or so after we started the Americans were formally allied to us in these projects, they did not venture into detailed planning for many months to come. We were given a completely free hand by the British Joint Planning Staff without any interference from them. The only interference from which we suffered came at the hands of Churchill and then only indirectly, for we were answerable to General Sir Bernard Paget and General Sir Alan Brooke. On the British side, no-one ever contemplated the possibility of a major invasion before the Spring of 1943, but we were nevertheless required immediately to begin the detailed planning for 'Round Up' in that year. The first priority however was 'Sledgehammer', the emergency small-scale invasion in 1942 which was to be entirely British, and which we all fervently hoped would never come to pass. Mercifully, it never did. It would have been an horrific failure.

The first thing which had to be decided was where the invasion was to take place, and even in the context of a 'Sledgehammer' operation the basic factors were the same. There were three areas for consideration. As we saw it, in ascending order of preference, there was Cherbourg and the Cotentin peninsula; there was the short Pas de Calais crossing, and there was the vast area of the Normandy beaches. We never seriously considered the area from the mouth of the River Somme to the northern estuary of the River Seine, which was the one contemplated in the Marshall Memorandum. It was neither a large continuous stretch of sandy beaches, nor was it provided with large port facilities. The only sizeable port was Dieppe, a direct assault on which, as later events tragically confirmed, was correctly considered to be suicidal. Combined Operations HQ had also given some thought to the larger question, though their efforts were more concentrated upon small-scale raids.

Now whatever Mountbatten may have later believed or persuaded himself, he was not, to begin with, a supporter of the Normandy beaches. As a deep sea sailor he was naturally more attracted to the early capture and use of a port big enough to cope with shipping of deep draught. He was at this time all in favour of going for Cherbourg. Moreover, there were strong arguments in favour of the Cotentin peninsula and Cherbourg if there was to be a limited invasion, to placate the Russians, with the main purpose of creating a foothold in France for later development the following year. A sealing-off at the neck of the peninsula would not be so much of a disadvantage in the short term. By contrast there were obvious reasons for the selection of the shortest sea crossing towards the Pas de Calais. It meant easier air cover and a quicker sea journey and turnround of shipping. If the intention of 'Sledgehammer' operation was to engage a large body of enemy forces to meet the Russian demand for a relief of pressure, then this was the place, because it was far and away the most heavily defended and had behind it the major part of the enemy's mobile reserve formations. But this strong defence made the area a daunting prospect for a direct assault. Turning to the Normandy beaches on the other hand raised as many questions as it raised certain advantages. The idea of landing on open beaches was still novel and untried, although Combined Operations HQ had been experimenting with and practising this type of assault landings on the West Coast of Scotland. However, large scale landings over the beaches gave promise of a quicker breakthrough after the initial coastal defences had been overcome.

It is my genuine belief that it was an inestimable advantage in the early stages of detailed planning to make use of junior officers who could visualize the harsh reality of this kind of war, particularly if they knew what it was like to have bullets whizzing over their heads and shells bursting all round them as they leapt out of their assault craft. It was all very well for the Eisenhowers of this world to draft papers sitting comfortably at a desk inside a peaceful office. Of course most of the top British commanders knew what the reality was, and General Sir Alan Brooke in particular was able to look at any plan in the light of what it would mean to the soldiers who were being called on to lead the assault. To begin with, the Americans simply had no idea. It is understandable therefore that the British Army Chiefs were constantly critical of airy-fairy plans which took no account of the reality of a strongly opposed landing. The Americans moreover were bad and pre-conditioned listeners. If one substitutes the word 'American' for the words 'Harvard Man', the old adage current in smart and sophisticated circles becomes 'You can always tell an American, but you can't tell him much'.

Mountbatten was a totally different sort of person from the American 'top brass', but in his way equally difficult. Tall, good looking, with a charismatic personality which dominated any group of which he formed a part, he possessed so much self-confidence that at times it led him to an obstinate refusal to see merit in the ideas of others. He had every right to be self-confident. At the age of forty-one he had fought at sea with such gallantry and courage that his exploits as Captain (Destroyers) were legendary. He was a close personal friend of HM King George VI and had completely won over Winston Churchill by his bravery and forceful personality. To begin with, his assumption of control of Combined Operations Headquarters was regarded with suspicion by the heads of the three established arms of the Services, and the staff officers who had to deal with their counterparts were to some extent infected with this inter-Service rivalry.

There was another aspect of Combined Operations HQ which caused some resentment with us, and that was the atmosphere of 'High Society' which characterized many of the staff. This feeling on our part was perhaps symptomatic of a general belief held by those who were not officers in the Household Cavalry or the Brigade of Guards or the crack Cavalry Regiments, that these privileged persons were somewhat over-conscious of an innate superiority. In reality, the young cadet who went to the Royal Military Academy at Woolwich was more likely to reach the very top ranks than anyone else. General Sir Alan Brooke, for example, was a Gunner from the RMA. Offhand it is difficult to think of anyone who made Field Marshal in the war who came from a Cavalry Regiment or the Brigade of Guards other than Harold Alexander, and he was an Irish Guardsman, who, along with the Scots and the Welsh were regarded as the more humble professionals compared with the aristocratic types or gifted amateurs from the Grenadier Guards or the Coldstream. Two of our greatest commanders were infantry men, namely Montgomery and Slim. Slim in particular was highly regarded by the volunteer army, for he had entered the First World War as a bank clerk turned private soldier in the Birmingham City Battalion of the Royal Warwickshire Regiment. He was the citizen soldier 'par excellence'. None of us in our little group of planners had any pretensions to be members of the aristocracy or of the Guards or Cavalry Clubs. Two of us were lawyers in civilian life, two were Regular Army gunners, two were Corps officers of the Regular Army, and at the head was an under-privileged Highlander.

The team at once got down to the task of considering first the Cotentin peninsula and Cherbourg. It was plainly an area which could be sealed off by the enemy so as to prevent any development of an initially successful landing. It was too long a sea journey, and could not be given any air support. We spent no time on this as a viable proposition for a full-scale invasion in 1943. We then considered the short Channel crossing, which had many obvious attractions, particularly to the Air Force and the Movements experts who were concerned with shipping. There were two ports, Calais and Boulogne, which were of course familiar to us all, and Boulogne had a small stretch of flat sandy beach on the northern side of the town. In between these two ports there was a long extent of high cliff with Cap Gris Nez the prominent feature. Further to the north of Calais there were the sandy beaches and dunes of Dunkirk with their painful memories of 1940. The ports were small, but would have to be seized before any substantial number of men or sufficient quantity of arms and equipment could be landed in the salient. At this time there was no known precedent for a direct frontal attack on a port other than the entry of the Navy into Zeebrugge in the First World War. It was obvious however that there would have to be a three-pronged attack with equal thrusts on each side of an attempt to get into the port itself. This presented a formidable task, for the open beaches, backed as they were by high dunes or rising ground or seafront buildings, could be covered by murderous crossfire from well-sited machine guns. Field artillery and mortar shelling would render in addition any successful landing virtually impossible unless all these defensive outposts and positions could be wiped out by heavy and persistent bombardment from sea and air. The whole of the Pas de Calais area was known to be heavily defended, and the hinterland was occupied by large number of troops and many armoured formations. These could quickly be brought up to deal with any landings which might have overcome and penetrated the coastal defensive positions. Rapid build up and reinforcement of the initial assault was vital.

Thus the dominant factor was the size of the invasion force. This in turn depended upon the shipping and transportation which could be made available. Our Q (Movements) Staff and Combined Operations HQ made a preliminary study which took quite a few days, and the early reports were that we would be unable to land more than about three thousand men in the first assault. In fact a further and more detailed report from us through General Paget and from Combined Operations HQ through Mountbatten to the Chiefs of Staff Committee on 8 May, 1942, put the figure at four thousand men. This figure was accepted by Churchill, and led him at this later date to focus his attention yet again on Norway. But in March he was all for an attack in the Pas de Calais area.

This figure of four thousand men was less than one third of the strength of one division, and would be smaller than one brigade group. Even in the first wave it would be necessary to have, for example, Engineers for demolition and breaking down operations, and the infantry had to have reserve ammunition; and anti-tank and light anti-aircraft guns had also to be landed early. The initial assault required the continuing back up of supporting forces and adequate supplies. What tended to be forgotten was that a second or even a third instalment of shipping had to be available to continue with the landing before what remained of the first were got back for reloading, and then the second lot had to be brought back. This question of turnround was as important as the availability for the initial landings. The woefully inadequate shipping facility meant that we could only advise that any attempt, however limited, in the year 1942 would be quite impossible.

According to Alan Brooke's diary, there was a meeting of the Chiefs of Staff Committee on 10 March which was the first one at which Mountbatten attended. It was then decided to investigate the possibility of a landing in the area of Calais which would be preceded by and accompanied by a contest in the air between the British and German Air Forces. This should draw off sufficient of the German Air Force to achieve some slight relief for the Russians, who were pressing all the time for a major offensive by the British and Americans. We had already done sufficient work on a short crossing assault to enable General Paget to be fully briefed when he attended the Chiefs of Staff Committee meeting on 28 March. It is interesting to note that on this occasion Mountbatten was still arguing in favour of an attack on Cherbourg, and had to be convinced by General Paget and Air Marshal Sholto Douglas that the Army and Air Force planners had concluded that Cherbourg was a hopeless proposition. At this time Parliament, the Press and the public were clamouring for a 'Second Front — Now', without knowledge of the enormous difficulties which made it impossible. General Marshall and Eisenhower, who had been promoted to Major General that very same day, were kept fully informed, but, again, being totally uninstructed, would not readily accept the British point of view. General Sir Alan Brooke had in fact taken over the chairmanship of the Chiefs of Staff Committee on 5 March, but had put General Paget in charge of detailed planning as early as 3 January. He and we in our turn were kept informed of what was going on in Washington. We knew, therefore, that at any moment the Marshall-Eisenhower paper would be put to us, and so had done a lot of work on the possibility of a full-scale invasion in the spring of 1943. We did not know, however, that General Marshall had persuaded President Roosevelt that a small bridge-head invasion could be done by British forces with American back up if the Russian situation required it in 1942. Nor did we learn until later that Roosevelt had rashly promised Molotov that the Russians could expect a Second Front later in the year.

Our preliminary work on the possibility of a major invasion proceeded on very different lines from those contained in the Marshall Memorandum, which he and Harry Hopkins brought to Churchill and the British Chiefs of Staff after their arrival in England on 5 April 1942. To begin with, we never seriously considered the Dieppe-Le Havre area, and we then worked backwards from a minimum force to estimate the minimum requirement of shipping, whereas the Marshall plan merely plucked a whole lot of figures out of the sky without any reference to reality. We had of course to assume that the provision of ships and landing craft would be sufficiently increased to enable this minimum force to be landed, supplied and reinforced.

The size of a minimum force was largely conditioned by the place of the landing and the strength of the defences and availability of quick enemy reinforcement. We were gradually more and more convinced that the best target area was the Normandy beaches, which were extensive and very flat. The hinterland was not nearly so strongly defended nor backed by reserve formations as was the Calais area. By a strange coincidence I knew these beaches very well, having attended Caen University for a short time before going up to Cambridge, and having each weekend gone down to the seaside. Before I could make use of this private knowledge, Combined Operations HQ without any reference to us, sent off some reconnaissance parties of commandos who paddled ashore in the dark from rubber boats. Combined Ops obviously fancied themselves at this sort of thing. On 23 June, 1940, the day after France had capitulated, a party of one hundred and twenty commandos had landed on the beaches of Boulogne, all to no purpose, as these were virtually deserted. A number of men lost their way on the journey back to England and were arrested as deserters by the Military Police! This time there were no such disasters. The information which this little party brought back, plus aerial reconnaissance photographs, became the authoritative version of topographical detail. I was able, in a smug and offhand fashion, to tell our own team that the information was correct. In particular, I could confirm that the tide ebbed and flowed at a very fast pace, but the water was never more than shallow even at high tide.

The more we examined the problems and weighed the various factors, the more it seemed that the Normandy beaches provided the best point for a large-scale invasion. This was a considered and persistent view, and I am absolutely satisfied that General Paget was persuaded of this. I know that Generals Alan Brooke and Paget argued with General Marshall in June 1942 that the Pas de Calais was the only area for a limited 'Sledgehammer' attack which would cause sufficient reaction from the Germans to be of any assistance to the Russians. I know also that they were both strongly opposed to this with the few resources then available. But it was a different problem altogether when a large-scale invasion had to be considered. It is extremely puzzling that in June 1942, Lieutenant-General Morgan, the Chief of Staff to the Supreme Allied Commander (COSSAC), when reviewing the planning which had gone before, referred to adverse criticism of an invasion operation centred in British Home Forces Headquarters emanating from senior officers who had gravitated there, and claimed that the Pas de Calais had been a first choice. Either these later arrivals at GHQ (whoever they were) or Lieutenant-General Morgan, or both, must have completely misunderstood the conclusions we had arrived at over a year earlier. Certainly General George Marshall understood and, as I recall, accepted our preference for the Normandy beaches. He also came to appreciate that it would only be a practicable operation if an enormous increase in shipping and landing craft could be organized, although neither he nor Eisenhower could have appreciated at this time that they would have to spend the next two years trying to get sufficient craft out of the clutches of Admiral King, the tight-fisted and anti-British US Naval Chief of Staff. In this they failed, and the British were the major providers of landing craft as well as naval vessels when it came to the actual invasion. This is a fact about which the Americans were never told, and which the British never boasted about.

The Marshall Memorandum was presented to the British Chiefs of Staff on 8 April, 1942. It envisaged a major offensive to be launched in the area south of Boulogne and down to Le Havre at the mouth of the River Seine. For this the force was to consist of forty-eight Divisions, eighteen or which were to be British. The number of combat aircraft involved were to be 5,800 of which 2,550 were to be British. No less than 7,000 landing craft would be required. In the event, when the invasion did actually take place in June 1944 we had to manage with far less. The target date for this mammoth operation was set at 1 April, 1943 which the British Chiefs of Staff persuaded the Americans to put back one month to the 1 May, 1943. When this plan filtered down to us after a joint meeting on 14 April between the British and American representatives, the whole thing seemed to us to border on fantasy.

As a result of the view held by Marshall and Eisenhower that a large-scale invasion of Europe was inevitable, General Marshall had already arranged for a buildup of American troops in England. The plan for this was code named 'Bolero'. Both of them, however, realized that there would be far too few American servicemen available for a limited 'Sledgehammer' operation in 1942. An American Headquarters was set up in London for the European Theatre of Operations United States Army (ETOUSA). After his promotion to Major-General, Eisenhower was made Commanding General of ETOUSA, but did not come to London until 26 May. In the meantime the Combined Commanders, who in January were the Commander-in-Chief of Home Forces, the Naval Commander-in-Chief Portsmouth and the RAF Commander-in-Chief Fighter Command, had added to their number the Commanding General ETOUSA. This was the first ever joint Allied

Command, a fact which is rarely remembered and not generally known. To begin with, Eisenhower must have been represented by his deputy, whose name after all these years I cannot recall.

By the time Eisenhower effectively took over his American command and was promoted Lieutenant-General (three star), the situation had changed dramatically for the worse. The Japanese were sweeping on from Singapore into Burma; the Germans had advanced through Russia down to the Black Sea; in the first six months of the year 1942 German U-boats had sunk over four million tons of allied shipping, and in the Western Desert and the Mediterranean the British suffered disaster after disaster. Small wonder then that the Combined Commanders could offer little or no hope to Molotov of any immediate landing on the shores of occupied France. Eisenhower and George Marshall were pressing as hard as they could for a huge increase in assault craft, without which they had come to realize that plans for an invasion of Europe were no more than a pipe dream. All this made our planning seem theoretical. But we were compelled by the pressure exerted on the British and American leaders by the Russians to continue our studies, and from time to time to come up with briefs with which the Allied Chiefs of Staff could meet this pressure.

By the time the Marshall Memorandum was presented to the British Chiefs of Staff we had been working for two months on plans for a major invasion of Europe. Whereas in the past all landing on the Continent had been effected in orderly fashion through ports with all units coming ashore complete with all their equipment, assault landings on beaches created a totally different problem. Even the initial landings could not be limited to assaulting infantry. There had to be an element of specialist or support troops. In the secondary stage of the assault landings there had to be some service and base units, which would have to be phased in as soon as practicable. Thus, if one was planning for a landing on what was called a one-divisional front, it would not do to land first of all the infantry, followed by artillery, then engineers, then signals, then medical units, then transport units and so on and so forth, as one would do if an army was advancing in orderly fashion.

In those days the Army was in theory organized in multiples of threes. There were three infantry battalions in a brigade, three brigades in a division, three divisions in a corps and three corps in an army. In practice a corps might, however, consist of only two divisions, and similarly an army might consist of only two corps. In each division there were divisional troops additional to those in each brigade, such as engineers, medical and transport units, who were allotted to and came under direct control of the divisional commanders headquarters. Similarly each corps and each army had its own corps and army troops. The strength and type of every unit from an infantry platoon up to a complete army was set out in what was called its war establishment. One could therefore work out the total number of men, armaments, equipment and vehicles in a complete army. We had concluded that on a one-divisional front it would be necessary to land at least two brigade groups in the initial assault, to be followed by a third to complete the first division and then a fourth brigade group, the start of the follow-up. There would have to be enough landing craft for four brigade groups to be landed before the first reloading on a turnround could be contemplated. Now the actual composition of a brigade group would be made up of the normal complement of infantry, or armour in the case of an armoured brigade, and in addition an element of assault engineers and specialist artillery and other support troops. The actual composition of a brigade group would have to be decided by a senior formation commander, but we had to have some ready reckoner yardstick in order to make a rough estimate of the shipping required to land a division, together with an appropriate element of corps and army troops. I made a suggestion which appealed to Brigadier McNab and Brigadier Buckle, that if we totalled up the complete war establishments of an army of three corps and nine divisions, and, imagining a layered cake with the infantry at the top and the army base units at the bottom, took a one-ninth slice right through the cake, we could arrive at a 'divisional slice' which would provide a rough idea of what would be required for an assault by one division. Of course there would be no need to land one-ninth of an Army Base Workshops or one-ninth of an Army Base Hospital. On the other hand, an assaulting division would have more than a normal complement of specialist engineers and supporting artillery, and what was gained on the roundabouts could well be lost on the swings. As a test and a check we made up two specimen brigade groups and multiplied by three in each case to make up a complete divisional landing.

The figures turned out to be remarkably similar to the 'divisional slice' figures. Thereafter for planning purposes we were able to use these calculations and to work out what shipping was required for a one-divisional assault, and doubling and trebling the requirement for a two-divisional assault and a three-divisional assault.

Although Lieutenant-General Morgan of COSSAC acknowledged the value of these preliminary studies when he and his staff (of whom I was one) took over the planning for operation 'Overlord' as it became known, General Montgomery would have none of it, and arrogantly ignored everything which had previously been done. This total inability to recognize that anyone other than he and his chosen few knew the answers was one of his greatest faults. When operation 'Husky', the landing in Sicily, was being planned, an offer to fly me out to Cairo with the files of our studies was brusquely refused. In the event, the later planners had to do a lot of unnecessary groundwork, all of which had been done before. When he took over 'Overlord', he rejected everything which COSSAC had done, and not only almost drove his staff into mental and physical breakdowns, but humiliated Lieutenant-General Morgan and made of him an embittered enemy. As I was there at each stage with each set-up, I used at times to get furiously angry at this dreadful waste of experience and mental energy. When his 'desert boys' used to complain of exhaustion, I had no sympathy for them. It was all the fault of their revered and beloved leader.

In fact the only difference which Montgomery introduced into 'Overlord' was to widen the front and to increase the size of the assaulting forces. In this he was of course right. But in 1942 and 1943 the plans were circumscribed by the amount of shipping available. If the shipping could only cope with a one-divisional front, then the plan had to be for a one-divisional front. If a one-divisional front was suicidal, then those that made the ultimate decision would be bound to advise against such a limited and futile exercise.

It is interesting to bear in mind the actual composition of the British and Canadian assault force on 6 June, 1944, two years after our initial planning was taking place. For 'Overlord', the assault was conducted by ten Infantry Brigades, two SS Commando Brigades and four Armoured Brigades, together with appropriate corps and army troops. The Brigade Group was the basic formation, and the total assault force was landed in three waves of shipping on three successive tides. In terms of Brigade Groups, the landings were six, five and five in successive waves and in terms of Divisions a little more than six in total. The American assault force was approximately the same. The British sector consisted of three beaches, each of which was approximately a one-divisional front, and the American sector was two beaches, again each of approximately a front for one division. The Americans pushed more divisions through on the second and third waves, and landed rather more than six divisions on their two beaches. Thus the initial assault by the Allied forces was carried out by twelve divisions on a five-divisional front. When the Combined Commanders handed over the planning to COSSAC, we had estimated that an invasion could not be contemplated with less than ten divisions on a three-divisional front. COSSAC thought that we were unduly pessimistic. Montgomery would have said, if he had bothered to read our papers, that we were too optimistic. But at least we were much nearer the final mark than the COSSAC plan.

However, what is much more interesting is that the final 'Overlord' plan was based on the Brigade Group just as we had envisaged it. Except for the introduction of the specialized tanks for laying track on sand and mud, and for exploding mines and explosive charges, and for 'swimming' ashore, none of which had been invented in 1942, the composition of a Brigade Group was very similar. The rough yardstick of the 'divisional slice' proved remarkably accurate, and the calculations of the total amount of shipping required to lift one division with the appropriate element of corps and army and other specialist troops never had to be altered. Why the whole thing had to be done all over again without any reference to, or at least acknowledgement of what had been done before, was a complete mystery to me.

Professionally educated and nurtured as I was in the common law of England, I knew the value of precedent. The English legal system proceeds upon the basis that any problem has probably been considered before, and that the right answer is already there if one looks for it in the decisions previously arrived at. I was utterly dismayed at the appalling narrow-mindedness displayed by a succession of professional top commanders and their planning staffs, who could see nothing good in what someone else had done before. The resultant waste of time and effort was prodigious. In my own case, the more experienced and knowledgeable I became and the more senior my rank, the less I was permitted to contribute. By the time Montgomery and his 'desert boys' took over in January 1944, I was pushed completely into the background, watching with growing cynicism the huge effort being expended to obtain an answer which was already previously discovered. Only once, in a moment of crisis, was my help sought, but of that more later.

4

THE GREAT MEN IN PERSON

The first of the great men involved in the Allied War effort with whom I came into contact was General Sir Alan Brooke. I did not see him face to face more than once or twice. He was for the most part the 'all-powerful' head of the Army lurking in the background. The power that he exerted over his subordinates even at long distance was quite phenomenal, and no-one who was junior to him could escape a feeling almost akin to fear when in his presence. If he passed by in a corridor, we all — even generals — instinctively froze to attention and pressed against he wall until he had gone by. He looked severe and seemed to project an aura of majesty. And later on, when I joined General Montgomery's Headquarters, it was generally known that 'Monty' would never dare to do anything if it was something of which 'Brookie' would not approve, whereas he cared not a fig for the opinion of anyone else, not even Winston Churchill himself. Montgomery considered that Brooke was 'the greatest soldier — soldier, sailor or airman — produced by any country taking part in the last war'. Although the American Chiefs of Staff were usually unable to keep pace with the rapidity of his thought and spoken delivery, and were therefore suspicious of him, he dominated the British Chiefs of Staff Committee. For all his somewhat brash self-confidence, Mountbatten recognized Brooke's supremacy, and once said to a member of his staff that if Brooke disagreed with any of his suggestions it would be impossible to get the support of any of the other members of the COS, whereas if Brooke did agree, then his suggestion would inevitably be adopted.

Giving, as he did, the impression of machine-like efficiency, it came as a great surprise to learn that privately Alan Brooke was a man of great sensitivity, devoted to his wife and children, who, whenever he could get a few hours of leave, spent them in the country in the study of nature and watching and photographing any shy or rare birds that he was able to identify. It was interesting to realize that in his case he just had to find from time to time an opportunity to relax, and to gain refreshment of strength from a communion with nature and in a quiet worship of the Deity in whom he passionately believed.

Winston Churchill on the other hand never found it necessary to resort to any relaxation throughout the years in which he guided the destiny of the nation. He had, nevertheless, an unbounding energy and a variety of talent which he could exercise whenever he was not in government office. Thus he wrote books by the dozen: could paint as well as any Academician, and even became a competent bricklayer, building a wall in his garden during the years before the Second World War broke out, when the staid and orthodox Tories drove him into the political wilderness.

Sir Archibald Sinclair
Minister for Air

Imperial War Museum

My first meeting with Churchill was quite accidental. One evening I bumped into Sir Archibald Sinclair, the Secretary of State for Air. It was at the entrance of the War Cabinet building. For a moment we looked at each other, I recognized him at once; he obviously wondering where he had seen me before, though, of course, not in uniform. I reminded him that he and I had spoken on the same platform in the Liberal cause when he was the Leader of the Party and I was one of the young Liberals fulminating against the inadequacy of Neville Chamberlain and his Government. At that moment the great man himself came upon the scene. Now, 'Archie' Sinclair and Winston were close personal friends. They had known each other from their early days as young politicians, and had for a short time served together in France in the First World War. As I came to attention and snapped a smart salute, came the words 'Hmph, Archie and who is this young man?' 'One of my pre-war young Liberals,' was the reply. Turning to me, the Prime Minister observed that he himself had been a Liberal in his earlier years. 'Oh, yes, sir,' said I, 'and in 1906 at Dundee you made a great speech lambasting the Tories and derided them for "distilling Imperialism by the pint pot".' 'Oh, you know about that, do you?' and then, nudging me in the ribs and with a twinkle in his eye, he said, 'Do you know, it doesn't matter what you call yourself, as long as you are sure you can do the job better than anyone else!' How right he was!

Although whenever the occasion called for it Churchill could make a magnificent speech, inspiring his audience with measured, orotund phrase, he was not in my opinion a natural orator. He worked hard in the preparation of what he was going to say, and no doubt rehearsed in his mind over and over again the choice of words. I would think from what I have learned that even the phrase he used from time to time in committee or in private conversation would have been thought out in advance. As a natural orator he did not compare with David Lloyd George, who, without doubt, was the greatest of such kind whom I ever heard. In his case the words came pouring out as if straight from the heart. He held his audience spellbound, and even though in reality he may not have believed in everything he said, his listeners were led to think so. Perhaps, like many of his kind, he had the gift of persuading himself of the genuineness of what he was saying while he was saying it.

I have a clear and lasting memory of an occasion in the summer of 1929 when I, as a young undergraduate, joined Lloyd George, Leader of the Liberal Party, to launch a crusade in the General Election with the proud boast 'We can conquer unemployment'. I have no doubt that we could have made a good shot at it, but the electors for the most part did not agree. Lloyd George held meetings all the way from Land's End to John O'Groats. The pilgrimage began on a gorgeous day, with occasional white clouds scudding swiftly across a clear blue sky. There on the cliff top he stood with a cloak around his shoulders, his silvery locks blowing in the wind and declaiming to a group of perhaps thirty or forty gathered round him. He was so magnificent and so compelling that if he had asked us to go down on our knees and pray for the blessing of the Almighty God upon our endeavours, we would no doubt have done so.

Lloyd George was short in stature, and so also, to my great surprise when I met him, was Winston Churchill. And then I think of other great and successful men who were physically small — Napoleon Bonaparte, Nelson, Montgomery are names that instantly occur to one. Does the subconscious mind, I wonder, seek to compensate for lack of inches by an aggressiveness of temperament and a motivation to conquer and overcome? And do tall men, by reason of superiority in height, rely subconsciously on this fact to render unnecessary any desire to exercise superiority in the conscious field of endeavour?

One day there came my way an instance of Churchill's direct interference with his military advisers, in language which revealed his fondness for the prepared and theatrical phrase. It was his practice to go to bed very late and to stay there after breakfast in the morning. Propped up against the pillows, he read the papers and documents submitted to him and then, letting his fertile imagination roam and his desire for aggressive action take control, would write out in his own hand a short paper which always required immediate attention and which generally by reply resulted in a carefully compiled report to indicate the impossibility of his proposal. We in our little group thought that the Combined Commanders had succeeded in demonstrating the suicidal nature of any attack in the Pas de Calais area during the summer of 1942, and that such an idea could be forgotten. But we were wrong. There came to me an instruction to prepare a brief for the Combined Commanders and the Chiefs of Staff to deal with one of the Prime Minister's early morning effusions. By the time the document reached me it was in copy typed form, but there at the foot were the magic initials W.S.C.

I can see it now in my mind's eye. It went something like this, and I can certainly remember some of the actual words:

> 'Pray consider an immediate attack upon the enemy held positions in the area of the Pas de Calais. I envisage a fleet of transports escorted across the narrow seas, driven ashore and beached upon the sands under the sheltering protection of the cliffs which rise above. Then debouching from these grounded ships I see hundreds of lightly-clad and lightly-armed troops scrambling overboard and hastily advancing towards the foe, supported by many pieces of cannon.'

It was this splendid phrase 'many pieces of cannon' that struck me then and still does, as Churchill at his magnificent best. But alas, my good friend Denis Kelly, who acted as researcher and amenuensis for Churchill in the production of the war histories, was able to find only an edited and prosaic version of the original memorandum, which is as it appears officially for posterity. However the original form of words does not deserve to be lost for ever. And if ever a concept merited the observation 'C'est magnifique, mais ce n'est pas la guerre', it was this. No doubt if Churchill had been the Earl of Cardigan, he would himself have led the Charge of the Light Brigade straight at the mouths of the many pieces of cannon ranged against them.

Two years later I was privileged to be told privately of another one of Churchill's gems and of an incident in the War Cabinet, which I cannot believe is protected all these years later by the Official Secrets Act. If it is, I will nevertheless take the risk of whatever strictures may come my way, for it is too good never to be disclosed. The Assistant Secretary to the Secretary of the War Cabinet was at that time T.L. Rowan as I knew him before he became Sir Leslie Rowan. When I first went up to Cambridge he was a hockey 'Blue', and we met as fellow members of the Hawks Club. Now although code names for offensive operations were devised by the military staff and approved by Churchill in his capacity as Minister of Defence, anything or any weapon which involved the safety of the Realm was a matter for the Home Office, or Ministry of Home Security as it was called at that time. Someone decided that the V2, the long range rocket which, privately, all those in the know positively dreaded and which the RAF so gallantly by their bombing put back for two years, should be given the code name of 'Big Ben'.

On this particular day, as Leslie Rowan told it, Churchill came to the War Cabinet meeting in a foul temper, and rounded on the little bespectacled Herbert Morrison with the words — 'Pray inform me, Mr Secretary, who it was who thought fit to give to this foul and odious weapon the name of the clock whose chimes ring out across the Empire?' Tension was quickly relieved when Ernest Bevin shifted his huge bulk in his chair and said 'Quite agree, Prime Minister — should have called it "Big Bugger".'

General Sir Harold Alexander

Imperial War Museum

One of my American counterparts once said to me, 'We like your General Alexander, he's a real English gentleman, but this guy Monty — goddam it, he's too much like us.' General Alexander left Britain to take over an Army command in Burma on 5 March, 1942. Before that, although officially he was GOC Southern Command based at Salisbury, he was also nominated Commander of what was known alternatively as Force X or Force 110. Whereas General Paget was the designated Commander of a European invasion force, any lesser expedition or major raiding offensive was the responsibility of General Alexander and not of Mountbatten, who had at this time only just taken over at Combined Operations HQ. In February, some bright spark at the War Office thought that this mythical Force X should be brought to life in the form of the First Guards Brigade with the task of recapturing Alderney in the Channel Islands, an extremely hazardous and utterly pointless exercise. As the Guards Brigade was under GHQ Home Forces command, General Paget, when he heard of this scheme instructed us, his planning staff, to find out what was going on. General Alexander equally was interested to know what his mythical Force X was being called upon to do.

So, a few days before Alexander left for Burma, a demonstration and planing exercise was laid on in a vast room in what had previously been the Northumberland Hotel and was now an annexe of the War Office. There we found a huge model of the island made of papier mache, laboriously built up from aerial reconnaissance photographs, with every house and every little cottage most realistically constructed, and the greens and the browns of the island's colours accurately representing the view of an aircraft flying overhead. The Brigade Commander was a little Welsh Guards Officer, whose name escapes me and which in any event is best forgotten. As we gathered round marvelling at this miraculous exhibition of a model maker's art, there entered General Alexander himself. 'Good morning, gentlemen; now Buggins-Snooks (or whatever his name was), tell me what your plan is.' The Brigade Commander then went to the model and detailed the deployment of his assaulting force on first one little beach and then another and then another, and so on round most of the island. Alexander listened intently without interrupting. To even the simplest soul among us, the plan, to say the least, appeared to be a passport to disaster. Alexander then said, 'You must forgive me, but I'm not at my best this morning and I do want to make sure I've taken it all in. Do you mind if I check back to see if I have got it right.' Then he went through the whole plan in the same order. 'Now take this beach. You did not say that you would put in two companies initially, following up with another two companies,' (which in fact was exactly what he had said) 'but as I understood it you preferred a stronger thrust with three companies, with one company immediately in reserve.' (which was what he had not said). And so he went round the island, pretending that he had misunderstood the absurdities and remodelling the whole thing to turn it into something sensible and viable. The Brigade Commander could have been publicly criticized, he could have been made to look a fool, but Alexander was able to deal with a potentially embarrassing situation without a moment's hesitation, with a complete grasp of every tactical detail and to leave the Brigade Commander with the comforting thought that he and the General really thought alike, and that the amendments were as much his as they were the General's. It was a superb performance on Alexander's part. It was only a minor incident, and a small occasion in a vast panorama of war, but it marked him out in my experience as one of the great men.

However not even the hand of genius could make the planned operation worthy of any serious consideration. We were able to forget about it, but the nightmare lived on and the sorely tried and overworked Alan Brooke was still resisting this madcap scheme right up to the end of May 1942, as his diary indicates. Mercifully, he was ultimately successful in his resistance, and the plan was quietly dropped. This was largely due to the substitution by Combined Operations HQ and the Canadians of the disastrous raid on Dieppe.

General George Marshall was the first of the top American Army Chiefs whom I was privileged to meet. It would have been on a day in the second week of April 1942. We in the planning section were initially prejudiced against him because of the Marshall Memorandum which we regarded as ridiculous, and when it was made known to us that a meeting had been arranged between the British Chiefs of Staff and the Combined Commanders and General Marshall and I think Colonel Wedemeyer for the purpose of studying the work which had been done, we were prepared for the worst. As far as I recall it, the presentation of the plans took place in the same large room at the Northumberland Avenue annexe where the Alderney plan had been examined. Brigadier McNab outlined the pros and cons of the various areas, using large-scale maps of the different salients under consideration, which, in deference to General Marshall's own expressed preference, included the area between Dieppe and Le Havre, which we had not seriously considered.

The summaries were excellently delivered and easily assimilated. After a short pause General Marshall went up to the maps and said in his slow, softly-spoken Virginian drawl — 'I say there', and put his finger, not, as we expected, on his own and Eisenhower's original choice, but on the Normandy beaches. No doubt he was privately not conceding an inch, but was wise enough to realize that if the British were to be persuaded to go along with offensive action later in the year, they had better be humoured by an expression of preference for their own choice for a major assault, so as to give the impression that the Americans would go along with British thinking. He certainly was all for encouraging America's new allies to be more vigorous in their approach. Moreover, he understood that the Normandy beaches was our preference for a full-scale invasion, and that if the American pressure for a limited 'Sledgehammer' operation in 1942 was still a possible option, the preference for the Normandy beaches in 1943 was an irrelevant consideration. The requirements for a limited bridgehead assault were quite different. Cherbourg and the Cotentin peninsula would then assume top priority in American eyes. The British Chiefs of Staff would no doubt continue to press for the Pas de Calais if a 'Sledgehammer' operation was forced upon them. But neither of these were realistic possibilities for a major offensive. From that moment Marshall was no longer the ogre, but a hero. I doubt if there was ever any official minute or record of this incident. We were greatly heartened to have General Marshall's agreement and support, and if our planning section had continued to be in active existence right up to March 1943, when COSSAC took over, a lot of further work could have been avoided, and there would have been no misunderstanding of the original planning conclusions such as there was on the part of Lieutenant-General Morgan and his staff.

I never met General Marshall again, but that first impression of his ability gained at that meeting was enhanced by his later involvement in the strategy for the liberation of Europe. Whereas when he returned to Washington he was still far too optimistic as to the ability of American troops to face the Germans and of the possibility of a major offensive in the Spring of 1943, he developed a firm grasp of realities and appreciated early on that any idea of an unprepared, inadequately mounted and supplied assault in 1942 was suicidal, and would only have gone along with it if President Roosevelt had ordered it in order to honour his rash and foolish promise to Molotov and Stalin. Mercifully he was not called upon to do so, and was able to devote his energies to the build up in England of a massive force of men, armaments and equipment, and to prise out of Admiral King's clutches a substantial fleet of assault craft and ships. And then, after the successful conclusion of the war, he used his great gifts and powers of organization to lead the programme for aid and recovery in devastated Europe. He never achieved his most cherished ambition, which was to be the Supreme Allied Commander in the field, in which capacity there is no doubt that he would have been a conspicuous success. He had all the necessary resources for his particular style which depended on the sheer weight and volume of the forces at his disposal. His greatest fault was a total inability to appreciate the value of the strategy of peripheral pressure, as favoured by the British.

Major General Dwight Eisenhower

Imperial War Museum

General Eisenhower, on the other hand, was a great disappointment as a strategist and military commander, partly no doubt because he was totally lacking in experience of command of troops in conditions of war. However, with hindsight it must be true that he was the right man for the job of Supreme Allied Commander, even though few of us thought so at the time. The job as it turned out called for gifts of diplomacy and political expertise rather than the art of making war. It involved the ability to recognize the advantages or the weaknesses of the views put forward by those who were far more experienced than he in the exercise of military command. In much the same way, in the profession of the law the best judge may well not be the man most learned in the law, but the one who can detect and reject the spurious and act upon the assistance given by the advocate who knows what he is talking about, and can produce the right answer.

Everyone who had any dealings with Eisenhower spoke of his charm of personality. This was undoubtedly his greatest asset. It was impossible to dislike the man. When I first met him, prepared as I was to be extremely critical of him as the actual author of the original Marshall Memorandum, I was completely disarmed by the infectious grin spreading over his round and cheerful countenance, and the hand out-stretched to the mere Major who was introduced to him as one of the British planners working on the logistics of an European invasion.

Eisenhower first came to England on 26 May, 1942, and stayed until 3 June. He had been sent over with General Arnold, the Chief of the US Air Force, by General Marshall in order to make a more detailed study of the state of progress of a planned invasion of Europe. He was by now a Major-General, but not yet appointed as Commanding General of ETOUSA. One of his first tasks was to examine the way in which 'Bolero' was working, and to see if there could be a speeding-up of the arrival of the American forces. Although the ultimate responsibility for the allocation of accommodation was vested in the Directorate of Quartering at the War Office, the one officer who had the power of saying whether this area or that area might be required for British and Canadian troops and which area could in consequence by allotted to Americans was Major General Humfrey Gale, the Major-General in Charge of Administration at GHQ Home Forces. I suppose because I had been his personal choice to join the planning staff, he thought it a good idea for his young Major to be in attendance when he and Major-General Eisenhower discussed the quartering arrangements for the US troops. This was how I came to be introduced to this new rising star in the US Army hierarchy. Now to be really cynical, it must be said that both of them in other and more humble walks of life would have made a success of being a door-to-door salesman. Each possessed the gift of 'charming a bird off a tree', whether the bird in question was worth the effort or not. Each must have recognized the counterpart in the other, and they took to each other at once. In consequence it was no surprise to me that, when General Eisenhower was put in command of Allied Force Headquarters, Humfrey Gale became his Chief Administrative Officer. Then, when Eisenhower set up his Supreme Headquarters Allied Expeditionary Force (SHAEF), Humfrey Gale was personally selected by him to be his Chief Administrative Officer and promoted to the rank of Lieutenant-General. He was the only senior British officer to be so individually selected. Air Chief Marshal Tedder was appointed by agreement between Roosevelt and Churchill to be Deputy Commander to Eisenhower.

Montgomery thought nothing of Humfrey Gale, could be studiously offensive to him, and on one occasion made it a condition that a joint meeting of SHAEF top officers and British and American top officers could only take place if Humfrey Gale was not present and his own Chief Administrative Officer, Major-General Miles Graham was. This attitude, although partly dictated by his belief that the only officers with ability were those selected by him, was also born of the mistaken belief that Gale was largely responsible for persuading Eisenhower to reject Montgomery's proposal to permit a drive after the breakout from Normandy at the end of August 1944 right up to the Rhine by a limited British force, supported administratively by all the combined Allied resources in supply and transport. In fact, as I know, for I had to carry out a staff study which demonstrated that Montgomery's plan was logistically feasible, it was Miles Graham and his own Chief of Staff, Major-General Francis ('Freddie') de Guingand who were unwilling to support him. For my own part I could never understand how Miles Graham earned Montgomery's esteem and de Guingand's admiration. On the other hand, de Guingand was a superlative and magnificent Chief of Staff to Montgomery, and one of the big blots on Montgomery's record was the shameful way he let de Guingand leave his Headquarters at the end of May 1945, when he had worn himself out and brought himself to the verge of physical and mental breakdown in the service of his Commander-in-Chief. Instead of losing his job to another, he should have been given a long period of leave and brought back to join his Commander-in-Chief in the enjoyment of the fruits of victory. That this was not done was extraordinary and not a bit typical, because as a rule Montgomery was completely supportive of his own staff.

In the course of Eisenhower's first visit to England his main task was to assess the progress in preparation for an invasion of Europe. It must have been quickly apparent to him that Churchill had by now, as a result of our briefing of the Combined Commanders for the meeting of 15 May, been diverted from thoughts of any form of invasion of Europe for the time being. Eisenhower would not have known, for he never met him during his visit, that Churchill was already thinking of some other place for offensive action. Norway came back into his reckoning, and when the British Chiefs of Staff headed him off that, North Africa later took its place.

At the end of his visit Eisenhower reported back that the preparations for an invasion of Europe in 1943 were woefully inadequate and that the British had no sense of purpose in that regard. In fact the month of June 1942 saw the relationship between the British and Americans strained and stretched almost to breaking-point. It was only the personal friendship between them and the admiration each felt for the other that enabled Churchill and Roosevelt to overcome the mutual suspicion which existed between the British and American Service Chiefs, to build upon the shaking foundations of the Allied war effort and to create the beginnings of a firm and lasting edifice.

Eisenhower, still a Major-General, first met Winston Churchill at a dinner party in the White House during the visit of the British to Washington in June 1942. He came back to London on 14 June as a Lieutenant-General (three stars) to take over as Commanding General, ETOUSA. We were given to understand that this meant that he was designated as the Commanding General of an American force in the event of offensive action. As such he was, of course, the American member of the Combined Commanders, attending their meetings whenever he was in England, and reporting back to General Marshall at frequent intervals. As each succeeding week went by, the prospect of launching a cross-Channel invasion, however limited in scope, became more and more remote. On 24 July, Churchill and Roosevelt agreed that there would be no operation across the Channel in the year 1942, and that the Allied war effort would be directed towards an invasion of North Africa in the late Autumn. This in turn meant that an invasion of Europe in 1943 would not be possible. In consequence our planning was put into cold storage, and some of us were transferred to the planning and execution of Operation 'Torch', as it became known. Fortunately Eisenhower was given the job of Supreme Commander for that operation, and so he was no longer a carping critic in our midst.

Although the Allied resources were now fully committed to the North African venture, General George Marshall and, to begin with, Lieutenant-General Eisenhower both regarded this as no more than a side-show, and were determined that as soon as was practicable a major Allied invasion of Europe would take place. Neither the set-up of the Combined Commanders nor the GHQ planning staff was wound up. Brigadier McNab went off to join the British First Army, and later was killed in action in North Africa. Major-General Neville Brownjohn was put in as a sort of caretaker head of the planners who were left behind. The Combined Commanders continued to meet sporadically. Their last meeting was on 1 March 1943, and their task and the work already done by our planning staff was handed over to the Headquarters of Chief of Staff Supreme Allied Commander (COSSAC) at the end of that month. I personally rejoined the planners about a week later after a temporary change of scene, not in North Africa, but in Kent. The Winter was spent as a staff officer on the Headquarters of the 53rd (Welsh) Division.

It was in the month of November 1942, during this period, that I first made contact with Montgomery, although only in indirect fashion. He had already left South Eastern Command some months earlier to take over command of the Eighth Army, but when I joined HQ 53rd (Welsh) Division I had to deal with confidential matters concerning officers, and in that capacity I inherited some of the sequels of his purges of those officers whom he regarded as inefficient and ripe for sacking. He was particularly severe on Territorial Army officers who had by seniority and not by merit become Lieutenant-Colonels in command of infantry battalions. If an officer received an adverse report he was entitled to appeal to the Army Council. One such officer did just that, and complained that the General had only seen him for two minutes in the officers' mess. When this appeal was passed to him for his comments, Montgomery wrote — 'Quite right. This was sufficient.' This was a good illustration of his manner — a terse comment, delivered in staccato, short sentences with supreme confidence in his own judgement. The maddening thing about the little man was that he was nearly always right.

Lieut. General Bernard Montgomery

Imperial War Museum

In South Eastern Army, as he called the Command, Montgomery, in accordance with his oft expressed views, saw his primary task as that of building up morale. Some of his ideas were hugely unpopular. Officers, for example, did not take kindly to the need to go for a short cross-country run before breakfast. To the other ranks he was merely the cause of a frantic whitewashing, painting and cleaning-up exercise, so that on inspection he would have no cause for complaint at the state of their accommodation. It is interesting to speculate whether, if fate had not intervened with the death in accident of General

Gott, the original choice to take over as Commander-in-Chief of the Eighth Army, Montgomery would have advanced beyond the command of the First Army in the invasion of North Africa. His method and his style depended for their acceptance and approval upon a prior demonstration of success in battle. After Alamein, for which he prepared with an insistence on numerical superiority and near-certainty of victory, his Staff officers would work themselves to the bone, confident that faith and trust were mutual, and the troops responded to his personal visits with the knowledge that the cocky little fellow had said he would win and had done so. Morale requires a confidence in a leader which has been demonstrated to be justifiable.

Those of us who served under him and with him — all ranks, high and low — were intensely loyal to him, valuing his clear-sightedness, his infectious self-confidence, and above all his ability, to use his own words, 'to deliver the goods'. We were prepared to overlook his vanity and his terseness, which could verge on downright rudeness, all of which made him intensely disliked by those whose paths he crossed. In the end, given the opportunity as he was to lead victorious armies in different theatres of war, he emerged and remains in history as a great man and a first-class, cautious commander who would never take unnecessary risks and never rashly sacrifice the life of one single man.

5

THE FIRST ALLIED ENDEAVOUR

In order to understand how the first joint Allied operation ('Torch', the landing in North Africa) came about, it is necessary to recapitulate on some of the ups and downs of the British and American relationship in the late spring and early summer of 1942. The Americans arrived in London on 5 April, 1942, with the Marshall Memorandum. This, as has already been described, was no more than a pipe-dream of colossal proportions, produced in a mood of totally unjustifiable self-confidence. General Marshall, first on his own with the British Chiefs of Staff, and then jointly with Harry Hopkins at a meeting of the Defence Committee on the night of 14.15 April, produced and argued for his plan. An initial response was prepared in outline by the War Office Joint Planning Staff, which pointed out the general and basic problems involved in any cross-Channel operation. This was handed to General Marshall before the midnight meeting of the Defence Committee.

By the end of this momentous meeting the Americans were assured that their proposals for offensive action in Europe, possibly in 1942 and more certainly in 1943, were accepted in principle. The enormous difficulties involved were indicated by General Sir Alan Brooke, who also argued for American assistance in the Middle East and the Indian Ocean. Hopkins and Churchill were both euphoric about a 'noble brotherhood of arms'. Moreover, the optimistic General Marshall read more into what was only an agreement in principle, and ought to have realized from the discussions which had already taken place that the British would produce a number of firmly-based critical observations. It was however understood and agreed that there must be an immediate introduction of US troops and equipment in Britain. This operation was given the code name 'Bolero' and, for their part, the Americans pursued it vigorously and with success. It was further agreed that plans for an invasion of Europe should be undertaken by the British in conjunction with the Americans. In the event, no participation by US officers took place for many many weeks, and of course the British GHQ Planning team had been hard at work for two months, and were already in a position to come up with some devastating conclusions. We were told by General Paget that he and the other two Combined Commanders required an updated analysis dealing with the implications of the Marshall plan for presentation by them to the British Chiefs of Staff.

Thus it was that on 8 may the Chiefs of Staff received the joint report of the GHQ Planning Staff and Combined Operations HQ that, with the shipping available no more than 4,000 troops could be landed at one time. In the circumstances any operation, however restricted in scope, was quite out of the question. At this time, the Chiefs of Staff were beset with far greater problems than dealing politely but firmly with ill-conceived and fantastic notions of an invasion or even limited attack on the enemy in France. Quite apart from the troubles in the Middle East, in Burma and the Indian Ocean, the Naval Chiefs were now burdened, as the result of political pressure by the Russians, with the provision of arms and equipment by sea to the Arctic port of Murmansk. From the end of April to the beginning of June, the escorted convoys of merchant ships ploughed on in the face of sustained enemy attack by sea and air in the course of which staggering losses of men, ships and the material which they carried were suffered. For all this sacrificial endeavour, no word of appreciation came from the brutal, surly and self-centred Stalin. He and Molotov were only interested in the opening-up of a Second Front.

On 13 May the British Chiefs of Staff were able to bury the stupid plan for an attack on Alderney. In its place, Combined Operations HQ through Mountbatten produced a suggestion for a large raid on Dieppe, partly to force the Germans to commit their French-based aircraft to battle, which would help the Russians a bit, and partly to experiment with the new techniques for landing on open beaches which had been practised on the sands of the West Coast of Scotland. This was of small concern to the Americans, who were only just beginning to learn of the hazards to be overcome through the necessity of assaulting the Japanese enemy on the sandy beaches of the atolls and islands of the Pacific Ocean.

In view of the statistical information we had provided for the Combined Commanders, they and General Sir Alan Brooke declined to be associated with any plans for an attack on Dieppe, which was so obviously a hare-brained scheme. Even after years of meticulous research, no historian seems to have unearthed any reliable evidence as to who gave Mountbatten the go-ahead. It was probably Churchill, who was being egged on by the Labour Party members of the War Cabinet to do something to satisfy the public cries for a Second Front. As neither Brooke nor Paget would assign any British troops, and as the Canadians stationed in England were getting very restless and thirsting for action, Mountbatten was able to enlist the support of General MacNaughton, who provided a force of some 5,000 Canadians. In the event, the operation turned out to be an unmitigated disaster.

There was a meeting of the British Combined Commanders on 15 May. In view of the complete acceptance of the report to the Chiefs of Staff by the Committee, and by General Sir Alan Brooke in particular, which had been tendered a week earlier, the Commanders were confident that there would be no likelihood of a 'Sledgehammer' operation in 1942. Of course, they were not to foresee the actions of President Roosevelt in this regard. However, the Combined Commanders being their employers, the GHQ Planning Staff found themselves no longer under any pressure. General Paget indicated that they were now to be concerned only to revise and update the plans for 'Round Up' in 1943. Nor did he require the Planning Staff to be housed any longer in Storey's Gate in close proximity to the War Rooms, and by the end of May there was a move just across the road to a house in Queen Anne's Gate, which in peacetime had been the lovely and luxurious home of the Marquis of Bute. Brigadier McNab relinquished his appointment and his acting rank, and went off to command a battalion of his Highland regiment. Brigadier Buckle moved to a Corps Headquarters and was replaced by Brigadier Dick Ritchie. For some weeks there was no head of staff, and it was in the late summer that Major-General Neville Brownjohn took on the overall control of GHQ

Plans.

At this time, although it was not the direct concern of the Planning Staff, we learnt that Combined Operations HQ had raised with the Prime Minister the notion of an artificial harbour at sea water edge to help with landings over the beaches. This notion was in fact the 'baby' of Captain Hughes-Hallett of the Royal Navy. Then on 30 May, Churchill sent his famous memorandum to Mountbatten or his deputy. This read, 'Piers for use on Beaches'. To CCO or deputy. 'They must float up and down with the tide. The anchor problem must be mastered. Let me have the best solution worked out. Don't argue the matter. The difficulties will argue for themselves.' It soon became obvious to those who studied the question that something far in advance of piers was required. In the end, two years later, a huge and immensely complicated structure was devised, built in sections, and then, three days after the landings on 6 June, 1944, towed across the Channel and constructed into an artificial harbour bigger than the port of Dover. The designing in detail of such a mammoth enterprise was far beyond the resources or the expertise of Combined Operations HQ so it was transferred and became the responsibility of the Royal Navy. At the outset of the war the Admiralty had taken over not only the largest hotel in Bath but also the buildings of Kingswood School at the top of Lansdown Hill, and it was there that the Naval and civilian structional engineers designed the artificial harbour, which was given the code name of 'Mulberry'. The code name was taken from the large mulberry tree which grew in the grounds at the front of the school. This marvellous project, without which a successful maintenance and buildup of the British and Canadian forces could never have been achieved, was entirely British in conception, design, manufacture and operation. The American people seem to have been quite unaware of this.

After the Americans left for Washington on 17 April, reading too much into the agreement in principle, and despite General Marshall's private scepticism of British intentions, they must on their arrival back have painted too rosy a picture and given President Roosevelt the impression that the British were willing to undertake offensive operations later in the year. Although the British Chiefs of Staff and the Combined Commanders believed that it was understood that a 'Sledgehammer' operation was out of the question, Roosevelt when he saw Molotov promised action during the course of the next month or so. On 31 May, he sent a message to Churchill to the effect that he had promised the Russians that there would be a landing in France before the end of August. This message crossed with one from Churchill telling Roosevelt that Mountbatten was on his way to Washington. The purpose of this visit was to explain why an operation of the 'Sledgehammer' type would not be possible in 1942. Churchill also indicated a preference for an attack on Northern Norway. So effective was Mountbatten's argument that General Marshall and the American heads of staff were convinced that the British had no intention of acting in 1943 either. This belief was supported by the report from Lieutenant-General Eisenhower, who had taken over his command of ETOUSA on 26 May, that 'it is necessary to get a punch behind the job or we'll never be ready for spring 1943 to attack.'

Churchill, whose heart was never really in a cross-Channel attack at this stage, was also facing pressure in London, not only from Molotov but also from the Labour Party members of the Cabinet to open a 'Second Front now'. At a meeting of the British Chiefs of Staff on 5 June, it was again concluded that any form of offensive operation in the summer of 1942 was out of the question. On reporting to Churchill, he agreed. A day or two later, he in turn persuaded the War Cabinet that the answer to those who urged the opening of a Second Front to help Russia was that there could be no landing in France until the Germans suffered a further setback in Russia. The British effort in Europe was to be concentrated on the bombing of German towns by the RAF which was steadily increasing in weight and ferocity.

The receipt of Roosevelt's telegram with his promise to Molotov, must have shaken Churchill. It meant that Mountbatten's visit would only produce a conflict of views with those of Roosevelt and his Chiefs of Staff. The decisions that Churchill had been forced to take on the advice of the British Chiefs of Staff about the abandonment of 'Sledgehammer' in 1942 were in complete contradiction of the impression given to Harry Hopkins and General Marshall at the midnight Defence Committee meeting a fortnight earlier. The Americans were dismayed at Mountbatten's report, and understandably thought that, whereas they were honouring their part of the Allied agreement by sending vast quantities of men and equipment under operation 'Bolero', the British were reneging on their part. Thus the euphoria of a 'Noble brotherhood of arms' had rapidly vanished in an atmosphere of mutual suspicion and distrust. Within a few weeks of its successful launch the alliance was in grave danger of total disruption.

Churchill rightly felt impelled to go himself to see President Roosevelt, and to take his Army Chief Brooke so that both could explain the problems. The trip was made by Boeing Air Clipper the night of 17 June on the short haul from Scotland to a touchdown in Newfoundland and thence on to Washington. When Secretary for War Stimson and General Marshall learnt of the visit they believed that Churchill intended to try and talk Roosevelt out of a cross-Channel invasion altogether, and get his agreement to some other operation like Norway or possibly North Africa, a policy which Stimson described as a 'diversionary debauch'. They were desperately worried about what Roosevelt and Churchill might get up to if left alone, and so also for their part were Sir John Dill and Sir Alan Brooke. In the event, neither of the two great leaders was foolish enough to disregard the advice of their respective advisers who, after meeting with each other, each prepared to criticise the other's point of view, ultimately not only got to know and to like and to respect his opposite number, but to hammer out a joint Allied strategy. In retrospect, this meeting was of critical importance; it not only cleared the air but enabled the two nations to work out a harmonious system of planning and operational control for every subsequent endeavour. Nevertheless, once again each side failed to make sufficient allowance for the other's point of view, and misunderstood what precisely was the measure of agreement. The British thought that 'Sledgehammer' had been given a decent burial; the Americans thought it was still a possibility which the British had not abandoned altogether, and they certainly believed that there was a firm commitment for the spring of 1943.

In June and early July the British were inevitably having to concentrate all their thoughts and energies on the disastrous events in the Middle East. Rommel was driving back the Eighth Army and sweeping on to Alexandria and Cairo. But he outran his supply links and, in the face of a last-ditch but determined stand, ground to a halt some sixty miles short of Alexandria. By 11 July the panic was over. Churchill, true to form, now bounced back with further optimistic proposals. He resurrected yet again the idea of an invasion of Northern Norway. Any such operation was strictly speaking within the province of the Combined Commanders and GHQ Planning Staff. To the great relief of General Paget, who had bitter memories of the abortive expedition in April 1940, General Sir Alan Brooke persuaded Churchill to hand over the planning for this proposed venture to General McNaughton and the Canadian Army. So we at GHQ Plans were spared examination of this thankless task.

Some three of four weeks before this, the first American officers were attached to GHQ Plans. Colonel Archie Hamblen and Colonel Schwartz arrived at the planners' offices in Queen Anne's Gate one day, and in the morning were fully and carefully briefed about all that was involved and what staff studies had been undertaken. In the afternoon they were provided with our files. Even though the pressure had been lifted, the British planners worked right through from nine in the morning until seven in the evening with an hour off for lunch. It was therefore something of a surprise when at five o'clock there was a knock on my door, and two far senior and much older gentlemen rather sheepishly asked the young British Major if they could go now. One had to treat the request with dignity, and avoid any air of superiority. This was, however, a good example of how modest were the American officers of middle rank. I have no knowledge of where Colonel Schwartz fetched up, but Colonel Hamblen became a much valued and respected Brigadier-General on the staff of Allied Force Headquarters in Algiers. But then of course he had had a good training!

By the middle of July, Secretary Stimson and General Marshall had become even more anxious and more critical of the British. Reference to some of the American records and diaries reveals that the Alliance was now in even greater danger than it had been a few weeks earlier. General Marshall, who had begun to form a good opinion of General Sir Alan Brooke when they met and discussed strategy in Washington in June, now started to wonder if he might not be two-faced, saying one thing to the Americans yet not intending to carry out his promises. With reference to a telegram from London which indicated that the British War Cabinet were seeking to revive

'Gymnast' (the North Africa project) to the exclusion of attack in France, Stimson, in his diary for 10 July 1942, remarked that Marshall was 'tired of these constant decisions which do not stay made — and he proposed a showdown which I cordially endorsed. As the British won't go through with what they agreed to, we will turn our backs on them and take up war with Japan.' Together with Admiral King, these three were all in favour of presenting an ultimatum to Britain that if they would not launch an offensive against the Germans in France within a month or so, then the US would pull out of Europe and concentrate all its efforts against the Japanese in the Pacific. If it had not been for Roosevelt's moderating influence, this unmitigated disaster for the Alliance might well have come about. He agreed that some action against the Germans in 1942 was imperative; that if the British remained obdurate that this was not to be cross-Channel, then it must be somewhere else, such as 'Gymnast' in North Africa. He therefore sent Hopkins, General Marshall and Admiral King to London to present the American case. They arrived on 18 July, 1942, and whereas Hopkins was largely involved with Churchill, General Marshall and Admiral King began discussions with the British Chiefs of Staff on 20 July which, off and on, continued until the afternoon of 22 July.

In addition to the visiting trio, there were several other top American commanders in London at that time, all of whom were called in by General Marshall to advise and give their opinions. There was Lieutenant-General Eisenhower, the Commanding General of ETOUSA, General Spaatz, the Air Force Commander, Admiral Stark, the Navy Commander, and Major-General Mark Clark, who was later to be given command in North Africa. Furthermore there was Major-General Lucien Truscott, who had been attached to Combined Operations Headquarters in late June as the American representative of an integrated staff. Eisenhower, of course, had been and still was a determined protagonist for a cross-Channel attack in 1942. General Truscott had been persuaded, as he openly acknowledged, by some of the members of Mountbatten's headquarters who were as brash and over-optimistic as the Americans themselves, that some such operation was a reasonable proposition. This was irresponsible advice and contrary to Mountbatten's own acceptance of the conclusions of the three Services planners and their Chiefs. It was this confident attitude which led to the decision to entrust the disastrous attack on Dieppe a month or so later to a joint force of Canadians and British, planned and commanded by Combined Operations HQ. Of the 5,000 Canadians who took part, two-thirds became casualties. The Royal Air Force lost one hundred and six aircraft whereas the Luftwaffe lost only forty-eight, but at the time this staggering differential was totally masked by distorted British propaganda. Nevertheless, the enormous casualties suffered by the Canadians and also by the British force could not be disguised, and ought to have had a salutary effect on the American commanders who still hankered after a cross-Channel invasion in 1943 if not in 1942. Moreover, German Army records reveal that in 1942 there were forty-five German Divisions in Europe, and Hitler was actually transferring seven Divisions from the Russian front. None of these matters were available as factors in the discussions which took place towards the end of July, but they were all strongly confirmative of the opinion of the British planners, and accepted by the Chiefs of Staff that any operation in 1942, and particularly a direct assault on a heavily defended port, was suicidal.

Combined Operations Headquarters were taught a bitter lesson by the disaster of Dieppe. Major-General Lucien Truscott also learnt the hard way a few months later. In November 1942 he commanded the American attack on Port Liautey in Morocco. His subsequent criticism of the American planning and assault landing operations in North Africa was much more devastatingly critical than the British were ever prepared to voice. We had our private opinions, which we discreetly kept to ourselves. General Truscott was typical of the better type of American commander. Over-optimistic to begin with, he was big-hearted and fair-minded enough to recognize that the bull at the gate approach of the American commanders and staff was an invitation to failure in an insufficiently-prepared and mounted assault on enemy territory. Time after time in the months and years that followed, the Americans had to learn the hard way. To their everlasting credit, they learnt quickly and rarely failed twice.

Fortified by the opinions of Eisenhower and Truscott, General Marshall argued with persistence for an early attack on the enemy in France, with Cherbourg and the Cotentin peninsula as a first preference. According to those present, Admiral King took little part save to make it clear that he was only interested in fighting the Japs in the Pacific. General Sir Alan Brooke shouldered the main burden of trying to persuade General Marshall that his proposals were quite impractical, and that the British simply could not accept them. Marshall felt keenly that the British had reneged on a firm undertaking, whereas Brooke was pointing out that there had only been an agreement in principle, and that subsequent detailed study had established that it was not a feasible option. By 22 July it became obvious that the British Chiefs of Staff would not budge. In desperation the Americans were even prepared to launch an attack on Cherbourg with their own forces, but recognized that they could not assemble a sufficient force until October. In the end they were thwarted in this endeavour by their own Admiral Stark. In his opinion, an attack on Cherbourg and the Cotentin peninsula was too hazardous for shipping in autumn weather. By the afternoon of 22 July General Marshall had to conceded complete failure. Churchill and the British War Cabinet were informed, and Harry Hopkins cabled Roosevelt. Eisenhower noted in his diary that it was 'the blackest day in history'. The Americans were within an inch of pulling out of Europe and bringing the Alliance to a dismal end.

Mercifully, Roosevelt and Harry Hopkins had recognized that this was the likely result of the discussions; Hopkins had already been favourably disposed to accept Churchill's preference for an assault in North Africa, and Roosevelt had instructed the trio in advance that if 'Sledgehammer' was off, then somewhere else — probably 'Gymnast' — must take its place. Roosevelt had made it so clear to General Marshall that on no account was he to turn his back on Europe that Hopkins merely had to remind Marshall of his Commander-in-Chief's views to bring him to his senses and by 24 July, Hopkins, Marshall and reluctantly, King agreed that operation 'Gymnast' must be the Allied project for the autumn of 1942. Thus was the Alliance saved, and thus was born operation 'Torch', the name which Churchill on that historic day gave to this first joint endeavour on the part of Britain and the United States.

On 25 July, Roosevelt sent a cable to the effect that 'Torch' must take place not later than 30 October. It was agreed by Churchill, the British War Cabinet and Chiefs of Staff on the one side, and by General Marshall for the Americans that there would be a Supreme Commander who was to be American and a Deputy Supreme Commander who was to be British. In addition there was to be a British Task Force Commander for the Oran front and an American Task Force Commander for the Casablanca front, and the staff at Supreme Headquarters was to be an integrated one of British and American officers. General Marshall told Lieutenant-General Eisenhower that he was to be the Allied Supreme Commander and as such a full General. At the time of the memorandum of 24 July, the operation was designated to extend from Casablanca on the Atlantic coast of North Africa which, contrary to British opinion, was included in deference to the insistence of Admirals King and Stark that the Atlantic was essential for naval deployment, and in deference to British naval opinion previously expressed by Admiral Cunningham into the Mediterranean and along the North African coast to Algiers and Oran, and possibly even further east.

The memorandum, agreed as it was, nevertheless did not prevent considerable rumblings of dissent. Eisenhower was perhaps gratified by his new post and promotion, and in later years acknowledged that the British opinion about the impracticability of the 'Sledgehammer' operation was correct. He does not appear to have expressed any doubts or complaints, and indeed threw himself into the welding of a joint Allied headquarters which, continuing into Europe, was his greatest contribution to the successful outcome of the war. General Marshall on his return to the United States was motivated by the fear that 'Torch' would involve the Allies with so much effort, material, men and shipping that his wholehearted preference for an attack across the Channel would get lost and forgotten. He tried therefore with Stimson's support to persuade Roosevelt that 'Torch' would mean the end of 'Round Up' in 1943, and that events in Russia might still compel an intervention against Germany in Europe before the middle of September. However, on 30 July Roosevelt exercised his prerogative as Commander-in-Chief of US Forces, and stated that he decided that 'Torch' was to proceed, and to proceed at the earliest possible date. Whereas Eisenhower, as soon as he was appointed insisted on close co-operation between the British and American staff officers on Allied Headquarters, there was persistent disagreement between the Chiefs of Staff of both nations on the strategic and tactical details of the operation.

In the meantime, General Sir Alan Brooke saw General Paget on 25 July and informed him of the decisions reached the day before. 'Sledgehammer' was definitely off, and this meant that the GHQ Planning Staff could be stood down in so far as operations in Europe in 1942 were concerned. We, the planners, got the message the next day. We had in fact done nothing in detail after the report for the Chiefs of Staff presented on 8 May, which concluded that there was sufficient shipping for no more than a force of 4,000 men. We knew moreover that the Chiefs of Staff had decided that if a 'Sledgehammer' operation was forced upon us, the most suitable place for a limited area attack designed to involve German forces sufficiently to bring some help to the Russians would be the Pas de Calais area. It was only in this very restricted context that the Pas de Calais was given preference, and at a much later period Lieutenant-General Morgan, as Chief of Staff to Supreme Allied Commander (COSSAC), completely misunderstood the attitude of General Paget and the GHQ Planning Staff. This, in a sentence, was that for a large scale invasion the Normandy beaches would have to be the place, but that no such operation could reasonably be mounted before the early summer of 1943.

The hopes of the much-relieved planners, that we might now get some well-earned leave, were not fulfilled. Within a day or two of the decision to mount operation 'Torch' under the supreme command of General Eisenhower, the War Office arranged for Norfolk House, a modern office block in St James's Square, to be at the disposal of Eisenhower, and to provide a Headquarters and facilities for those who were to plan the operation. There had never been a joint Allied headquarters before and the thing just developed in an entirely haphazard fashion. The first, or almost the first, occupants of the place were Major-General Neville Brownjohn and his four Majors from GHQ Plans. To begin with, we just sat about doing nothing. Within a day or two a semblance of organization became apparent. I have no recollection of seeing General Eisenhower about the place. No doubt he was using his ETOUSA headquarters office for the purpose of assembling the senior members of his team. Gradually a motley crowd of officers, Army, Navy and Air Force, both American and British appeared on the scene. There was, however, no sense of purpose and direction. Nor, as far as the British GHQ Planners were concerned, was there anything of value in our previous work for an operation which was totally different in conception.

General Eisenhower obtained Major-General Bedell Smith as his Chief of Staff, and to begin with they were concerned with the establishment of his staff. When 'Torch' was agreed in principle, Churchill had proposed General Alexander as both Deputy Allied Commander and as British Task Force Commander. Brooke wanted him as Task Force Commander. Both these proposals were dropped, as the situation in the Middle East was a much more pressing and immediate problem, and Churchill and Brooke were already planning to fly out to Cairo and sort things out on the spot. There were at least two months before 'Torch' could be launched, and in the meantime it was up to Eisenhower to get things moving. It was however decided that Lieutenant-General Montgomery was to be the Commander of the British Task Force. This decision was changed a few days later when Montgomery was appointed to take command of the Eighth Army in the desert war. Lieutenant General Kenneth Anderson took his place for 'Torch'.

It became obvious very early on that an invasion of North Africa not only presented great difficulties logistically in the conveyance over the seas of a planned force of 300,000 men and their arms and equipment some 1,500 miles from Britain and 3,000 miles from the United States, but also politically. Gibraltar would have to be used as a staging post and assembly point, and if the Spanish, who, though technically neutral, were notoriously pro-German, got wind of the plan all element of surprise would have vanished. Moreover, in Morocco and Algeria, both French colonies, there were substantial forces, now neutral and under the Vichy Government headed by Marshal Petain. Apart from a quarter of a million men, there were five hundred aircraft and in particular a powerful fleet, whose officers were bitterly resentful of the British attack in June 1940 on their warships at Mers-el Kebir in Algeria and Dakar in Morocco. That the Vichy French would resist an invasion was taken for granted, but it was hoped that this would be only half-hearted, particularly if it was an American operation and it was expected that political negotiation would lead to passive resistance if not actual acquiescence. Consequently, although Eisenhower was engaged upon the integration of the members of staff below top level, the command structure of his headquarters became largely American. Not only was his Chief of Staff the American Bedell Smith, but his Deputy was not British as originally intended, but the American Mark Clark. As the major part of the naval forces and the shipping were British, the Navy Commander was first of all Admiral Bertram Ramsay of Dunkirk fame, and then Admiral Sir Andrew Cunningham, who had so distinguished himself in all the naval operations in the Mediterranean. In the event all the forces, Navy, Army and Air Force were commanded separately by Americans for the Atlantic coast landings and by British for the Mediterranean landings, and Eisenhower and Mark Clark controlled the whole operation from headquarters in Gibraltar.

Major General Mark Clark

Imperial War Museum

Major-General Humfrey Gale became the Chief Administrative Officer at Allied Force Headquarters (AFHQ). He was however largely concerned with the logistical planning and build up which was almost entirely an Admiralty, War Office and Ministry of War Transport operation, and spent most of his time in Whitehall rather than Norfolk House. Gale and

Bedell Smith remained in London until well after the landings took place, and indeed neither was at Gibraltar with Eisenhower and Mark Clark, and joined up again after AFHQ was established in Algiers. As it turned out, it was vitally important for Eisenhower to have firm links with Whitehall and the British Foreign Office because of the increasingly political aspect of the whole affair, an area in which Eisenhower was more adept than the purely military side. His strategic control, or lack of it, of the military aspect of the campaign has earned as much criticism as praise has rightly been bestowed on his political and diplomatic handling of quirky and difficult top commanders of the different nations.

There was very little detailed planning on the administrative side at Eisenhower's Headquarters in Norfolk House. This meant that there was no involvement of the GHQ Planning Staff, and within a week or so we were 'put on ice' and, to pursue the metaphor, gradually melted away. One, perhaps two, became part of the British element in Eisenhower's integrated staff. There was an interesting example of how his policy of complete integration worked in practice when I first met Major-General Mark Clark. One day, getting into the lift ('elevator' to the Americans) there was this tall, rangy and much senior officer already in the lift. With outstretched hand he shook mine, and 'Howdy, Major; Clark's the name' was his greeting. It is just possible that the more reserved type of British General might have said 'Good morning' to a young Major, whether he was British or American. Then there was the well authenticated tale of how General Eisenhower felt compelled to give one of his American Staff officers the sack because of an offensive remark. 'But sir,' said the man, 'I only called him a son of a bitch.' 'No,' said Eisenhower, 'you called him a British son of a bitch.'

In the belief that everything was fixed for 'Torch', Churchill and Alan Brooke set off first to Cairo and thence to Moscow to see how the Middle East forces were faring, to restructure the command there, with Alexander as Commander-in-Chief and Montgomery as Commander of the Eighth Army, and then to explain to Stalin what Britain was doing to fight the Germans, and to try and pacify his constant and carping criticism. They left London on 31 July, and returned on 24 August to find that the planning for operation 'Torch' was in a state of chaos, and that there was no agreed strategic purpose or objective.

Notwithstanding Roosevelt's firm instruction to General Marshall and the American Chiefs of Staff that 'Torch' must take place by 30 October, the Americans were still smarting with indignation at the way they believed the British had reneged on a firm agreement on strategy reached on 8 April. They retaliated by interpreting the Combined Chiefs of Staff memorandum which authorized the Allied landings in North Africa as meaning that the United States could concentrate on the Pacific as there was no requirement to build up American forces for invasion of Europe. Sir John Dill reported that the Americans felt that they had been let down, and they showed little interest in 'Torch'. So whatever Eisenhower may have felt and believed, he was becoming more and more isolated from active support by his superiors in Washington. The alliance was beginning to disintegrate yet again. This indecision and grudging acquiescence in Roosevelt's instruction to get on with 'Torch' soon showed itself in a somewhat acrimonious debate as to what 'Torch' was supposed to be and what its purpose was.

When the original 'Gymnast' had been mooted, it envisaged an invasion of Morocco from the Atlantic. But as soon as 'Torch' took its place, British naval opinion, largely expressed by Admiral Cunningham, was that the Casablanca operation would be of little value in the strategic context, whereas seizure of Mediterranean ports such as Oran, Algiers and Bone would be far more helpful in freeing the whole area from German and Italian action on land, sea and air. The Americans were convinced that operations in the Mediterranean were not of great importance in the war against Germany, and that the British preference for this area was prompted by the desire to keep open the seas for access to the dominions of India and Burma and South Africa and the Colonies of Africa and the Far East. The American Chiefs of Staff were not in the least interested in a successful landing in North Africa as a prelude to further exploitation against Italy. They would carry on with 'Torch' because they had been ordered to do so, but it would have to be limited to the Atlantic coast of Morocco.

There was therefore at this time a curious change of role on the part of the Allies. Whereas right up to 24 July the Americans had been enthusiastically pressing for early action against the Germans and the British were those who argued for delay, now it was the British who pressed for early action and the Americans who showed no keenness to launch an offensive. No doubt they were beginning to understand that any amphibious operation launched over vast distances at sea with the objective of landing troops in the face of enemy opposition, even if half-hearted, was nothing like anything they had ever experienced before. Their troops were raw and untried in battle, and there was the disaster of Dieppe to remind them how easy it was to court disaster. On the other hand the British had learnt by experience that a well-prepared expedition amply protected by superior naval forces and with air superiority was likely to succeed. Indeed, Admiral Cunningham even advocated a direct assault on Bizerta in Tunisia, hundreds of miles further east than Algiers.

As soon as Churchill got back from Moscow and learnt of this indecision and disagreement, he cabled Roosevelt with a proposal that the landings should take place on 14 October, a fortnight earlier than Roosevelt had originally ordered. This was in contradiction to the messages which the British Chiefs of Staff, in order to pacify and help the Americans had sent, suggesting that the operation might be postponed until a date in November. The Americans were entirely unco-operative and wished to alter the whole project and to go back to the very first idea, which was to establish a base at Casablanca, and to cut out all the Mediterranean objectives altogether. Eisenhower now joined with Churchill and the British Chiefs of Staff in urging the adoption of the plan which had been agreed at the end of the discussions between 22 and 24 July. There was not much else that Eisenhower could do, for, after all, he had been appointed Supreme Commander for just that purpose. It may well have been Eisenhower's insistence, being General Marshall's 'favourite son', that led the Americans to abandon their opposition to the Mediterranean aspect. The British Chiefs of Staff had all the best arguments on their side, and were able to point out that an Atlantic coast landing was far more hazardous than attacks on the ports of Algeria. Indeed, when Churchill some months later saw the size of the rollers sweeping in from the Atlantic on to the sandy beaches he marvelled how any troops could land at all. In fact the experts correctly advised that the ocean was relatively calm about one day in four. Churchill put forward to Roosevelt a counter-suggestion that the Casablanca attack should be abandoned in favour of an all-out combined attack on the Algerian ports in the Mediterranean.

For the first few days of September this battle of the plans was waged by cablegrams across the Atlantic. The dispute was resolved on 5 September, when a cable arrived from Roosevelt agreeing to a compromise previously suggested by General Sir Alan Brooke. This was that the assault on Casablanca would be reduced in size so as to release sufficient landing craft to enable 10,000 British and American troops to be landed at Algiers, and for the British to drop the idea of going for Bone as well as Oran and Algiers.

At Norfolk House, none of the officers who were assembling there were told any of the details of the acute disagreement between the Allied chiefs, but we knew that there was a lot of trouble and that there might not be any British expedition, wherever its precise destination was to be. Then we learnt that operation 'Torch' was on, and involved British participation in landings in North Africa. It was, however, impressed on those of us who had acquired this much knowledge that the whole operation was to be planned with the utmost secrecy, and that the slightest of leaks could easily jeopardize everything. There was the further source of great anxiety, as we learnt later, that the use of Gibraltar as a staging post, particularly for the assembly of boxed aircraft, might indicate to Spanish and German spies that something big was afoot. Moreover, the Germans might persuade the Spanish to interfere with the use of Gibraltar. In the event, none of these fears were realized.

By the middle of September the planning of this vast Allied enterprise was in full swing. There was not much to do at Norfolk House on the administrative (logistics) side. The logistical aspect was under the supervision of Major-General Humfrey Gale as the newly appointed Chief Administrative Officer, but in detail was the responsibility of the Admiralty and the War Office. There had however to be a small section at Allied Force Headquarters (AFHQ), consisting of both British and United States officers. One of the American members was Colonel Archie Hamblen, not yet a Brigadier-General, but as modest, self-effacing and charming as he had been when we first met. There was room for only one member of our GHQ Planning Staff, and Major George Hodnett, who was later promoted to Lieutenant-Colonel, was the one who was selected. He took the instruction as to complete secrecy so seriously that, although he worked in a room next to mine and we travelled together every day to and from our billets at Latimer Court, Hammersmith, he insisted that I must not speak to him at all about the operation. I never did. But Colonel Archie Hamblen was a little more realistic, and would from time to time chat to me about specific problems. Moreover the 'top brass' must have thought that I was a good security risk, because a month or so later I was sent off with Brigadier Head (later to be Minister of Defence and a Viscount) from Combined Operations HQ to instruct the British Army Corps and Divisional Commanders in the logistic problems of an advance from Oran and Algiers to Bone and Bizerta. As a mere Major I felt highly embarrassed, but they took it all in good part and seemed to be interested in what I had to say.

This was another illustration of the fundamental differences between the British and the Americans. A British Major-General (two stars) or Lieutenant-General (three stars) would listen courteously to what a junior officer had to say. I doubt if any American of corresponding rank at the early stages of their entry into the war would have thought that they could be told anything by anyone, let alone a junior officer. The opportunity to attempt the impossible was never given to me. By now all contact with my American counterparts had come to an end, and as soon as Operation 'Torch' was launched it was decided that I had better spend the next three or four months at a more down-to-earth headquarters, and so this period was spent in the entirely British context of the 53rd (Welsh) Division. There were no American officers there to work with, and curiously no Welshmen either. The Divisional Headquarters was commanded by an Ulsterman, and the rest of the Staff were either English or Scots.

6

SUCCESS AND FAILURE IN THE ALLIED ENDEAVOUR

Operation 'Torch' was a compromise which, under American pressure, was a retreat from the original British proposal to attack as far east as Bone and as near as possible to Bizerta in order to get a foothold in Tunisia, and to deny to the enemy the use of that country as a base. The British hoped that General Montgomery's Eighth Army would be able to drive Rommel's Afrika Korps and the Italians back into a trap, with the British First Army blocking his retreat by advancing to meet the Eighth Army in Tripoli. The whole of the North African Mediterranean seaboard would then be in Allied hands.

Although in the short term the operation was a resounding success, like most compromises the plan failed in its major objective. The battle of Alamein began on 23 October, and ended with victory on 5 November. The convoys for 'Torch' were then at sea and nearing their destinations. On 8 November the Allied troops landed at Oran and Algiers. The Germans did not begin substantially to build up their forces and in particular to develop airfields in Tunisia until the middle of December. Over a month had gone by since the landings, and yet the Germans were not finally kicked out of Tunisia until the middle of May 1943. In the meantime they had built up strong forces and turned Tunisia into a stronghold from which only bitter and prolonged fighting led to their ultimate dislodgement and defeat. This six months' delay had a profound effect on Allied plans for an invasion of Europe in 1943.

What went wrong? The eastern limb of the pincer movement began with success at Alamein. There was thereafter a failure of the Eighth Army to cut off Rommel's retreat and to annihilate his forces. This was largely due to long periods of heavy and incessant rain which completely bogged down the British armour and support transport, both along the coastal route and an inward sweep round through the desert. General Montgomery was reporting regularly to General Sir Alan Brooke that not only was he bogged down but that he was faced with administrative problems. His forward troops were some six or seven hundred miles ahead of their main base, and the arrangements for supply were not sufficient to keep up with such a speedy and lengthy advance. Nevertheless the Eighth Army did make a stage by stage move forward, forcing Rommel back on to his defence lines at El Agheila by the middle of December. Tripoli was captured on 23 January 1943. These British forces had done as much as could reasonably have been expected of them. The real disappointment was the failure of the Allied forces to get into and to occupy Tunisia. For this there were three reasons, all of which point to the Americans as the most involved.

The main reason why the concept of a sweeping advance into Tunisia was not realized was the inexcusable delay throughout the whole of the month of August in implementing Roosevelt's instruction that Operation 'Torch' must be mounted and launched before 30 October. For this delay, as has already been described, the Americans were entirely responsible. Once the final firm decision was made on 5 September, it took two months to prepare and launch this colossal expedition. If the landings had been at the beginning of or even in the middle of October, there would have been at least three weeks more in which to mount a drive eastwards. On the other hand in mitigation, the delay in fact introduced the welcome bonus politically of the accidental presence of Admiral Darlan, Petain's deputy, in Algeria at the actual time of the invasion. The next reason was the rejection of Admiral Cunningham's experienced advice that there should be a landing as far east as Bone. He knew the Mediterranean area better than anyone, and had been consistently successful in the naval war in that sea. It was his firm opinion that the Royal Navy would be able to provide sufficient protecting escorts for such a landing. If there had been one, then of course the advance forces would have been some two hundred miles nearer to Tunisia. The third reason, which General Sir Alan Brooke regarded as the most serious, was that

General Eisenhower was too much involved in the political aspects of the operation and, from lack of experience in high military command, failed to obey the elementary precept of rapid exploitation of success derived from surprise. There is no doubt that the Germans were taken completely by surprise when the Allies landed at and captured Oran and Algiers.

Alan Brooke did not suggest that the political aspect was not a vital factor. He complained at the time that either Eisenhower or his deputy Mark Clark could have concentrated on the military aspect and the other have concentrated on the political aspect. In the event there was no rapid thrust eastwards. The situation in the French territories of Morocco, Algeria and Tunisia was complicated. After the capitulation of the French in June 1940, Marshal Petain became the head of the French Government which was located in Vichy. The Germans were content to leave the southern half of France unoccupied as they had the control of the whole seaboard in the Channel, and the use of the ports of Brest and St Nazaire for their naval forces to continue the war against Britain. The larger part of the powerful French Navy was at Toulon in the Mediterranean where the French admirals maintained a strict neutrality, but they also had battleships at Mers-el-Kebir in Algeria, and a battleship and cruisers at Dakar on the Atlantic coast of Senegal. The French Navy officers could not forget nor forgive the British action in June 1940 in rounding on their former allies by sinking three battleships at Mers-el-Kebir and greatly damaging other warships at Dakar. These officers were not, as Churchill feared, acquiescent with Petain's capitulation, but bitterly resented the attack on their ships, which was based on an unjustified fear that these naval forces might fall into German hands. The Army high command in French North Africa was loyal to Marshal Petain and by no means enamoured of the British.

On the other hand the Americans were hopeful that the French Army and Navy commanders in North Africa would not too strongly oppose an American invasion and might even be persuaded to connive at it, for friendly relations between the United States and Vichy France had existed since June 1940. Admiral Leahy, who was in November 1942 the Chairman of the American Joint Chiefs of Staff, had been the United States Ambassador at Vichy in 1940 and 1941. It was their opinion that American troops would be as much welcomed as the British would be resented.

In consequence, steps were taken discreetly and secretly to sound out the reactions of the French to some sort of invasion by the Americans. One of the key figures was General Giraud. He was a French General, who after being taken prisoner by the Germans in 1940 was imprisoned in a fortified castle but had managed to escape, and returned to Vichy France as something of a hero. It was thought that Giraud could be used as a figurehead and focus for anti-German elements among the French officers, to stifle any fierce reaction to an American invasion, and indeed where possible to get a degree of connivance. In the middle of October, Robert Murphy, the United States Agent General in Algiers, requested that a high-ranking American officer should be sent to Algiers to have secret talks with French officers, including General Juin, the Commander-in-Chief. Major-General Mark Clark undertook this secret mission by air to Gibraltar and then by submarine. He was nearly captured by the local gendarmerie but managed to escape, and returned with a report that the omens were favourable for a degree of active co-operation, and that Giraud might well come out openly as the leader of a breakaway force which could actively support an invasion by American troops.

Buoyed up with these hopes, the command was given for the convoy to set sail from America on the 24 October, to cross the Atlantic Ocean, and to aim for Casablanca with a very large American force under the command of Major General Patton. The other convoy escorted by British naval forces, consisting of transports carrying United States and British troops later left the estuary of the River Clyde in Scotland, crossed the eastern Atlantic and went through the Straits of Gibraltar towards Oran and Algiers. Bedell Smith and Humfrey Gale, the two Allied Chief Staff Officers, stayed in London to manage the base operation, while Eisenhower and Mark Clark flew out to Gibraltar on 2 November to direct operations from their Headquarters there. General Giraud was taken by submarine and thence by air to join Eisenhower at Gibraltar. The two huge convoys escaped German attack either by submarine or from aircraft until the very end of the voyage, when one transport was torpedoed, but the soldiers transferred themselves to the landing craft and ultimately landed safely only a day behind their schedule. Not one man was lost while the ships sailed towards their different destinations.

The proposed American landings at and to the north and the south of Casablanca ran into difficulties, as the British had always feared that they would. There were three separate areas for the Atlantic coast assault. It was the northern assault force under Major-General Truscott that suffered the worst. After the campaign he complained that the operation was inadequately and too optimistically planned and the troops so inexperienced that his part in the operation nearly ended in disaster. It was impossible to land at all to begin with, and when the Atlantic waves subsided a little and the order to land was given, many of the landing craft were overturned and capsized. Contrary to Admiral Leahy's advice in Washington, the French put up a fierce resistance. This was particularly true of Casablanca itself. The naval forces were engaged in a furious exchange of gunfire, and once Major-General George Patton did manage to get his large force ashore and assembled for attack on Casablanca they failed to capture the town even after three days of bitter fighting. However, on the fourth day the French agreed to an armistice. At Algiers, although they lost two destroyers in the engagement, the British naval forces were able to protect the landing parties who were all put safely ashore on the beaches to the east of the town, and then the Navy engaged the harbour defences and overcame them. Both airfields were captured, and Royal Air Force fighters were flown in from Gibraltar. There was however none of the connivance or token resistance which they had been led to expect. The only reason why the town was surrendered was because Admiral Darlan happened to be there on a private visit, and as soon as he realized the force of the Allied attack gave permission to General Juin to arrange for a local ceasefire. Further to the west at Oran, there again the American troops, having been successfully landed by the Royal Navy ships, then ran into strong resistance by the French. The port was only captured after two days of fierce fighting.

On his arrival in Algiers, having impudently demanded from General Eisenhower the command of all the French forces in North Africa, Giraud found himself completely ignored. The officers were loyal to Marshal Petain and the Vichy Government, and would accept orders only from the Marshal or his deputy Admiral Darlan.

So Darlan became the key to the whole situation. The day

after his instruction to General Juin to negotiate a local ceasefire in Algiers, Darlan began to have second thoughts about the effectiveness of the Allied landings and the legality of his own actions. When confronted by Major-General Mark Clark, who had flown in from Gibraltar, Darlan at first declined to take any steps to negotiate a general armistice. He reluctantly agreed when Mark Clark threatened him with arrest. The arch-collaborator Pierre Laval pressed Petain into ordering a disclaimer. Darlan tried to renege on his undertaking, but Mark Clark refused to let him do so. It was quite a tricky situation. These problems were resolved by the action of the Germans in repudiating the armistice with the Vichy Government, and overrunning the whole of unoccupied France. There was now nothing more than a puppet Vichy Government, and Petain was no longer an effective Head of State. So Darlan ordered the end of resistance throughout Algeria and Morocco. His writ did not run in Tunisia where the Germans began to land airborne troops. Fortunately for the Allies, the French Admiral in Toulon, acting on his own initiative, took his fleet out of the inner harbour and scuttled all his ships before the Germans could get hold of them.

Eisenhower himself flew to Algiers on 13 November, established Allied Force Headquarters there and made an agreement with Darlan, recognizing him as Head of State in North Africa and General Giraud as Commander-in-Chief of all French Forces. It was a risky move on Eisenhower's part, for Darlan was regarded with suspicion, and the move caused some dismay and raised some doubts both in Washington and London. General de Gaulle and the Free French headquarters in London made a lot of fuss. They wanted to get in on the act, but in the eyes of the French admirals and generals de Gaulle was just a jumped-up junior officer. As everyone agreed in the end, Eisenhower had no other option but to make a deal with Darlan, for the Allied troops were not numerous enough or strong enough to battle against organized French resistance if the French with their superior forces had turned against the invaders.

Preoccupied as he was with all these political manoeuvres, Eisenhower did not order any advance in strength on Tunisia. Lieutenant-General Kenneth Anderson commanded the British First Army and the associated American troops in the Algiers area. But this Eastern Task Force, as it was called, was nowhere near fully landed, and its supply and transport services could not support any major advance. Nevertheless Anderson arranged a push eastwards with as much strength as he could muster. Bougie had fallen to the Royal Navy three days after the initial landings, and a contingent of commandos and infantry had been landed at Bone. All the Allied forces which moved eastwards by sea or land from Algeria were subject to constant attack from German aircraft now based in Tunisia. This small force pushed on, but there was no concerted drive or Allied effort to support them or to reinforce them.

By the end of November the forward elements of the First Army reached the mountainous region of Tunisia. Here they were halted by the resistance from a gathering army of Germans and Italians. An attempt was made to occupy some of the high ground, but a small reinforcement by American troops was not sufficient to give adequate strength to the Allied force, and on 1 December a German attack drove them back from the position they had reached. The initial success of the Allied landings three weeks earlier had not been exploited. It was now a stalemate and the initiative was lost, not to be regained for months to come.

It had always been part of General Sir Alan Brooke's strategic plan, with which Winston Churchill originally agreed, to clear the Germans and Italians out of North Africa, open up the whole of the Mediterranean, then invade first Sicily and after that the southern part of Italy, so as to strike at the Germans in the weakest part of the Axis. On his appointment as Allied Force Commander-in-Chief, Eisenhower had been completely converted to the priority of the Mediterranean strategic plan. The only difference of opinion which he and Mark Clark held was that they preferred an invasion and occupation of Sardinia, rather than Sicily and the toe of Italy. This was because, being nearer to the continent, it would provide a base for Allied bombers to strike at Germany. On the other hand, the American Joint Chiefs of Staff in Washington, and General Marshall in particular, were still resentful of having been ordered into Operation 'Torch' against their will, and took the earliest opportunity to argue for the closing down of the North Africa project and the restoration of the priority of a cross-Channel invasion of France to attack the Germans.

Suddenly, to the dismay of Brooke and Eisenhower, Winston

Churchill joined in giving the same opinion as General Marshall. Bedell Smith passed on to Eisenhower the intimation that it was being said in Washington and London that the Allied forces in North Africa could be reduced and made available for invasion elsewhere. For once Eisenhower displayed real anger, and sent back a message that it was by no means all over bar the shouting: there was a lot of hard fighting to be done and as he put it ' . . . For God's sake let's get one job done at a time.' So it was now Eisenhower and Brooke ranged together against a very powerful lobby of opposing views.

This dispute was settled for the time being by the unhappy result of the last battle of the year. Eisenhower at last ordered a major thrust against the German positions in the mountains of Tunisia. The operation was timed to begin on 21 December, and was entrusted to part of Lieutenant-General Anderson's First Army with American and French troops added. But this motley Allied force was not properly co-ordinated, was inadequately supported and supplied, and continuous rain meant that all roads and lines of communication were a sea of mud. The Royal Air Force was greatly hampered by poor airfields and was almost entirely grounded. This Task Force was up against strongly entrenched positions firmly held by experienced crack troops of the German Army who had been flown in, making an Axis army more than 50,000 strong. The operation was doomed to failure from the start, and on Christmas Eve Eisenhower called it off and the situation reverted to stalemate. So by the end of the year, Operation 'Torch', which had begun so successfully, now ground to a halt and the initiative once lost had not been regained. During the next six weeks, action on both sides was confined to skirmishing at no more than Brigade strength, probing and testing the defences but suffering quite a lot of casualties in the process.

However, this was not the end of defeat and near-disaster for the Allied Force. When the spring weather returned and the mud dried out, Field Marshal Rommel, the Commander-in-Chief of the German and Italian forces in Tunisia, struck where the Allies were weakest. The United States 2nd Corps had been put under Lieutenant-General Anderson and became part of the Eastern Task Force. General Eisenhower was now the Supreme Allied Commander. Under him, in addition to the newly-created United States Fifth Army whose Commanding

General was Mark Clark, was General Sir Harold Alexander, who was in overall command of the British First and Eighth Armies which made up 18 Army Group. These two British Armies were miles and miles apart, with Montgomery's Eighth Army now firmly based in Tripoli and preparing to move forward to attack the Mareth defence line.

Rommel correctly calculated that he had a week or two in hand before Montgomery would assault this very strong defensive position. On 14 February, 1943, Rommel launched an offensive in the other direction against US 2 Corps, who were spread out across the plain between Gafsa and Fondouk with the Kasserine Pass behind them. The US 1st Armoured Division was dispersed behind forward infantry units. Neither the American soldiers nor their commanders had any experience of war and they were quickly overrun, the tanks knocked out and a huge wedge driven right through, into and beyond the Kasserine Pass. The only solid resistance of any kind was provided by a hastily organized little British force based on a motorized battalion under command of Lieutenant-Colonel Gore. Although gallantly creating some valuable delay in the German advance, 'Gore Force' was pushed aside and the way was clear for Rommel to turn northwards and to cut off and annihilate a large part of the Eastern Task Force. On 20 February General Alexander took over active command, correctly read Rommel's intention and, seeing the situation as desperately serious, called on Montgomery and the Eighth Army for help. The British responded quickly and, although not fully dispositioned for an impromptu assault, moved forward with sufficient strength to attack the Axis forces from the other direction, and led Rommel to halt his thrust. Knowing the power of the Eighth Army he decided to withdraw, which he did on 26 February with great skill, and lost only nine tanks in the course of the whole operation.

The Americans had been roundly defeated and their confidence badly shaken. In early March, Eisenhower moved Major-General Patton to take over command of US 2 Corps, and with his vigorous approach and forward-thrusting attitude to war quickly restored the morale of the troops under him. This was the first time the Americans had received a bloody nose. It taught them a lesson, and they learnt very quickly. On 17 March the 2nd Corps went on the offensive, captured Gafsa, and was only held up in difficult territory at El Guettar. Patton spoke of his admiration for the magnificent US soldiers and what they did in this small attack. There was never a word of appreciation for the British Eighth Army, whose rescue operation prevented the whole of the US 2 Corps being cut off and taken into captivity. Without the British, there would not have been any American troops for Patton to enthuse about.

The British Eighth Army in the meantime was fighting its way forward step by step, and the gap between the two Armies was gradually closing. On 5 April, after the successful battle of Wadi Akarit, the Eighth Army broke through into central Tunisia, and the next day the US 2 Corps and the British 10th Corps linked up. The Axis forces were now encircled. The Eighth Army advanced along the coast line. On 10 April Sfax was captured, and Sousse fell two days later. The Eighth Army now consolidated its gains and started to open up the ports, whilst the main thrust to finish off the campaign was entrusted to Anderson's First Army. For this purpose the 7th Armoured Division (the 'Desert Rats'), the 4th Indian Division and a Guards Brigade, all well-seasoned and successful troops, were transferred from the Eighth to the First Army on 20 April. In the vanguard was the 7th Armoured Division, and on 7 May the 11th Hussars entered Tunis.

The *coup de grace* was administered by the British 10th Corps headed by the New Zealand Division under Lieutenant-General Freyberg V.C., D.S.O. at the battle of Enfidaville on 12 May. Field Marshal Rommel having previously returned to Germany, it was left to General Von Arnim to surrender the remaining troops of the once-famed Afrika Korps. The whole of North Africa was now in Allied hands, and the way was clear for the next great offensive by the Allies, the invasion of Sicily and the south of Italy. The campaign so successfully launched had dragged on for six months, and the long protracted effort was justification for General George Marshall's fears that the Mediterranean strategy might be such a drain on shipping, men and equipment that his preferred choice of an attack across the English Channel would for the time being be pushed right out of the reckoning. On the other hand, one of the great benefits that resulted was the creation by General Eisenhower of a successful and happily-welded Allied Force Headquarters. The American and British Staff officers worked well together, however much the top commanders on each side may have disagreed with, and at times actively disliked each other.

7

THE ALLIED GRAND DESIGN

The difficulties in the way of hammering out an agreed Allied strategy were not made any less by the differences of opinion which existed between the British Chiefs of Staff among themselves and also, for their part, between the American Chiefs of Staff. The United States Chiefs of Staff were all technically under the overall command of the President as Commander-in-Chief of all Forces, who on occasion personally exercised his prerogative and gave a direct order overruling their decisions. In the British system the ultimate authority was the War Cabinet, presided over by Churchill as Prime Minister, but in practice the War Cabinet rarely if ever took a view contrary to the advice of the Service Chiefs, which may have been arrived at either as a result of Churchill's insistence or on many occasions in spite of his personal opinion. Churchill was always scrupulous in his observance of the British democratic system, which was in marked contrast to the autocratic powers given to an American President.

In the case of the British the differences were contained within their own four-man committee, of which General Sir Alan Brooke was the chairman. He was consistently against any premature invasion of Europe and was in favour of a peripheral strategy of attacking the Axis powers from the North African and Egyptian bases. Air Chief Marshal Portal advocated the giving of complete priority to a heavy and persistent air bombing assault on German industry and economic power. Admiral Sir Dudley Pound and his top Navy advisers considered that they must concentrate all their resources in coping with the German U-boat menace and the occasional breakout of powerful surface raiders. Vice-Admiral Mountbatten had had his earlier enthusiasm for the dominance of combined operations considerably dampened by the disaster of Dieppe, but he still believed that the one area where combined operations techniques could best be utilized was in a cross-Channel invasion of France.

Combined Chiefs of Staff (CCS) was the term used for the Chiefs of Staff of both countries meeting together. Although they might and did meet together in different parts of the world they had a permanent headquarters and secretariat in Washington. Here the British Chiefs of Staff were represented by their relevant deputies under the leadership of Field Marshal Sir John Dill, who had been appointed as a British representative attached to the US Joint Chiefs of Staff Committee. He had no executive power, but played a key role in putting the British Chiefs of Staff opinions and explaining, which he frequently did with firmness, courtesy and conviction, why the British were opposed to this or that proposal. He would also relay to the British what the American viewpoint was. When the Combined Chiefs of Staff did meet they would issue a joint paper or communiqué, which was supposed to represent either an agreed or compromise policy which would be binding on both nations.

The American equivalent of the British Chiefs of Staff was the Joint Chiefs of Staff Committee. Here the dominant personality was General George Marshall. He always advocated the build up of US forces in Britain for the purpose of mounting an Allied invasion across the English Channel, and resolutely opposed Brooke's strategy of the peripheral attack, and only consented to it when ordered to do so by President Roosevelt. The Navy member was Admiral King, the Commander-in-Chief and Chief of Naval Operations. In his opinion the Combined Chiefs of Staff had no jurisdiction over the US Navy, which was entirely his prerogative to dispose. The only theatre of war he was prepared to recognize was the Pacific Ocean, and any contribution to escort duty of American troops crossing the Atlantic or landing craft for an invasion was reluctantly made at the desperate appeal from General Marshall. It was the Japanese who were the enemy that his ships were required to fight, and all landing craft were primarily and almost exclusively to be used for that purpose. Marshall and Eisenhower had to use all their powers of persuasion to get him to make any contribution at all to an invasion of Europe. In his membership of the Combined Chiefs of Staff he remained awkward and obstructive, and his whole approach was coloured by an attitude towards the Royal Navy which amounted almost to a contemptuous dislike. It is a regrettable fact that his contribution to a harmonious Allied war effort was always grudging and inadequate.

General Arnold was Chief of Army Air Force. As the air war in the Pacific was largely conducted by US Navy airplanes operating from aircraft carriers, the demand on the US Army Air Force was relatively small. This meant that General Arnold saw his first priority as the build up of a massive bomber force in Britain for continuous aerial offensive against Germany working in tandem with British Bomber Command. Inevitably therefore, he and Air Chief Marshal Portal shared the same views and adopted the same approach. Whereas Brooke and Marshall in the Army context and Dudley Pound and King in the Navy context were protagonists of different strategic concepts, the two Air members of the Combined Chiefs of Staff worked together in complete harmony. In view of these five or six different and conflicting attitudes, both within the two nations' own Chiefs of Staff Committees and when assembled together as a Combined Committee, it is remarkable that the Allied war effort was as successful as it turned out to be.

The disagreements and difficulties over Operation 'Torch' were only temporarily overcome by Roosevelt ordering the US Joint Chiefs of Staff to get on with it. The British view put forward by Brooke and supported up to a point by Eisenhower was for an exploitation to the full of the initial successful landings. The American view put forward by Marshall was that in no way was any extension of the war in the Mediterranean going to hinder or put back an invasion of the continent across the English Channel. As soon as the Allied forces were established at the three landing areas in North Africa, and before there was any exploitation at all, signs of dissension began to show themselves both in London and in Washington. Winston Churchill was disagreeing with General Brooke, and General Marshall was disagreeing with his military planners. Churchill suddenly swung away from extension of the North African campaign, and quite surprisingly began to press for a cross-Channel invasion in 1943. This was no doubt largely due to his personal foolish promise to Stalin when they had met in

Moscow in August, that the British and Americans could be relied on to open up a second front in the summer of the next year.

The United States planning staffs reached the conclusion that the British strategy of exploiting the acquisition of bases in North Africa was the best of three options. The planners rejected the notion that a massive air bombing attack could itself be decisive. There had to be a campaign on land somewhere, but with their recently acquired knowledge of the difficulties of a seaborne invasion against heavily defended territory and the lamentable shortage of shipping, they concluded that it was not feasible to mount a large scale assault across the Channel for a long time to come. General Marshall refused to accept the advice of his planners, and remained resolute for his own policy.

In London, Brooke was engaged in verbal battle with his Prime Minister. On 19 November Churchill sent a minute to the British Chiefs of Staff, complaining that he never intended the Anglo-American army to be stuck in North Africa, and suggested closing down the Mediterranean campaign in the early summer of 1943, so as to be able to launch Operation 'Round Up' across the English Channel later in the year. Brooke stoutly resisted this. A week later Churchill changed his mind again. In a strategic study paper dated 25 November he referred to the conquering of North Africa and the use of the acquired bases in the Mediterranean in order 'to strike at the underbelly of the Axis' as the paramount task. General Sir Alan Brooke knew too much of Winston Churchill's mercurial changes of mood to assume that he had won the debate. How right he was. In the beginning of December Churchill changed course yet once more, and referred to the promise given to Stalin to open up a Second Front. Brooke successfully argued against this, pointing out that any such promise was made privately and personally without reference to or consultation with the Chiefs of Staff.

To make his position even more difficult, on 11 December General Brooke received a cablegram from Field Marshal Sir John Dill, reporting that General Marshall wished to close down operations in the Mediterranean and to concentrate all resources on a cross-Channel invasion. At this time Marshall had learnt that Churchill was thinking along similar lines, and said to Dill how much this had pleased him. Dill passed this information on to Churchill. So for once and, as it turned out, for a very short time only, Brooke was isolated and faced by an alliance of his own political master with General Marshall. However, the British Chiefs of Staff were working on a paper which argued the preference for the Mediterranean strategy, rejecting the cross-Channel strategy in the immediate foreseeable future. This paper was produced on 15 December, and the next day Churchill was compelled to accept the logic of this argument, which in truth mirrored his own thinking from which he had temporarily been diverted as the result of his personal euphoric promise to Stalin. So that was the end of Churchill's temporary desertion to the American strategic point of view.

At the end of November, and before all this strategic debate reached its climax, Churchill had raised with Roosevelt the need for another meeting of political leaders with their military advisers. They agreed to meet. Stalin was invited to join them, but as he was busy directing Russian operations from his headquarters in Moscow he found it impossible to attend. The constant shifting and changing direction of the views of Churchill in relation to General Brooke and General Marshall, and Marshall's rejection of his own planners' conclusions, and with Roosevelt temporarily detaching himself from these disputed opinions made it an opportune if not critical time for a full discussion with expert advice and factual basis. Just before Christmas it was decided to have another top level conference — this time at Casablanca in the middle of January 1943.

The British went to the Conference, known as 'Symbol', well-prepared. Their Joint Planning Staff had produced a paper which set out the stark choice between on the one hand a concentration of all resources for operation 'Round Up', which was a doubtful proposition for 1943, and would mean the giving up of the Mediterranean campaign and losing the advantages to be gained therefrom; or on the other hand the exploitation and development of the 'Torch' landings, which in turn would definitely put back 'Round Up'. On the 31 December the British Chiefs of Staff produced their own strategic appreciation and an order of preference for the various types of operation which had to be considered. This was sent to Washington, so the Americans ought to have been fully aware of the arguments with which they would be faced. The top priority was given to the struggle with the German U-boat campaign; the second was the intensification of the bomber offensive against Germany. So the

Navy Chief of Staff and the Air Chief of Staff obtained a unanimous agreement on their own preferences. Equally the Army Chief of Staff, General Brooke, got the whole-hearted support of his colleagues for his Mediterranean strategy, which ranked third in their agreed order of priority. The war in the Pacific and in Burma and the Far East got an honourable mention as, naturally, did the continuation of military supplies to Russia. But, no doubt to the dismay of General Marshall in particular, offensive operations across the English Channel, even of a limited 'Sledgehammer' variety were put right down to the bottom of the list, only to be contemplated if there was a dramatic weakening of German defensive power.

When they arrived at Casablanca, the British Service Chiefs were backed by their planning staffs and a large secretariat and a statistical and calculatory organization, all housed in a small sea-going liner which had been converted into a headquarters vessel with elaborate cipher and communications facilities. It has to be remembered that all this was long before the day of the computer and electronic technology and the microchip. Everything had to be done by the human brain referring to and relying upon human storage and human assessment. The work which had been done by GHQ Planning Staff in conjunction with Combined Operations HQ, and the factual basis for our reports to the Combined Commanders and the Chiefs of Staff were not wasted. The details of how many ships were wanted for this or that could be ascertained quickly and accurately. Thus the British were able to produce chapter and verse in support of their propositions and in response to American arguments. Alan Brooke relied heavily on his personal Staff Officer, Brigadier Guy Stewart, the brilliant young Director of Plans at the War Office. Stewart tragically lost his life when flying back to England, leaving a widow and a son Robin then aged five and now a highly successful Queen's Counsel.

By contrast, the Americans were hopelessly unprepared and were at a grave disadvantage. They had none of this backup organization, and indeed General Marshall would have been landed with planning conclusions with which he disagreed if he had had recourse to such detailed advice. In a sense, this was typical of the American set-up. Right from the start, and going back to the Marshall Memorandum, the American Joint Chiefs of Staff were conditioned to think big in broad terms without any reference to the facts. Thus General Marshall had great organizational ability in assembling men and equipment in the mass. He could ensure that a huge striking force could be assembled in Britain, but with only the vaguest concept of how and where it could actually be used, except to say that it must be used to defeat the Germans on the Continent of Europe, and that quickly.

As has already been observed, the Joint Chiefs of Staff rarely, if ever, arrived at a concerted view based on a true joint service assessment and policy. The Navy under Admiral King was beholden to no one except the President of the United States in the last resort. There was little if any joint planning. Thus, at Guadalcanal the US Navy put ashore a large contingent of marines without any logistic support or any planned administrative backup. In the event the US Army had to come to the rescue with some hastily-provided arrangements for supply and maintenance.

General Marshall had some reason to believe that Churchill would prove an ally in pressing for an early cross-Channel invasion. Churchill must have found it embarrassing to make a personal choice between two conflicting strategic options. Emotionally, and with the inspiration of the continental victories won in the eighteenth century by his ancestor, the great John Churchill, Duke of Marlborough, allied to a fierce desire to get British troops back into France to avenge the disasters of 1940, he must have longed for an invasion by the Allies across the Channel. Moreover, he was haunted by the promise he had made to Stalin and by Roosevelt's even more foolish promise to Molotov, that the British and Americans would open up a Second Front against the Germans in France. On the other hand his own dramatic analogy of the crocodile made German-occupied north west Europe the hard and vicious snout of the Axis creature, and Sicily and Italy the soft underbelly where a mortal blow could more easily be delivered. Nevertheless, in spite of his own restless, questing spirit Churchill was open to reasoned argument when it came to final decision on priorities. He was therefore not committed to Marshall's point of view.

From all accounts, President Roosevelt was strangely noncommittal at the 'Symbol' Conference, leaving it to General Marshall to shoulder the burden of establishing the American position. The President could also rely on Admiral King to make the Pacific war against Japan the top, indeed the only priority, so far as the US Navy was concerned. Such personal preference as Roosevelt had would have been in favour of 'Round Up', if only because this was what was desired by General Marshall and Secretary for War Stimson. The President too was conditioned by the undertaking he had given to Molotov six months earlier.

General Marshall was accompanied by Brigadier General Wedemeyer, the head of the Operational Plans Division, who was there to support his chief, notwithstanding that the more junior members of his own staff, linked as they were to the American members of Allied Force Headquarters in Algiers, had come to recognize the cogency of the British case. Wedemeyer was not attracted to the British attitude. He was one of the strongest believers in the false American opinion that all British strategy was geared to a minimum of involvement while Germany and Russia exhausted themselves, leaving Britain to be the controlling power in Europe and the head of a resurrected Empire all over the world. He was never as open-minded and generous-hearted as Eisenhower, who was completely weaned away from such views by the sheer force of events and his contact with the British Chiefs of Staff. He did, however, get on with Mountbatten, who later took him as Deputy in South East Asia Command.

As Marshall and Wedemeyer fought for their policy they became more and more isolated. Surprisingly, Admiral King was prepared to agree with General Brooke's argument, and Roosevelt himself began to show an interest in further Mediterranean development. In the end, General Marshall accepted the British point of view largely because General Eisenhower came in with the statement that his experience of 'Torch' indicated that the amount of assault craft required for a major seaborne invasion was considerably more than the planners envisaged, and the opening-up of the Mediterranean would release a lot of shipping which would contribute to the ultimate requirement for 'Round Up', a requirement which could not possibly be met by the summer of 1943. So operation 'Round Up' was put on standby. 'Sledgehammer' still remained as a fall-back in 1943, should there be any dramatic weakening of the German forces. The main offensive action for the year was to be the clearing of the Axis forces from Tunisia followed by an invasion of Sicily, to be called Operation 'Husky', and which if successful might lead to an assault upon southern Italy. The aim would be to knock Italy out of the war.

In his report to the US War Department Plans Division, General Eisenhower stated that the decisions reached at Casablanca were realistically the only viable options for 1943, and he put the earliest date for a 'Round Up' type of operation as August of the following year. This pessimistic view made a Mediterranean campaign the one area where the Allies could exercise the imperative requirements of offensive action in 1943. There still remained one item of acute dispute between the Allies. The British wished the allocation of assault craft to the Pacific to be halted, arguing that it had been previously agreed that the war against Japan should be defensive only until after Germany had been defeated. Admiral King would have none of this, and wanted to know what the British would do to help in the Far East once victory had been won in Europe, largely as the result of the American contribution. A compromise was eventually reached which proposed that operations against Japan in the Far East and the Pacific should continue as planned to maintain pressure and to keep the initiative so that a full scale offensive could be mounted once Germany was defeated, but that any development of the war against Japan should not prejudice the ability of the Allies to mount a decisive offensive against the Germans if the opportunity presented itself in 1943. Both the British and the Americans, and Admiral King in particular were happy with this statement of strategic intention. Indeed King was sufficiently mollified so as to be a little more co-operative in the allocation of landing craft of Europe. But this generous outlook did not last for long.

Finally and most importantly, it was agreed to create an Allied organization for control, planning and training for cross-Channel operations. There was agreement that it was not sufficient merely to keep 'Round Up' and 'Sledgehammer' on standby. Active steps would have to be taken to ensure that the Allies were sufficiently prepared and organized to mount an invasion should it be necessary and possible in 1943; and in any event in 1944. It was consequently decided that there should be for this purpose a Supreme Allied Commander, but that it was premature to nominate any particular person for this appointment. It was therefore agreed in the meantime to create the post of Chief of

Staff to Supreme Allied Commander (COSSAC) and under him an Allied integrated staff. An Englishman, Lieutenant-General Frederick Morgan was appointed to this position with an American, Brigadier-General Barker as Deputy. A few weeks later, this body began to assemble at Norfolk House in St James's Square, where planning for Operation 'Torch' had taken place.

The directive from the Combined Chiefs of Staff was clear and simple. The objective was to defeat the German fighting forces in North West Europe. There were to be three planned operations. The 'Sledgehammer' emergency type to take advantage of a German collapse was renamed 'Rankin'. There was to be a major deception plan, code named 'Starkey', the object of which was to deceive the Germans into thinking that large scale preparations were being made for an invasion across the Channel in 1943 or thereafter, which would keep their army formations in situation and not transferable to other theatres of war. The massive invasion designed to defeat the German fighting forces if they were still in full trim was to be planned for the spring of 1944, and the code name 'Round Up' was later replaced by Churchill himself by the title of 'Overlord', the name which remained for the great Allied endeavour ultimately launched on D-Day, 6 June 1944.

The 'Symbol' Conference at Casablanca broke up on 24 January, 1943, and the political leaders and their Chiefs of Staff dispersed, the Americans to Washington, Churchill and Brooke to Cairo, and the rest of the British to London. Generals Marshall and Wedemeyer returned deflated, and felt themselves defeated by the British. In the Mediterranean, Eisenhower was now designated Supreme Allied Commander. General Alexander, in addition to commanding the British 18th Army Group, was to be Eisenhower's deputy. With Alexander in this position, the effective overall military command was in the hands of a first-class and highly experienced Army commander, who by his attractive personality and courteous manner achieved the willing co-operation of the American generals. He was also able to bring some sense of order and purpose into the working of the integrated Allied staff officers who, for all their anxiety to be genuinely co-operative, suffered the inevitable confusion to be found when fully trained and experienced British officers were working alongside Americans who had not yet learned the discipline of detailed planning. Major 'Robbie' Crichton, a

Liverpool barrister who was later to be Sir Robertson Crichton, a Judge of the High court, used to say what a difference was made by the arrival of General Alexander. 'Robbie' was doubly enthusiastic about Allied Force Headquarters because it was there that he met his future wife Margaret, an American officer — an excellent example of an Anglo-American alliance!

The overall Air command was given to Air Chief Marshal Tedder and the overall Naval command to Admiral Sir Andrew Cunningham, the much-admired and successful commander of the Royal Navy in the Mediterranean theatre of war. It was undoubtedly a triumph for the British to have all the top key command positions. But this agreement also made the best use of the various talents available. As Supreme Commander, Eisenhower was able to exercise his great skills in the political field. There were constant problems which resulted from the original introduction of General Giraud as prospective head of the French forces. Eisenhower regarded Giraud as the natural successor as leader of the French in North Africa after the assassination of Admiral Darlan on Christmas Eve 1942. De Gaulle as head of the Free French Forces in London claimed superiority. Churchill began a process of reconciliation between the two which appeared to result in what was referred to as 'a shotgun marriage'. It was not in reality very successful, and Eisenhower had to exercise great tact and skill in dealings with Giraud so as not to cause too much offence to de Gaulle.

At the beginning of February, the planning for the invasion of Sicily (Operation 'Husky') was put in train even though the Germans were firmly entrenched in Tunisia, not to be finally eliminated until the middle of May. For this operation a Western Task Force was to be drawn from a newly-created US Seventh Army, to whom an additional Corps had been allotted under General Montgomery. Montgomery was fully engaged in the campaign in North Africa, and Patton had to be taken away from the American preparations for 'Husky' to take over the demoralized US 2 Corps in Tunisia. He did not return to command of the Seventh Army and the Eastern Task Force until the middle of May, although the invasion of Sicily was planned for the beginning of July.

General Montgomery and General Patton first met for a matter of a few hours at the victory celebrations at Tripoli on 4 February. Thereafter each had his own job to do, first in North

Africa and then in commanding the separate task forces for the invasion of Sicily. The co-ordination of the whole operation was the responsibility of Eisenhower as Supreme Commander, but in practice was done by General Alexander, who, now that he was Deputy Supreme Commander, still doubled as Commander-in-Chief of an Army Group, now the 15th, not the 18th. It was during this time that the respective staff officers of the two nations were not only in regular contact with each other, but were in a position to make their own judgements of their own and each other's top commanders. Whereas two of the senior staff officers, Major-Generals Bedell Smith, Eisenhower's Chief of Staff, and de Guingand, Montgomery's Chief of Staff, hit it off together from the start and throughout the next two years, and whereas everyone liked and admired General Alexander, it cannot be said that Montgomery was liked by the American staff officers nor Patton by the British staff officers.

Major General F. de Guingand

A VERY GOOD YES MAN

The trouble with 'Freddy' de Guingand was that basically he was too nice a man and tended to overlook the obvious faults and weaknesses of others. He was excessively loyal to his own staff, and to his own Commander in particular. Even after the war was over, he still thought it very amusing that Montgomery held Bedell Smith to a light-hearted bet that he would be entitled to the private use of an American 'Flying Fortress' aircraft if the Eighth Army, as in fact they did, were to capture Sfax before the middle of April. In reality, 'Monty's' insistence on the honouring of the wager created a very serious amount of friction between him and Eisenhower which required the personal intervention of General Brooke to be smoothed over. Brooke privately expressed his feeling of sadness that Montgomery, for whom he had great admiration, was not liked by the Americans, and he himself recorded that Montgomery needed firm handling and a resounding 'ticking-off' if he had been guilty of tactless or overbearing behaviour. It was to the credit of both of them that when these occasions did occur, Brooke did not hesitate to deliver, and Montgomery for his part to accept with good grace.

Both Patton and Montgomery were strong characters who could be truculent and abrasive. Both men had a firm religious belief which fitted well with the conviction that the Nazis were pagans and Hitler was Antichrist. Montgomery was brought up in an austere and simple Protestant background. He was essentially a dedicated professional soldier, with little or no culture. It is doubtful if he ever read anything other than military text books and the Bible. Patton was a more cultured and widely-read man whose tastes ranged from Kipling to the Koran, and his religious outlook was developed in a romantic Roman Catholic tradition. Both men were conceited, and both were convinced that they alone knew the answers to any military problem. To this extent they were similar, but their answers were governed by an entirely different approach. Patton was all for thrusting forward regardless of the risk of being thrown off-balance, aiming to obtain a momentum which could not be stopped. Montgomery was governed by an intention never to be caught off-balance. He would attack only after intense artillery preparation and aerial bombardment, then come to grips, finally waiting until the enemy was off-balance, bringing up reserves to put to flight a weary and disorganized foe. Montgomery's tactics were right for any situation, Patton's wrong if he came up against a strong and well-organized defence. As it happened, Patton was lucky in the roles given to him, and was always able to thrust against an enemy of insufficient strength to halt the momentum of his progress, so he had no failures and was able to achieve spectacular success. Montgomery had much the more difficult conditions to cope with; he was equally successful, but sometimes only after long periods when success seemed to be in the balance, and when those accustomed to Patton's striking achievements failed to understand either the conditions or Montgomery's tactics.

Lieut. General George S. Patton

Imperial War Museum

It was during the Sicily campaign that General Patton displayed an unfortunate aspect of his naturally impetuous behaviour. Dropping in one day at a field hospital where there were a large number of seriously wounded men, he saw an American soldier sitting on a box, apparently quite unharmed. When this man replied in answer to the General's enquiry that there was nothing wrong with him, but that he could not take being shot at, and thereupon burst into tears, Patton then slapped him across the face with his glove and ordered him to go back to his unit. Patton justified his conduct by saying that he recognized that it was a case of hysteria for which a slap on the face was a recognized treatment. However, those who saw it happen considered that he lost his temper. Whatever the explanation, it was extremely foolish behaviour, bound to be misunderstood, and in fact created such a furore that, after the campaign came to an end, General Eisenhower had to discipline and downgrade him, and put Major-General Omar N. Bradley above him. Although Bradley was considerably junior to Patton, he retained this acquired seniority for the rest of the war.

In France, General Patton was to prove a dashing commander, but at times a reluctant if not actually disobedient member of Eisenhower's higher command structure. He was always highly critical of General Montgomery, and on occasion blamed both General Bradley and General Eisenhower for weakly giving way to Montgomery's point of view when this was not to Patton's liking. All in all, Patton may well have been a great and successful general in the field, but his contribution to the harmonious working of the alliance of the British and American armies was sadly lacking.

The planning for 'Husky', which went on in his absence, was at variance with Montgomery's experienced opinion. As soon as he finished the Eighth Army campaign in Tunisia, he was able to devote all his efforts to the use of his Task Force in their part of the invasion. He was able to persuade the Allied Commanders-in-Chief to revamp the plan; as a result the US Seventh Army was to be more concentrated in its landing operations and to abandon landings to the west, so that there was a more closely-linked and concerted Allied punch along the southern and south-eastern coast of the island. It was a most complicated operation, which involved the sailing of separate convoys from a number of different fronts on the North African coast. But the Royal Navy did its work well, and the vast majority of the ships arrived at the right place at the right time. The landings went according to plan on 10 July, and apart from a certain amount of confusion in the airborne assault in which a lot of unnecessary casualties were suffered, the invasion was successfully begun. Montgomery's Task Force had the most difficult task, and gradually inched their way forward. Patton's Seventh Army made the more spectacular advance up through the centre of the island along the western coast and on to the north-east. Messina fell to the American troops on 16 August: they were joined by the British the next day, and all was over and the invasion successfully concluded.

So successful had been the earlier stages of Operation 'Husky' that Eisenhower, who had previously resisted all Churchill's pressure for a landing on the mainland of Italy and the capture of Rome, now felt able to make the decision to invade Italy itself. However, when it came to assessing the capabilities of the Allied forces to do so, he reluctantly came to the conclusion that shortage of shipping and landing craft would render such an operation impossible before September. Nevertheless, his decision to invade received unexpected support from the political upheaval in Italy. On 25 July the Italian Army Commanders took control and persuaded the King to have Mussolini arrested, and Marshal Badoglio was appointed head of Government in his place.

On the day that Sicily was finally conquered Marshal Badoglio put out peace feelers, but although the Italians ceased to be an effective enemy, they were powerless in the hands of the Germans. There was virtually no opposition to the British landings in early September across the Straits of Messina. It was a different story at Salerno, where the American Fifth Army under General Mark Clark were faced with fierce resistance, and for days it was touch-and-go whether they would be thrown back into the sea. But Mark Clark managed desperately to hang on, and in due course made a bridgehead for an advance first on Naples and then in the direction of Rome.

The Germans had reacted quickly to the collapse of their Axis partner and to the Allied invasion. Military control of most of Italy was assumed, and reinforcements hastily brought in. All further advance by the Allied armies was either delayed or completely held up. Throughout October, November and December, bitter fighting went on in worsening weather and appalling conditions. It was disappointingly slow progress, and Rome was not reached by the end of the year. General Alexander, in overall command of all Allied forces, was never able to realize his ambition of overcoming all German resistance, striking through the passes in the mountains of north-east Italy and Jugoslavia, and making for Vienna. If he had been able to do so, the whole map of postwar Europe would have been different. There may well have been no 'Iron Curtain' and no Berlin Wall. Because of American insistence that the Mediterranean campaign was a side-show, and their foolish decision to withdraw seven divisions and transfer them to 'Overlord' when manpower was never the critical factor in the cross-Channel assault, Alexander was denied the resources to defeat the German armies. After the war was over, it transpired that Hitler and the High Command feared more than anything else being cut off from, and being denied the vital mineral resources of the Balkans.

As it was, Alexander had to yield preference to an Allied invasion of North West Europe which, although the Combined Chiefs of Staff directive was issued in February 1943, could not be mounted at the earliest before the late spring of 1944. Unhappily, the Americans dithered and dallied for months after the issue of the February directive. They stupidly concentrated most of their energies in an effort to defeat British strategic desires and to denigrate the Mediterranean campaign, without at the same time taking any steps to ensure that the cross-Channel invasion was firmly accepted by the US Navy chiefs and provided with a top command structure, instead of merely relying on a planning staff to work out ideas for some mythical creature known as the Supreme Commander designate. In the event, when Eisenhower was ultimately given this position, the plans presented to him were constrained and conditioned by a woeful lack of practical provision by the American Joint Chiefs of Staff. All in all their performance throughout 1943 was pretty poor and sadly distorted by an unreasonable distrust of British strategy, and an unfair assumption that Britain was more interested in acquiring the hegemony of Europe rather than the total defeat of Hitler and his myrmidons.

8

THE PLANNING FOR OPERATION 'OVERLORD' — FIRST PHASE

Lieutenant-General Frederick Morgan and the staff of COSSAC began assembling at Norfolk House at the beginning of March 1943. It was at a time when the US forces in Tunisia were only just beginning to recover from their disaster at the Kasserine gap, and before Major-General Patton had taken a grip of the situation and restored the morale of the shattered US 2 Corps. The American members of the COSSAC staff were understandably subdued. Moreover they had no experience of planning either in a broad strategic context, or, what was more important, in actual detail. The British team for their part, although experienced in general terms, were unversed in the problems of a seaborne invasion across the English Channel.

Fortunately, however, General Morgan was aware of all the work which had been done in this field by the British GHQ planners, and had access to the files which had accumulated and the staff studies which had been prepared for the reports to the Combined Commanders, and from them to the British Chiefs of Staff in April and May of the previous year. On the other hand, it was unfortunate that to begin with there was no-one available to explain or to enlarge upon this mass of paper and detailed working. Morgan had to read it all for himself, and undoubtedly obtained a wrong impression of the general conclusions reached by the planners. Too late, as it turned out, somebody at the War Office must have taken the trouble to track down the whereabouts of at least one member of the original little planning group, for out of the blue I was posted as a Lieutenant-Colonel back to GHQ Home Forces. The intention was that a posting should have been made to COSSAC, but by the beginning of April all the vacancies had been filled, and GHQ Home Forces was by now to provide the nucleus of the overall Army headquarters for an Expeditionary Force when the invasion was actually launched. So, although most of the next two months or so was spent as effectively a member of the COSSAC team, my true position was that of a founder member of the administrative side under Brigadier Randle ('Gerry') Feilden of what became Headquarters 21 Army Group in July 1943. This was a personal stroke of good fortune, because ultimately COSSAC was absorbed into Supreme Headquarters Allied Expeditionary Force (SHAEF), which in the British logistics context was a useless, unnecessary organization; whereas HQ 21 Army Group, when General Montgomery was appointed to command, became the planning and executive supreme headquarters for the whole of the Anglo-American initial assault upon the continent of Europe.

The build up of US troops and equipment under 'Bolero' had dried up while 'Torch' was being planned and carried out, but resumed again after the decisions reached at the Casablanca conference. Major-General Humfrey Gale being now with Eisenhower at AFHQ in Algiers, it fell to Brigadier Feilden, promoted to Major-General when HQ 21 Army Group was formed, and Lieutenant-Colonel Charles Hardie to make all the allocations of territory and the quartering arrangements both for the British formations and for the American forces as they began to pour in again. This kept them fully occupied. At this time there was no involvement by GHQ Home Forces in any of the planning of how, when and where the British and American troops would be employed.

Although Lieutenant-General Morgan paid tribute to all the work which had been done by the planning staffs of GHQ Home Forces and Combined Operations Headquarters, he was completely mistaken in thinking that the Pas de Calais was the preferred area for a seaborne invasion. It was the considered view of everyone involved in the planning exercise during the first half of 1942 that the Pas de Calais was the one area where a 'Sledgehammer' type of operation could achieve the objective of engaging substantial German forces, and particularly the Luftwaffe, if there had to be such a suicidal gesture to help the Russians. For a large-scale invasion, the planners had opted for the Normandy beaches, while Mountbatten, whatever his staff at Combined Operations HQ may have felt, was personally all for Cherbourg and the Cotentin peninsula. In his Report as Supreme Commander to the Combined Chiefs of Staff after the war was over, Eisenhower referred to the informal discussions which took place in June and July 1942 between the Combined Commanders, of whom he was one, when the work of the planners led to a clear conclusion that the Normandy region offered the greatest chance of success in an invasion of Europe.

Morgan and the COSSAC staff were faced with problems resulting from the three types of operation which they had been directed to consider. The 'Rankin' (former 'Sledgehammer') operation was the immediate priority if something had to be done in 1943. If it was, then it had to be somewhere where it could be launched quickly and with such forces, however inadequate, as were available. But as it was a precondition that the German armies should be on the verge of collapse before this operation could take place, no one really bothered with it very much. It was obvious from the way the Germans were fighting in Tunisia and with Italy at this time still in the war, that this precondition was unlikely to be fulfilled. In any event, the promises made by Churchill and Roosevelt to Stalin and Molotov about opening up a Second Front had largely lost their significance once it became apparent that the substantial Allied invasion of North Africa was fully occupying a sizeable portion of the German armies. Stalin was temporarily pacified by the proposals for an 'underbelly' attack in the Mediterranean. The 'Starkey' operation was a deception plan designed to indicate to the Germans that an invasion would be made at a place where in fact it would not be made. It could not therefore be put in train until the area for actual invasion was chosen.

The COSSAC staff soon learnt what the GHQ planners had previously discovered, which was that it was useless to come to any firm conclusion until an adequate supply of landing craft and shipping could be guaranteed. The size of the invasion force was entirely conditioned by the number of ships available. My own recollection of the month of April 1943 is that to me there was a depressing atmosphere of *déja vu*, and if the anthem of the English football crowds had then been written I should have been singing 'Here we go, Here we go, Here we go', not as a paean of victory, but a funeral dirge. By the beginning of May,

Morgan and his staff had got nowhere beyond a realization of the enormity of the problem. My American counterpart was totally bemused.

Fortunately it had been arranged between Churchill, once he had recovered from a severe attack of pneumonia, and Roosevelt that another top-level conference should take place. At long last the Royal Navy, assisted by very long range aircraft and by Royal Air Force Coastal Command, was winning the battle against the German U-boats. A major factor in this success, which mystified and worried Admiral Doenitz, was a much-improved British radar system. After a disastrous month in March 1943 when the Allied losses of merchant shipping exceeded half a million tons, there was a dramatic and steady downturn in the number of ships lost in the Atlantic. The time was ripe therefore in Churchill's mind for a reappraisement of the Allied strategic position and objectives. The conference was intended by Churchill and General Brooke to involve a finalizing of plans for the Mediterranean and discussion as to what, if anything, should be done to drive the Japanese out of Burma now that General Slim and the British 14th Army had halted the drive towards India. As soon as the conference was mooted, the Americans prepared themselves for a showdown with the British. They had no intention of being again roundly defeated in argument as they had been at Casablanca.

The conference, named 'Trident', was held in Washington between 12 and 25 May 1943. It began with the representatives of the two nations poles apart. The US Chiefs of Staff were still opposed to further operations in the Mediterranean, notwithstanding the resounding victory in Tunisia, which culminated on the very day that the conference began with the surrender of all the German and Italian forces in North Africa. Admiral King was going far beyond the agreement made at Casablanca about the war against Japan by draining off more and more resources, particularly ships and landing craft for use in the Pacific. Roosevelt and Marshall had been persuaded earlier in the year by Generalissimo and Madame Chiang Kai-Shek that more help should be given to the Chinese in their struggle against the Japanese occupation, and that operations in Burma should be stepped up and co-ordinated with the Chinese forces under the American General Stillwell. In contradiction to a policy of further land operations in the

Mediterranean, the Americans believed that the effect of continuous and heavy bombing by Allied air forces would be far more effective in reducing the German capacity to defend France, Italy and the Balkans. In this they were supported by Air Chief Marshal Portal, the British Chief of Air Staff, and Air Chief Marshal Tedder, Eisenhower's Air Operations Commander-in-Chief. Churchill and General Brooke were faced with a formidable task in presenting their objections, and their adherence to their policy of exploiting the Allied success in North Africa. Eisenhower had agreed to an invasion of Sicily, but was not prepared to commit himself further without General Marshall's concurrence.

The argument and discussion went on for days. During the conference Churchill made agreement more doubtful, by advocating a Danubian Confederation to take the place of the former Austro-Hungarian Empire, and a Balkan Confederation after the war was over. All the suspicions which Roosevelt and his Chiefs of Staff harboured with regard to British motives in pursuing a Mediterranean campaign were restored with increased strength, and General Brooke had to defend his strategy with all the power at his command. The planning staffs of both nations were ordered to produce papers in consultation with each other on facts and figures, but representing the views of their masters.

During most of the conference sessions the two sides physically faced each other, with the Chiefs of Staff supported behind them by a phalanx of planners and advisers. Each session resulted in stalemate, and agreement in the end was only reached when the Combined Chiefs met alone to exercise their own judgement without acting as advocates for the strategy put forward by their staff officers.

When the planners met to prepare their papers they had recourse to the statistics and calculations which were made in Washington. It transpired later that, without consultation with those at COSSAC or British GHQ Home Forces or Combined Operations HQ, they made at least one fundamental error, in assessing the capacity of a Tank Landing Ship at thirty tanks. This was in actuality the figure of stowage in transit. When loading for use in an assault landing, the true figure was twenty-five. This mistake spoiled much of the calculations for months to come, and was one reason why Eisenhower had to bang the table in January and February 1944 to force the Combined Chiefs of Staff to increase the requirement for shipping before 'Overlord' could take place.

By the end of the Conference both nations were tolerably satisfied, though neither had achieved all that they had set out to do. General Marshall was persuaded to give some latitude to Eisenhower to progress further than an invasion of Sicily, and for himself to accompany General Brooke to Algiers to assess the situation on the spot. But this grudging concession was made only on the basis that no exploitation of the Sicily operation could take place without the consent of the Combined Chiefs of Staff, and that four squadrons of heavy bombers and seven experienced Army divisions must be withdrawn and made available for operations in North West Europe. The Americans stuck to their viewpoint that in addition to the war against Japan a cross-Channel invasion remained top priority in Allied joint strategy. The British were not opposed to this, but required a realistic appreciation of what was required and what could be done.

Within limits, Operation 'Overlord' was firmly accepted. It was to be planned with the objective, no longer so specific as to defeat the German forces in North West Europe, but to secure a lodgement on the continent from which further offensive operations could be carried out. The target date was fixed at 1 May, 1944. An assessment was made of the forces required within the constraint of the probable availability of shipping, and an outline plan was embodied in the final concluded agreement. Lieutenant-General Morgan and the COSSAC staff were now given a firm directive, but one which severely limited the scope of their planning. When Eisenhower and Montgomery rejected the ultimate COSSAC plan in January 1944, they, and Montgomery in particular, never acknowledged the degree to which Morgan had had his hands tied from the start by the Combined Chiefs of Staff. Montgomery was gratuitously offensive about the whole thing.

The 'Trident' plan, if it can so be called, required five infantry divisions for a simultaneously loaded assault, associated with two airborne divisions and a further two infantry divisions in an immediate follow-up. Thereafter, twenty divisions had to be available for build up into the lodgement area: it was further decided that reinforcements were to arrive direct from the United States at the rate of three to five divisions a month, up to a total of one hundred divisions. Thus the force to be available for the securing of the lodgement area amounted to twenty-nine divisions, of which two were to be airborne, and all of which were to be based in the United Kingdom. Nothing was said in the directive about the area to be selected for invasion, nor was the total figure of troops involved translated into terms of an appropriate shipping requirement.

By comparison, the report to the Combined Commanders in May 1942 estimated that the minimum assault force should be one of ten divisions and a three-divisional front, which, when Morgan first had a look at it, he considered to be an overestimate of the size of the assault force required. In 1942 we had been trying to assess the necessary weight behind the initial punch as a basic factor to determine the amount of shipping required. We never got as far as an analysis of the spread of the assault landings; if we had, we may well have thought in terms of a five-divisional front, which is what Eisenhower and Montgomery ultimately decided was essential. Obviously five divisions assaulting at the same time require more landing craft than three, unless the other two are simultaneously loaded to be put through as an immediate follow-up. The 'Trident' directive referred to 'five Infantry Divisions (simultaneously loaded in landing craft)', and it is possible that the Washington planners deliberately left open whether or not to use all five divisions at the same time on a five-divisional front. In his Report to the CCS, Eisenhower referred to the plan as a three-divisional one. In the event the final COSSAC plan, because of the geographical limitations imposed by the area selected, opted for a three-divisional front. It was this narrow-fronted attack which earned the criticism which it received later on. When General Brooke handed over the directive to Lieutenant-General Morgan he is reported to have said, 'Well, there it is. It won't work but you must bloody well make it.'

In saying what he did, Brooke was well aware of the estimate of shipping required which had been made to the Combined Commanders a year earlier. He knew also that the planners in Washington during 'Trident' had queried the earlier conclusions as an overestimate of the number of landing craft which would be needed, but he may well not have realized that the 'Trident' planners had made the unfortunate error with reference to Tank Landing Ships. But much more serious was the actual and projected situation with regard to the amount of shipping for a Cross-Channel operation.

Following the Casablanca Conference, the British had made in March 1943 a request that more Landing Ships (Tank) (LST) should be built in American shipyards for use in North West Europe in an 'Overlord' assault. Admiral King, resiling from his co-operative mood and reverting to type, rejected the request out of hand. It has to be borne in mind that, whereas the original design for two of the three types of landing craft were British, the facilities for construction in the United Kingdom were severely limited. In the United States there was a far greater capacity; there were many more shipyards and many more skilled shipwrights and labourers. In consequence, the British plans and drawings were handed over to the Americans. Once the building of these craft was begun, Admiral King assumed control of the lot and maintained a tight-fisted grip over their allocation and disposal for the whole of the time the United States was in the war. In 1943 more than 19,000 assault craft were built in the American shipyards. King agreed to allot only one thousand of this number for use in Europe. The maximum capacity of British shipyards was about 350 a month, which would produce a total of 4,000 by May 1944. Even with the addition of the American 1,000, a total of 5,000 specialist ships could only lift three divisions. On this basis, the 'Trident' directive was really no more than 'pie in the sky'.

It is interesting to note that already in May 1943 the planners were thinking in terms of using airborne troops in the first stages of assault. In 1942, the British GHQ and Combined Operations Staffs had not got far enough with detailed planning to consider whether or not to do so. The successful use of paratroops by the Germans in Crete and again in Tunisia in November and December 1942 provided a useful precedent. The first time that the Allied nations made use of airborne forces was in operation 'Husky', the planning for which was going on contemporaneously with the 'Trident' Conference in Washington. The actual deployment in Sicily was not very successful, and there were many casualties in both men and aircraft. However, the British Airborne formations under Lieutenant-General 'Boy' Browning learnt many useful lessons from this somewhat unhappy operation which were of great assistance to the COSSAC staff, and from which much profit was drawn when it came to the vitally important role of the Airborne Divisions in Normandy on D-Day, 6 June, 1944.

When Brooke handed over the 'Trident' directive to Morgan and the COSSAC staff at the beginning of June 1943, the target date of 1 May, 1944 meant that there was less than a year in which to plan the operation and to complete all the vast preparations necessary for the mounting of so huge an endeavour. As Morgan himself rightly said, 'Overlord' must be regarded as being already in train: and from the start everything must be geared up to be ready in time.

Another significant thing about the 'Trident' directive was that whereas it introduced the addition of airborne forces in the assault, there was no mention of armoured formations. When the invasion actually took place on 6 June, 1944, the initial deployment of specialist tanks was probably the most decisive factor in the success of the initial landings. These specialist armoured vehicles were entirely a British conception. At the time of the Allied success in breaching the German defensive system in Normandy, Field Marshal Rommel observed that he was surprised by the Allied use of specialized armoured vehicles in the early stages of the landings, and came to the conclusion that these were the result of American ingenuity. Nothing could be further from the truth. No doubt for purpose of comparison, Rommel had in mind the old-fashioned way in which the British armour had been used by the Eighth Army in the desert war before Montgomery abandoned the deployment of tanks in roaming penny packets and cavalry charges, and instead used them as static artillery in positions well forward of the Field and Medium Regiments. After the Battle of Alamein, General Brooke, himself a Gunner, light-heartedly expressed his pleasure that Montgomery, an Infantryman, had turned himself into a Gunner! But generally speaking, the British had never, before Montgomery's arrival, shown much understanding of the enormous scope which an adventurous use of armour could provide. The commanders were old fashioned and steeped in the traditions of the cavalry. Montgomery's use of the firepower of a tank sited defensively in a hull-down position contributed substantially to the devastating continuous hammering of the Germans, beginning with aerial bombardment and then taken up by the artillery, all of which, according to Rommel, brought about his defeat at Alamein.

The man responsible for the reliance upon the specialized tanks in operation 'Overlord' was Major-General Hobart, who had previously paid the penalty for being far too advanced in his theories of the handling of armoured formations but now he came into his own at last with the development of what were known to the British Army chiefs and planning staffs as 'Hobo's funnies'. He was a pioneer in the tactical use of armour, and as early as 1934, many of his ideas, though rejected by the orthodox and stereotyped British commanders, impressed the Germans, who used and developed his doctrines of tank warfare with such success in the *Blitzkrieg* of May 1940. The British War Office, Army Commanders and Chiefs of Staff considered Hobart to be a nuisance and had him posted to the Middle East before war was declared in September 1939. Based in Cairo, Hobart's restless inventive mind led to the creation of the 7th Armoured Division out of a motley collection of Tank battalions and cavalry armoured units. But when the desert war began, his superiors and fellow officers found his ideas too advanced and his brusque manner hard to stomach, and he was pushed into early retirement and occupied himself as a Corporal in the Home Guard in England. Most fortunately he was rescued from this by the personal intervention of Winston Churchill and General Sir Alan Brooke, who in March 1943 gave him command of a newly-created formation named the 79th Armoured Division.

When Hobart took up his new position, a scientist named Straussler had already converted five old obsolete Valentine tanks into amphibious vehicles known as DD (Duplex Drive), which were waterproofed, made to float and provided with a propellor, though not, to the dismay of the old sea salts at the Admiralty, with a rudder, and therefore in their minds not a viable piece of equipment. Hobart applied the design to Sherman tanks, demonstrated that they could 'swim' ashore, and so satisfied General Brooke of their viability and usefulness that in July 1943 he gave orders for 900 Sherman tanks to be converted to DD. But British production was very limited, and such a few having been altered, General Eisenhower, as the newly appointed Supreme Commander, agreed in January 1944 that they were essential and must be made available, and therefore arranged for a British engineer to take the plans and drawings to the United States, where American capacity led to the production of 300 of these amphibious vehicles within two months. No doubt because they were converted in American factories it was assumed that they had been devised and designed in the United States. But as happened time and time again, it was British ingenuity and inventiveness that produced the prototype. Sheer physical manufacturing capacity was the American contribution to this joint Allied endeavour.

Day by day, week by week and month by month during the rest of the year 1943, assisted by engineering experts and the facilities provided for him by Combined Operations HQ Hobart was applying his fertile mind to the problems of a seaborne invasion against a strongly defended enemy coast. His final list of 'funnies' used on D-Day, 1944, was most impressive. There were the AVRE, the generic title for various armoured vehicles handled by assault engineer units. These included tanks converted into flame-throwers for burning out an enemy esconced in concrete pill boxes; armoured bulldozers for clearing obstacles from the beaches, tanks with bridging equipment for getting across ditches and craters, and tanks which laid a steel mesh for getting over mud or soft sand. There was the CRAB, a tank carrying a revolving 'flail', mounted well-forward for beating a path through enemy minefields by exploding mines as it went forward,and the CDL, a tank with an armour-plated searchlight for dazzling and temporarily blinding defenders. Then there were tanks which had the turrets removed and which could be driven up against an obstacle so as to provide a ramp for other tanks to drive over. The only American contribution to all this, albeit a vitally important contribution, was the DUKW, an amphibious carrier of troops, equipment or supplies, which could act like a boat in the sea and drive on its wheels when on land.

Over three or four years of war the planning for invasion went through a change of emphasis, and the manner of mounting a seaborne assault was profoundly altered. Until 1942, although the British Expeditionary Force was mostly evacuated across the beaches of Dunkirk, even for an opposed landing it was a port to which the Navy and the Army would look. The main lesson of Dunkirk, repeated at Dieppe, was the vital necessity of local command of the air in order to give protective cover to troops as they landed. Air cover and naval protective escort thereafter were always the first priorities in the consideration of an assault against an enemy-held coastline.

In early 1942, the British GHQ planners introduced the concept of landings on beaches, a technique which the Americans were compelled to use when landing in the Pacific islands, which had no ports to speak of, but plenty of sand. A further development came with a reliance upon airborne forces either to protect a flank or to seize a key point. Later still there followed a partial swing back to the use of ports once landings had been made on the beaches, to provide a more adequate means of supply and reinforcement. If there was no port readily to hand, then an artificial harbour would have to be brought into being. Finally, in addition to the obvious prerequisite of a heavy and persistent barrage from aerial bombing and from the guns of warships off the coast, one of the lessons learned from the disastrous attack on Dieppe was that assaulting infantry must be preceded in the landing by armoured vehicles to deal with all the various types of obstacles and to break a way through the defences. Furthermore, there also had to be covering artillery fire immediately before and while the infantry went ashore. This close support was better provided by gunfire from tanks and self-propelled guns whilst still seaborne.

Operation 'Overlord' was, as General Morgan recognized, already in being from the end of June 1943. Not only was the 79th Armoured Division busily engaged in the design and the testing of the 'funnies', but Combined Operations HQ was rehearsing the use of landing craft both for landing and for embarkation. With Hobart and his engineers and Mountbatten and his staff working closely together, the contemplated use of heavy tracked vehicles created fresh problems. One was the necessary construction of concrete pathways known as 'hards', so that tanks would not get bogged down in sand or soft shingle as they were driven aboard. This was quickly put in hand at embarkation points all round the coast of England and Wales. As there was to be both an actual operation and a deception operation aimed at places somewhere from the coast of Belgium down to the ports of Brittany, it made no difference where assembly and embarkation points might be revealed to German aerial reconnaissance surveys. In fact the more there were, the greater the likelihood of confusion.

When Morgan and the COSSAC staff began a detailed examination of the possibility of and a place for a cross-Channel assault, it became clear that it was for him and him alone to make a final judgement in the light of previous planning studies, updated by the increasing experience gathered from the practice exercises and experiments of Combined Operations Headquarters. The COSSAC staff had to produce the information and the factual studies, and the Chief of Staff had to produce the ultimate evaluation.

Having absorbed all the material produced for him, Morgan began the task all over again, and started with an entirely fresh appraisement of the best place for an invasion of sufficient size and scope to meet the requirements of the 'Trident' directive, and even considered, though not for long, whether an invasion could be launched against the Belgian or Netherlands coast. The choice was narrowed down to somewhere on the French coast, extending from the Pas de Calais area down to Cherbourg and the Brittany ports. A major factor which the COSSAC staff had to bear in mind when selecting the place for lodgement was the provision of the necessary port facilities to cope with the subsequent influx of three to five divisions a month sailing direct across the Atlantic from the United States.

It was this particular factor which led Morgan and his staff to conclude that if the Pas de Calais was to be decided upon, the lodgement area would have to be extended northwards into Belgium so as to include the port of Antwerp, and in a south-westerly direction down to Le Havre at the mouth of the River Seine. If the ultimate objective of the lodgement was to obtain the use of Cherbourg and Brest, and St Lorient and St Nazaire in Brittany, then the only feasible area for the actual invasion landings was the Normandy beaches. A direct attack on Cherbourg or the Brittany ports was out of the question.

The examination proceeded upon lines similar to those adopted by the British GHQ planners over a year earlier, which were personally very familiar to me. The advantages of the short crossing towards the Pas de Calais were obvious — an easier task for air cover and for naval escort; a quicker turnround, and therefore a lesser requirement for shipping. The disadvantages were that this was the most heavily-defended part of the whole of North West Europe, and it was territory in which the fighter element of the German Air Force was largely concentrated. Furthermore, it was an area where the mobile reserves of armoured and infantry divisions were stationed for quick reinforcement of the defending formations. Moreover, the exits inland from the beaches were poor and presented difficulties for an enlargement of a beachhead. An attack against the Cotentin peninsula, with the object of securing the use of Cherbourg as a port, may well have been the easiest option, but invasion forces, even if successfully landed, could be bottled up in the peninsula by sealing off the neck, leaving them without much hope of breaking out. On the other hand, the Normandy beaches had many advantages — the beaches themselves were flat and very extensive, providing a high capacity for landing and disembarking, and were tolerably well-sheltered from the prevailing winds. The exits into the hinterland were good, and the 'bocage' country, with its pattern of small fields with hedges on high banks of earth, although more troublesome for invading armour, made it more defensible for invaders who had got ashore, and provided a difficult problem for the deployment of the enemy armoured units if they rushed up to come to the rescue of troops in static defence positions. The area was well away from the concentration of the Luftwaffe fighter squadrons, and was defended much more thinly and by troops of a lower quality than those in the Pas de Calais, which was where the Germans expected an Allied invasion to take place. The main disadvantage of the Normandy beaches was the extra length of the sea crossing, which meant that assault convoys were at risk for a greater period, which in turn called for more and stronger naval protective escorts than would be required in the shorter voyage. The biggest drawback was that the distance was such that Allied fighter aircraft would be operating at extreme range, which made it an imperative part of an plan that suitable territory for the construction of air landing strips and refuelling stops must be made available at the early stages of an invasion. The Navy and Air Force advisers were, however, of the opinion that these problems were not so great as to make the selection of the Normandy beaches wholly unsuitable.

As a result of all this study, Morgan came to the same conclusion that the Combined Commanders, on the advice of the GHQ Home Forces and Combined Operations planners, had reached a year earlier. An invasion force should be landed on the beaches of Normandy in the general area of Caen to Bayeux. The COSSAC plan was, however, bound to be different in that once a landing had been achieved, the objective was to include Cherbourg and the Brittany ports in the lodgement area. In its first outline form, the planned operation was for an assault by three infantry divisions, followed immediately by at least three brigade groups of armoured units, the actual landings to be preceded by aerial bombardment of the beach defences, and airborne forces to be utilized for certain key purposes once the aerial bombardment ceased.

The more that Morgan endeavoured to crystallize these general thoughts, the more difficult the whole problem seemed to be. He was well aware that there were strongly held critical and pessimistic views in certain quarters, and no doubt he recalled the words of General Brooke, that he had got to make an impossible job somehow work, when the 'Trident' directive was first handed to him. Although Morgan did not specifically name him as one of the doubting Thomases, it is probable that General Sir Bernard Paget, the Commander-in-Chief of British Home Forces, was one. As the Army member of the original Combined Commanders and as the one ear-marked for command of a British Expeditionary, he would have been strongly influenced by the conclusions of his own former planning staff that an invasion would have to be in much greater strength than that subsequently envisaged in the directive of COSSAC. As one of the authors of the original planning studies, I should, if asked for an opinion, have found it embarrassing to decide whether a new loyalty to the COSSAC staff under a directive from the Combined Chiefs of Staff required a change of view but the bigwigs were not interested in what a mere Lieutenant-Colonel might think, and never asked!

Lieutenant-General Morgan has put it on record that by the end of June 1943 he was extremely doubtful about the whole thing, and it was only after a very close examination of all the factors and of the arguments for and against an operation of this kind, which took place during a symposium held at the Combined Operations training school at Largs in West Scotland, that he and Mountbatten were sufficiently confident to go ahead, provided that certain conditions were met. These conditions were subsequently recognized and rationalized by the British Chiefs of Staff, but the American members of the Combined Chiefs of Staff tended to brush them aside, even though these conditions indicated a sensible and realistic approach to the over-optimistic nature of the CCS directive to COSSAC.

The first outline plan was sent by Morgan to the British Chiefs of Staff on 15 July, with a covering note which stated that in his opinion it was possible to undertake the operation on or about the target date with the forces specified, given a certain set of circumstances at the time. After the British Chiefs of Staff examined this first COSSAC plan, they set out a threefold set of circumstances. First, there had to be a substantial reduction in the strength of the German fighter aircraft force; second, there must be no more than twelve mobile divisions in northern France at the time, with a maximum possibility of no more than fifteen further divisions for build up within a period of two months; and third, the problem of maintenance of an invasion force over the beaches must be mastered, and would in an event require the construction of at least two synthetic harbours. This third condition led to an immediate intensive study of the 'Mulberry' harbour. In the event, the actual construction of two of these did not begin for several months to come. A British design was worked out, and this colossal enterprise was carried out entirely in British shipyards and factories. This was yet another instance of a vitally important contribution to the ultimate success of Operation 'Overlord' for which the British were never given the full credit.

The handing over of the plan to the British Chiefs of Staff, as Morgan rightly stressed in his covering note, called for a recognition that the preparations for this vast operation must be regarded as already in train. In fact this was true over a wide range of activity, embracing the conversion of specialized tanks, the construction of embarkation 'hards', the detailed designing of the 'Mulberry' harbours, the notion of undersea pipelines for carrying petrol ('gasoline' to the Americans), and many other matters. If all this active preparatory work had not been in hand when the COSSAC plan was first submitted, it would have been impossible to have launched the 'Overlord' invasion in June 1944. The US Joint Chiefs of Staff, and General Marshall in particular, should have recognized that all this was strong evidence that the British were taking seriously the Allied agreement to launch the invasion in the late spring of 1944. For their part, the Americans failed lamentably to appreciate that they were far from providing an adequate fleet of landing craft, which, as it turned out and as it always had been, was the one critical factor in getting the invasion off at the due date.

At the time that General Brooke and the other Chiefs of Staff were handed the COSSAC report and Morgan's covering note, they were heavily involved in the consideration of the way that Allied campaign in the Mediterranean was progressing, and what the prospects for the future were. The invasion of Sicily, successfully begun a few days earlier, was developing according to expectations; and ten days later there followed the arrest of Mussolini and the creation of a new military government in Italy under Marshal Badoglio. Understandably, therefore, the COSSAC plan took second place for the time being — it was, after all, nearly a year before the target date for the operation, and the Mediterranean campaign was burgeoning as General Brooke had always hoped. At Norfolk House the COSSAC planners were put on standby, and were not in fact required to put in any further, more detailed work for several weeks to come.

General Sir Alan Brooke, although fearful of a premature and inadequate invasion across the English Channel, was nevertheless loyal to the decisions reached by the Combined Chiefs of Staff, and took energetic steps to see that a British element of an Allied Expeditionary Force was fully enlisted, fully trained and properly equipped. His acceptance of the viability of Major-General Hobart's DD tanks and his order for 900 tanks to be converted were a case in point. He had already decided that the British part of the invasion army was to be called 21st Army Group, and this was officially brought to birth at the beginning of July 1943. The Army Group was to consist of a British 2nd Army and a 1st Army, based on the Canadians who had been stationed in the United Kingdom for two or three years training, waiting impatiently to be used. They had been given the unhappy task of providing the main force in the disastrous attack on Dieppe, which dampened their ardour a bit; and they also contributed a part of the Allied forces in the invasion of Italy. But now at last they were to be able to come into their own as partners in the great invasion armies, whenever the day was to be. Brooke moved General Sir Bernard Paget from Home Forces to be the first Commander-in-Chief of 21 Army Group. The new headquarters staff had been assembling for two or three months under the aegis of GHQ Home Forces, and were all transferred at a stroke of a pen to HQ 21 Army Group in name; but they physically remained at St Paul's School in

Hammersmith, from which the rump of GHQ Home Forces was turned out.

Whereas the staff at COSSAC were temporarily made metaphorically moribund, the members of the newly created Headquarters 21 Army Group were full of life and bursting with enthusiasm. Personally, a switch to the Q Staff meant the end of any participation in theoretical planning; in its place came an involvement in operational administration, which for the next six months or so meant a supervision and checking of all the multifarious aspects of preparing for the embarkation of the assaulting troops, and for the equipment and supply of a huge expeditionary force over the beaches with the aid of an artificial harbour. There was close co-operation with Combined Operations HQ in arranging for practice exercises in all the aspects of the embarkation and maintenance of a seaborne invasion army. Sadly, this meant an end for the time being of any contact with American counterparts. Except for a handful of US officers at COSSAC, the whole of the gathering forces from across the Atlantic Ocean were under the direction and control of ETOUSA, commanded by General J.L. Devers. Hundreds of thousands were quartered for the most part in the south-west of England in the counties of Devon, Cornwall, Wiltshire and Dorset, where they were knocked into shape and gradually built up into a well-equipped, well-trained army.

All this was down-to-earth practical soldiering. In the stratosphere of the higher direction of the war, the success of the Allied Forces in the Mediterranean was causing anxiety to General Marshall in Washington. It looked as if his worst fears about the diversion of the Allied war effort into the sideshow, as he saw it, of an Italian campaign might jeopardize the one great operation on which he had set his heart. The British Chiefs of Staff, and General Brooke in particular, were all for further exploitation of the invasion of Sicily, going even beyond a toehold in Italy, but General Marshall now had the support of War Secretary Stimson. The old man came back from a visit to London and Algiers with a firm conviction, resulting from his discussions with Lieutenant-General Morgan and the American members of the COSSAC staff, and even more so with Winston Churchill, that the British, though professing support for the 'Overlord' operation (which he erroneously and confusedly described as 'Roundhammer'), were in fact hoping that such a huge undertaking might not after all be necessary if all went as well as was hoped in Italy. He also warned Eisenhower that if the British had their way over the Mediterranean there would be no invasion of North West Europe in the late spring of 1944. This conversation placed Eisenhower in a difficult position, because he could not abandon an invasion of Italy now that it was a logical next step after Sicily. He was also acutely aware that it was due to the failure of the Americans to provide enough assault shipping that it was not possible to make further landings north of Rome, thereby to crush the Germans in a pincer, which was the sort of strategy for which General MacArthur had the resources, and which he executed with such effect and brilliance in the Pacific war against Japan.

The most that could be done was to put US forces under General Mark Clark in at Salerno. Much to the surprise of General Brooke and probably Eisenhower also, General Marshall now came out in support of an American landing at Salerno, but the British failed to appreciate the motives behind this apparent sudden change of heart. Marshall was all for a quick and successful entry into the southern end of the Italian mainland, because that was the limit of his concession to British strategic thinking and would mean that a Mediterranean campaign could reasonably by closed down, and all effort and resources switched to 'Overlord'. Stimson went even further than Marshall. Not only did he warn President Roosevelt that he thought that the British would try and avoid the 'Roundhammer' (sic) operation, but he advised that it was time that the Americans took over the control and command of the whole of the Allied Expeditionary Force. Previously it had been thought that this post would go to a British officer, and indeed Churchill had privately invited General Sir Alan Brooke, to his great delight, to take over this command. Stimson was, however, laying down the poison. No British leader was fit for this great task. Strains and stresses among the leaders of the two nations were again beginning to show.

There was urgent need for yet another top-level conference. This was arranged to be held at Quebec in August 1943, and given the name 'Quadrant'. The conference itself began on 15 August, but before that Churchill spent a couple of days with Roosevelt, who had by now received Stimson's forthright memorandum on the need for Roosevelt to assume the control of the Allied project for invasion, and to establish the principle of US Command of 'Overlord'. Roosevelt went all the way with his elderly War Secretary, and informed Churchill of his proposition that General Marshall should take over the Supreme Command. Notwithstanding his promise to Brooke, Churchill surprisingly acquiesced without demur. Indeed, he and Roosevelt entered into a horse-trading session on their own, covering a wide field of top-level appointments. Marshall was to be the Supreme Commander for Europe; Eisenhower was to return to Washington to take over as US Chief of Staff; Alexander was to be Commander-in-Chief Allied Forces in the Mediterranean; Montgomery was to come back to England and take over command of 21st Army Group from General Sir Bernard Paget; and, as a consolation prize for losing Supreme Command in Europe, Britain was to have the new appointment of Supreme Allied Commander in South East Asia, which Churchill had already decided was to be Mountbatten. Poor General Brooke was completely taken aback when Churchill told him of all these proposals, although Churchill recorded that he bore this shattering disappointment with 'soldierly dignity'. Brooke himself expressed one of his strongest-ever criticisms of Churchill, complaining that he was quite off-hand and never had a word of explanation or apology for his breach of promise. The only difference which was later made to all this pattern of top-level command was that Roosevelt changed his mind and declined to part with Marshall's services as Chief of Staff, and gave the Supreme Command to General Eisenhower instead.

In the early stages of the discussions between the members of the Combined Chiefs of Staff and their entourage, progress was negligible and at times acute tension was only too apparent. Although Brooke kept reiterating that the British were fully committed to 'Overlord', and were doing all that was required of them, as indeed they were, the Americans refused to budge an inch from their preconceived attitude, sparked off by Stimson's report to the President. They refused to accept Brooke's arguments in favour of further action in the Mediterranean, notwithstanding that Marshal Badoglio, through his emissaries in neutral embassies, was seeking to arrange complete capitulation of the Italian armed forces and an honourable peace, which would only come about if quick and strong Allied action prevented the Germans from acquiring full military control of most of Italy. There was an ominous stalemate which was only broken by Brooke's proposal for another off the record private session of the Combined Chiefs of Staff, when he said with brutal frankness that the trouble was due to the fact that neither side trusted the other, and it was time that the various differing points of view were examined on their merits. As the discussions developed over the next day or two, the British finally persuaded the Americans that they were serious in their support of 'Overlord', but failed to get Roosevelt and Marshall to agree to the contention that there should be a twenty-five per cent increase in the allotment of shipping so that the assault could be strengthened. Indeed, the sad feature of this period of time was the almost incredible naivety of the US Joint Chiefs of Staff in their assumption that all they had to do was pour men and equipment into Britain, and that the mounting of Operation 'Overlord' could take care of itself.

The only good thing that came out of the 'Quadrant' conference was the final communiqué, which indicated a full acceptance of the COSSAC plan and, to pacify Churchill and Brooke, the inclusion of the pre-conditions about enemy strength, a caveat which to the Americans was something not worth bothering about, in view of their belief that the sheer weight and size of the US forces would carry the day. The communiqué, supported by Marshall, stated that from the Allied resources in the Mediterranean sufficient men, equipment and shipping should be diverted to land an invasion force on the southern coast of France in the area of Toulon and Marseilles with the objective of driving northwards toward Brittany. For the first time mention was made of French forces; these were raised from those who had joined the Allies in Tunisia, and were organized and equipped by the Americans. This operation, code named 'Anvil', was to bedevil much of the strategic thought behind 'Overlord' and its detailed planning during the early months of 1944.

During the three months that followed the 'Quadrant' conference, the COSSAC staff got down to the detailed planning of Operation 'Overlord' and presented the final version at the end of November 1943. The British were hard at work with all the preparations involved in the launching of the greatest-ever seaborne invasion, whereas, except for the provision of the men and their equipment based in England, the Americans never raised a finger to prise any more assault shipping from the clutches of Admiral King. It was not until, very belatedly, when Eisenhower was told of his new command, that he and General Montgomery realized that the operation as planned was woefully inadequate and could only be made viable if there was a very large increase in shipping resources to provide a much greater punch in the initial landings.

9

THE PLANNING FOR OPERATION 'OVERLORD' SECOND PHASE

In the Autumn of 1943 or 'Fall' as the Americans would say, President Roosevelt realized that his political opponents would allege that in making Marshall the Supreme Commander in Europe he was kicking him upstairs; moreover there was a danger that General MacArthur, the conquering hero of the Pacific war, might be drafted as a formidable Presidential candidate in the Republican cause. Roosevelt therefore decided not to make any change in what his advisers referred to as a winning team. So Marshall, like Brooke, had his cherished desire of leading victorious Allied armies snatched away from him by his master, but he took it well and accepted the fact that it was better for him to stay where he was. That meant that Roosevelt could turn only to Eisenhower for the post of Supreme Commander, and in this he was strongly supported by Marshall himself, but he did not finally make up his mind until the end of November. Eisenhower, who was fully occupied with the Allied Command in Italy and the Mediterranean, was officially told of his new appointment at the beginning of December: it was to take effect on 1 January 1944. So there was still no effective leadership of Operation 'Overlord' while the year 1943 was ebbing to its close. This was a devastating disadvantage which nearly caused a disaster.

Quite apart from coping with the burden of all the preparations for a seaborne invasion and with the regular bombing of targets in Germany, the Allies and the British in particular had another problem to face. In April 1943, British secret agents with the help of the Polish underground movement had discovered that the Germans were developing weapons which were called 'Vergeltungswaffen', designated by the first letter V; there was V1, a pilotless jet-propelled aircraft carrying a bomb, and V2, a long-range rocket missile. In these days, accustomed as we are to thousands of jet aircraft flying all over the world, satellites stationed in the stratosphere circling with the turn of the earth, men living in space and men landing on the moon, we forget, if we ever knew, that the pioneering inventors and scientists in this great leap forward by mankind were either British or German.

The first successful flight in 1941 of a jet-propelled aircraft was one powered by a development of an engine designed by Frank Whittle, a Royal Air Force officer, which he had first invented a few years earlier. In the United Kingdom there was no production of these aircraft during the war years. The Germans, although starting later than Whittle, then moved ahead and contemplated putting jet aircraft into production in 1940. In fact they did not do so until the end of 1942, when the original Messerschmidt design had to be abandoned because of the impossibility of creating sufficient of a very highly specialized type of fuel required for its propulsion. The plans of a design for a long range rocket were presented to Hitler by Von Brauchitz in 1939, but mercifully for the future of the civilized world, they were at that time rejected. It was not until the end of the year 1942 that Hitler, advised by Speer, his great administrator of armament production, realized the potential of these two horrific weapons which could be used for indiscriminate targets anywhere in the South of England, and ordered their large-scale production. The long-range rocket missile had been developed and was being still further developed by Werner Von Braun, a brilliant scientist and engineer. When the war ended, he escaped arrest and possible trial as a war criminal by surrendering to the Americans who, preferring practical advantage to the administration of justice, took him to the United States where he was required to exercise his genius in the creation and development of the American contribution to the space age. For many years the Americans were able to harness their formidable capacity for manufacture to the inventive genius of those who came from other nations. Whittle was another who took his invention to the United States from his native Britain, where he had found himself increasingly frustrated in the years immediately following the end of the war.

In May 1943, a Royal Air Force reconnaissance pilot spotted a vast and peculiar collection of buildings at Peenemunde, later aerial photographs of which coupled with the information received through the underground spy channels enabled the British experts to identify as a massive research and development station for self-propelled aerial missiles. Ultimately, once the British War Cabinet realized the importance and threat of this establishment, the Royal Air Force launched a huge attack on the place with 600 bomber aircraft on 17 August, and did enormous damage, very nearly wrecking it completely. During the summer months aerial reconnaissance revealed a number of odd-looking things springing up along the French coastline, which appeared to be, as in fact they were, launching sites for missiles of some sort. They seemed to be sited so that a target area was either London or Portsmouth. Hitler had ordered ninety-six of these launching pads for the V1, the flying bomb. Some sixty or so of these sites were identified to begin with, and all were attacked and largely destroyed.

By December 1943, a total of seventy-three of these sites were put out of action, and the combined effect of this sustained bombing of the launching pads for the V1 and of the establishments for design and manufacture of the V2 rocket totally disrupted Hitler's plans for the use of his secret weapons. It is estimated that their use was put back by at least six months, and when it is remembered that their arrival in June 1944 over Southern England, particularly the V2 in the streets of London created havoc and near panic, the thought of what might have happened if they had been used at Christmastime 1943 hardly bears contemplation. When these bombs did finally land in Britain, the Allied armies were already established ashore in Normandy, and the British people were sustained in their anxiety by the knowledge that this aerial horror could not last for long.

At the end of November 1943, Lieutenant-General Morgan, in the name of the Supreme Commander, not yet officially named, issued directives to 21 Army Group and US First Army that they must be prepared to provide the forces for an invasion of the Normandy beaches in May 1944 in accordance with the plan approved by the Combined Chiefs of Staff. Except for the detailed planning of how the forces were to be assembled, conveyed and landed, many of the basic preparations were of course well advanced, and in fact the issue of the directive made no difference to the daily round at HQ 21 Army Group.

In Italy the bad weather, the difficulty of the terrain and the superb defensive quality of the German forces had led to a serious lapse in the Allied timetable for advance. General Brooke and Winston Churchill strongly resented the withdrawal of troops and equipment from the Mediterranean theatre of war for the purpose of bolstering up the forces required for Operation 'Overlord'. They pressed for an increase in support of Alexander's armies, but got nowhere. As Generalissimo Chiang Kai-Shek was constantly harping on the need to assist the Chinese Nationalist Army against the Japanese, and as Stalin, as a result of Russian successes against the Germans, was now in fact a powerful ally, it became necessary for the Americans and the British to have another top-level conference. This was held in two parts; at the end of November in Cairo with Chiang Kai-Shek as the third member, and at the beginning of December in Teheran with Stalin as the third member.

By the time of the Teheran conference, Britain had already lost the power to exercise any decisive role in Allied strategy. For the future, the conferences were dominated by Roosevelt and Stalin, and Churchill's dramatic contributions made little difference to the end result. Indeed, the extent to which Roosevelt thereafter leaned towards Stalin and away from Churchill was the greatest political disaster of the whole war. Roosevelt could never rid himself of the conviction that Britain was an imperialist power whose Empire must be broken up when fighting came to a stop. He and Harry Hopkins and, astonishingly enough, General Eisenhower, all believed that there was a special relationship with the Russian people because the United States and Russia were both 'free of the stigma of colonial empire-building by force'. Putting on one side the conduct of the Emperor Peter the Great and the Empress Catherine, that may have been true before the year 1943, but by the time the Russians had held off the German invasion, Stalin was already fixed in his determination to destroy the old balance of power in Europe, and increasingly to move towards the creation of a vast Soviet empire. Roosevelt and Hopkins both died before the blatant empire-building by force by the Russians became a fact, but Eisenhower, if he was able to take an honest dispassionate view when he became President of the United States, must have bitterly regretted the way he had foolishly misjudged Stalin and his generals, and the strategic decisions which let the Russians into Berlin and enabled them to overrun and virtually annexe East Germany, Czechoslovakia, Hungary and Poland. The British for their part never forgot that it was the cynical signing of the Russo-German treaty of non-aggression that provided Hitler with the assurance that he could safely invade Poland, which in turn led to the outbreak of war. Understanding the true nature of Stalin's objectives, Churchill was absolutely right in his desire to keep the Russians out of the Balkans and Austria.

It was at the Cairo conference that General Marshall privately told Eisenhower, a day or two before it was officially decided, that there was to be no change of US Chief of Staff, and that Eisenhower would be put forward as the Allied Supreme Commander. At Teheran, Stalin insisted that the British and Americans must demonstrate their commitment to Operation 'Overlord' by having a Supreme Commander in control, and after the end of the conference Roosevelt and Churchill agreed that his position should be given to General Eisenhower.

During the conference Stalin supported the Americans in their plan for an additional invasion of Southern France using the resources in men, equipment and shipping which were already there in the Mediterranean. This was ultimately agreed, albeit most reluctantly by Churchill and General Brooke, and the operation was given the code name 'Anvil'. It was never at that time appreciated by the Americans that the crafty Stalin was already aiming to direct the efforts of the other two Allied Nations towards a concentration against the western elements of the German forces, away from Vienna and the Balkans. The date for both operations was fixed for May 1944.

As soon as Eisenhower was advised of his new appointment, he asked for General Alexander as his Deputy, and Air Chief Marshal Tedder as his top airman; then, along with Lieutenant-General W. Bedell Smith as Chief of Staff and Lieutenant-General Humfrey Gale as Chief Administrative Officer, he would have with him the whole of his team of top brass from Allied Force Headquarters in the Mediterranean. However, Winston Churchill and General Brooke declined to take Alexander away from the direction of the Allied offensive in Italy. The ultimate arrangement was that Tedder became Eisenhower's Deputy, with special responsibility for co-ordination of British affairs and with the Allied Bomber Air Forces, which remained outside Eisenhower's area of control. The Naval Commander-in-Chief and the Air Commander-in-Chief were both British, namely Admiral Sir Bertram Ramsay and Air Chief Marshal Sir Trafford Leigh Mallory.

General Omar N. Bradley

Topham

This left the position of Army Commander-in-Chief unsolved. Obviously, if the invasion was a success and firmly established, that position would be undertaken by General Eisenhower himself. It was decided therefore that the planning and execution of the assault and bridgehead phases of the operation would be the responsibility of Headquarters 21 Army Group who, until there were sufficient American divisions to make up a US Army Group, would have US 1st Army under command. US 1st Army was to be under Lieutenant-General Omar N. Bradley, who would move up to be Commanding General of US 12 Army Group when it was formed. In view of his well-known successes and public recognition, as well as his actual experience of directing a seaborne invasion, it was thought that General Montgomery should take over command of HQ 21 Army Group from General Sir Bernard Paget. Thus, in effect, Montgomery was the Army Commander-in-Chief of the Allied armies for the

Imperial War Museum

Back Row, Left to Right: Lt. Gen. Omar Bradley, Admiral Ramsay, Air Chief Marshal Leigh Mallory, Lt. Gen. Bedell Smith.
Front row, Left to Right: Air Chief Marshal Tedder, General Eisenhower, General Montgomery.

first part of Operation 'Overlord'. Moreover it became his responsibility to plan the invasion, reporting to Eisenhower for ultimate approval. Lieutenant-General 'Freddie' Morgan was made Deputy Chief of Staff to Bedell Smith, and the COSSAC staff were all absorbed into Eisenhower's Supreme Headquarters Allied Expeditionary Force (SHAEF).

The announcement that General Montgomery was to take over command of 21 Army Group was made on Christmas Eve 1943. Before arriving in England on 2 January 1944, he had broken his air journey back from Italy at Marrakech to see Winston Churchill, who was recuperating from illness; he also saw Eisenhower and his Chief of Staff, and the three generals had a look at the COSSAC plan, and a short discussion about it. The immediate reaction of all three, with their experience of the Sicily and Salerno landings, was that the initial assault was on too narrow a front and with insufficient forces. As Eisenhower had to visit General Marshall and the US Joint Chiefs of Staff in Washington, he instructed Montgomery and Bedell Smith to make preliminary studies and to be prepared to discuss the plan when he arrived in England on 15 January.

When the news of Montgomery's appointment was announced, those at HQ 21 Army Group who knew what he was like expected a gigantic upheaval on his taking over. Well, there was an upheaval, but not quite as gigantic as was feared. Major-General 'Freddie' de Guingand, it was realized, would inevitably be brought back as Chief of Staff. This never caused any difficulty, except to Major-General Morgan (not the COSSAC one), who lost his job, as did quite a few other senior officers. The whole of the middle echelon of the existing staff had the highest regard for de Guingand, an admiration which increased as the months went by. Moreover, one of the things which held the Alliance of Britain and the United States together in spite of bickering and sniping at the top level was the way in which de Guingand, as Montgomery's Chief of Staff, worked happily with Bedell Smith as the Supreme Commander's Chief of Staff. The 'Brit' and the 'Yank' both had a mutual high regard for the other, and were close friends throughout the war.

A clutch of Brigadiers came with de Guingand. Among these were R.F.K. ('David') Belchem, E.T. ('Bill') Williams, Charles Richardson and Rim Lymer. The invading forces also included Major-General Charles Inglis as Chief Engineer, and

Major-General Richards as Chief Adviser Armoured Corps. The least satisfactory appointment was that of Major-General Miles Graham as Chief Administrative Officer, who, notwithstanding the praise he got from de Guingand and the reliance placed upon him by Montgomery, never earned any respect from the more junior administrative staff officers who formed his team. As some justification for criticism, there has sadly to be recorded the fact that he never once in eighteen months even spoke to a certain officer who was first his senior Lieutenant-Colonel, then full Colonel and finally Brigadier. This was no doubt true also of several others of his own staff. There can be no stronger complaint to be made of any senior officer that he never takes the trouble to meet, let alone to get to know his own more junior officers.

When all these 'Monty men' arrived, it was probably Lieutenant-Colonel Peter Foster, himself an earlier transfer to HQ 21 Army Group from the Eighth Army in the desert, and possessed of a mordant wit and biting turn of phrase, who observed 'Here they come, oozing conceit and with sand pouring out of their ears'. This may have been true of some, but certainly not of Charles Richardson, who became Brigadier (Plans) and in later years reached the rank of full General and Master-General of Ordnance, one of the top posts in the British Army. As a young man attending the Royal Military Academy at Woolwich he so distinguished himself that, after being commissioned in the Royal Engineers, he was one of three or four officers who were sent to Cambridge University, where all were highly successful either in sporting activity, or, in his case, with a first class honours degree. He was one of two really outstanding officers on the Headquarters staff, and although better qualified academically and in war experience, did not quite match the achievement of a very young Brigadier, Geoffrey ('George') Baker, who finished his army career as a Field Marshal and Chief of the Defence Staff. Perhaps this was because 'George' Baker was in the Royal Regiment of Artillery. Gunners generally did better than Sappers in reaching the very top!

Headquarters 21 Army Group was very large indeed. It was divided into Main Headquarters, which was where the Chief of Staff and his General Staff Brigadiers and the Chief Administrative Officer all operated, and Rear Headquarters, which consisted of all those in the Adjutant General's ('A')

Branch and Quartermaster General's ('Q') Branch together with the staff representatives of the various ancillary services. The senior and the head of Rear Headquarters was the newly-promoted Major-General Randle ('Gerry') Feilden, who ranked as a Deputy Quartermaster-General. Major-General Miles Graham was exceedingly fortunate to be supported by 'Gerry' Feilden as head of the actual working staff on the administrative side, just as he was to have as his link man at Main Headquarters Colonel Oliver Poole, a reserve officer from the Life Guards (incidentally, so was Miles Graham). At the end of the war Oliver Poole went into Parliament, and in due course became a highly successful businessman and, for a time, Chairman of the Conservative Party Organization, being rewarded with a Barony in the House of Lords. Another member of HQ 21 Army Group to reach the House of Lords, as a leading Liberal Party politician, was Frank Byers who was at this time 'George' Baker's grade one General Staff Officer in the rank of Lieutenant-Colonel.

It was probably a good thing, certainly for 'Gerry' Feilden himself and his collection of Lieutenant-Colonels, that he had served as a major on the 'Q' side at HQ 3rd Division, commanded by Major-General Bernard Montgomery in France during the Blitzkrieg and the evacuation through Dunkirk in 1940. So when the new Commander-in-Chief took over 21 Army Group in January 1944, there was already there one senior officer whom he knew and of whom he approved. Now, Montgomery was accustomed to refer to officers as 'chaps', and they were assessed according to a graded category. The highest accolade was that of 'a good chap'; there were not many of those. A 'proper chap' was one who could be entrusted with operational command according to rank, or a senior staff officer with a high degree of operational responsibility. Then there were 'clever chaps'. This could be mildly derogatory, meaning that, although very able, these officers might not measure up to important command in the field; but he also applied the description to those who had demonstrated that they had the brains, judgement, and ability to qualify as senior and middle grade staff officers. This latter category included a number who came into the Army from the legal and accountancy professions, or academic posts, or with business experience.

Within a day or two of his arrival, General Montgomery went

round both sections of Headquarters in order to meet all those officers down to the rank of Lieutenant-Colonel whom he did not already know. As his past history made plain, he was quite capable of forming a judgement of a man in the course of a few moments' conversation, and writing him off as 'useless', whatever others may have thought and however good his track record may have been. In his office, Major-General Feilden gathered the several Lieutenant-Colonels in the 'Q' branch to meet the great man and to wait with trepidation to find out whether they were acceptable or not. There was Colonel Val Duncan and Lieutenant-Colonel Donald Ross (the only Regular Army officer among them), both of the 'Q' (Movements) side. There were Lieutenant-Colonels Charles Hardie, Ralph Kilner Brown and Kenneth Cocks of 'Q' (Maintenance and Operations), and Lieutenant-Colonels Peter Foster and John Hobson of 'Q' (Equipment). Not in the group was Lieutenant-Colonel Humphrey Prideaux, another Regular officer who, as Major-General Feilden's Military Assistant and Co-ordinating Officer, presumably was outside the scope of any 'vetting' exercise. In came the little General, clutching with both hands the lapels of his tunic as was his wont, and, in his high pitched, clipped and staccato mode of speech, said 'Good morning, Feilden. These your clever chaps? All right are they? Very well, you can keep them.' And off he went. It was all rather like a bunch of entrants at a dog show being scrutinized, but at least none was disqualified for poor pedigree!

In after years, most of these 'clever chaps' justified the appellation in civilian life. Val Duncan became head of the vast mining and industrial empire, Rio Tinto Zinc Corporation; Charles Hardie was and still is a chartered accountant, holder of many directorships of companies in the City of London, and at one time was Chairman of British Overseas Airways; John Hobson became Attorney-General in the Conservative Government of Harold MacMillan, and died tragically early before attaining further advancement; Peter Foster and Ralph Kilner Brown both were made Judges of the High Court. All five were honoured with Knighthoods. If one adds also Humphrey Prideaux there were six such, because on resigning from the Army he took on the job of chairing the management of the Navy, Army and Air Force Institutes (NAAFI to all and sundry), as well as becoming a director in one or two large business organizations. In addition, one of the Majors in the 'Q' Branch in due course became Sir Paul Wright, at one time British Ambassador in Lebanon.

The volunteer soldiers who were appointed to middle-ranking positions on the staff of HQ 21 Army produced from their number quite an impressive array of those who after the war was over returned to civilian life and achieved the status of 'top brass' in their respective occupations. To those already mentioned there should be added 'Bill' Williams, who after leaving the Army combined an academic career as a Fellow of Balliol College, Oxford, with participation in a number of public offices for which he also was Knighted; and Raymond Mais, head of a large building and construction corporation, in his year a Lord Mayor of London, and the third staff officer at HQ 21 Army Group to be elevated to a peerage in the House of Lords.

By contrast, apart from Field Marshal Sir Geoffrey Baker and General Sir Charles Richardson, there were few of the Regular Army officers who reached higher rank than Major-General. One was Major-General Maurice Chilton, older and more senior than most, who did become General Sir Maurice Chilton by a combination of seniority and ability. Major-General Feilden left the Army, became Chairman of NAAFI and Senior Steward of the Jockey Club, and was made a Knight Commander of the Victorian Order for his part in the organization of the Coronation of Queen Elizabeth the Second. 'David' Belchem was a disappointment. Regarded by Montgomery and de Guingand, whose Deputy he was, as a brilliant first class staff officer and a highly successful regimental officer, he must have failed to have won the support of some influential people at the War Office, because he only made the rank of Major-General some time after the war was over, as the result of the personal selection of the Field Marshal. He took an early retirement to take up a position in industry. There must have been a flaw somewhere in his make-up, because his civilian career did not match up to his talents. Devastatingly good-looking, he possessed a charm which was irresistible to women, but, perhaps sparked by envy of his ability in this as in other fields, the more stuffy, old-fashioned males tended to be unkind in their opinion of him, epitomized in Peter Foster's invariable disparaging reference to 'that Belchem'.

On 2 January, 1944, Major-General de Guingand went over to Norfolk House, St James's Square, to discuss with Lieutenant-General Bedell Smith, now himself COSSAC, that is Chief of Staff to Supreme Allied Commander, and the newly appointed Deputy, Lieutenant-General 'Freddie' Morgan, who outlined the existing COSSAC plan for the invasion of Normandy. De Guingand's reaction was similar to that of Eisenhower and Montgomery when the plan was shown to them at Marrakech — too narrow a front and too few forces. But being the reasonable, fair-minded man he was, de Guingand recognized that Morgan and his staff had had to do the best they could with the resources made available to them, and gave them every credit for the enormous amount of thought, research and work which had been done. He also praised the manner in which the plan was presented to Montgomery a day or two later.

In marked contrast, Montgomery, in cavalier fashion, was contemptuously dismissive of the whole thing. His opinion was, as he repeated more than once in later years, that it was 'simply not an operation of war'. He could so easily have rejected the plan in a more courteous manner, but was quite incapable of seeing any good in other peoples' ideas, and tended to assume that only he knew the right answer. Moreover, he even introduced the ludicrous suggestion that there should be dispersed assaults all the way from Dieppe down to the Brittany ports, or at least landings on both sides of the Cotentin peninsula if it was too far to go down to Brest and St Nazaire. However, after detailed examination of Morgan's staff studies and a further presentation of plans, he abandoned these notions and accepted the COSSAC preference for the Normandy beaches. Nevertheless, the manner of his approach to all the work which had been done by the COSSAC staff permanently damaged his relationship with Morgan, who thereafter usually sided with those who criticized Montgomery's tactics. It is interesting to note that the 'anti-Monty' faction of SHAEF was headed by the two British, namely Air Chief Marshal Tedder and Lieutenant-General Morgan, whilst his strongest supporters, at any rate to begin with, were the two Americans, Lieutenant-Generals Bedell Smith and Omar N. Bradley. Tedder, though a great success when he was in control of the Air Forces under Eisenhower's command in North Africa and Sicily, suffered from a totally distorted view that Air Forces could win the war on their own, and that most British generals were incompetent, an opinion which carried considerable weight at SHAEF as he was Eisenhower's Deputy Supreme Commander.

Headquarters 21 Army Group remained at St Paul's School, Hammersmith, and to begin with SHAEF functioned at Norfolk House, as did the Naval and Air Force Commanders-in-Chief. After Eisenhower arrived from Washington in the middle of January, SHAEF moved to new headquarters at Bushey Park just outside London, and then later Admiral Ramsay took his staff to Southwick House, Portsmouth, and Air Chief Marshal Leigh-Mallory to Stanmore, while Lieutenant-General Omar N. Bradley, who to begin with was Commanding General 1st US Army and then in due course of 12 US Army Group, set up a skeleton Headquarters of the Army Group for planning purposes in London, and the operational Headquarters of 1st US Army at Plymouth. To add to this dispersal of the various headquarters, there was HQ 2 Tactical Air Force, the British element of the supporting air forces, which was at Uxbridge. Not merely because Montgomery was in charge and control of the assault phase, but because St Paul's School had a large lecture hall, all the subsequent Presentations of Plans took place there. The dispersal of all these different headquarters over such a wide area produced an untidy and inconvenient set-up, which involved a lot of travelling and moving about whenever it was necessary for the various Chiefs of Staff and other staff officers to meet.

From the start, Montgomery and de Guingand were faced with a decision as to whether or not there should be a fully integrated US and British staff at HQ 21 Army Group as there was at Allied Force HQ in Algiers, and was to be at SHAEF. There were two problems. The first was that in due course US 1st Army was to pass from Montgomery's command once Eisenhower assumed overall command and US 12 Army Group began to function operationally. Any American officers at 21 Army Group would then have to move over to US 12 Army Group, and there would then be gaps in the organization of 21 Army Group Headquarters. The other problem was caused by the fact that the administrative system and origins of supply and maintenance were different. The British, Canadian and European forces would all be the ultimate responsibility of the War Office, and all demands for equipment stores and supply and for reinforcement of personnel would be made through HQ 21 Army Group to the War Office. The American forces, who operated under a somewhat different system anyway, would in the first place be the responsibility of ETOUSA, based in England and then change to maintenance and provision directly from the United States.

In the face of these difficulties Bedell Smith and de Guingand worked out a compromise. In some branches of the staff there was full integration, but for the most part American officers were posted to work in parallel with British counterparts, so that each national representative could advise and assist the other with regard to the difference in organization and procedure. In view of the totally different and separate systems of logistic support, a complete self-contained echelon of administrative officers joined HQ 21 Army Group, and the Brigadier-General at the head was made deputy to the British Chief Administrative Officer (Major-General Miles Graham). In the planning stage, this joint staff at HQ 21 Army Group assumed control of the administrative requirements of both nations' armies.

Quite apart from the fact that the Americans referred to logistics and not to administration, they had long since abandoned the old-fashioned British triumvirate system of General Staff, Adjutant-General Staff and Quartermaster-General Staff. With much more common sense, they regarded all staff officers as General Staff, which in truth they were, and which the British should have recognized long ago. Formations in the US Army from the top down to a certain level operated with a Chief of Staff and a Deputy Chief of Staff, to whom all senior section staff officers were responsible. The staff was organized in four sections, G1 — Personnel; G2 — Intelligence; G3 — Plans and Training, and G4 — Supply. They did have an Adjutant-General on all superior headquarters, but he was an officer of junior status, responsible for compiling lists of casualties, losses of equipment and of prisoners of war and captured equipment. With the Americans there was no such thing as a separate chain of command for administrative staff officers, and the position of Chief Administrative Officer was created by Eisenhower at Allied Force Headquarters and at Supreme Headquarters Allied Expeditionary Force to provide a top general to co-ordinate and supervise the two different logistic systems of the Anglo-American forces. In the British set-up, because of the triumvirate system there was always a separation of power and responsibility between G staff on the one hand and A/Q staff on the other, with officers of equal rank in each branch. Without a Chief of Staff on American lines, as introduced by Montgomery, all British headquarters operated on the understanding that the senior officer on the General Staff would be the one to issue orders in the name of the General Officer commanding any particular formation.

Whilst all this reorganization of HQ 21 Army Group was going on, Montgomery and Bradley, Ramsay and Leigh-Mallory and their respective Chiefs of Staff were working out a new outline plan to take the place of the rejected COSSAC plan. Apart from the obvious necessity to enlarge the area for the purpose of adding weight to the assault, Montgomery from his own experience of Sicily and Italy was able to put his finger on a major weakness in the COSSAC plan. He was able rightly to say that the concept of leap-frogging a follow-up formation over the initial assault force would inevitably lead to confusion and chaos, with troops and vehicles getting all mixed up as the newly landed formations tried to make their way through those already there. This was a further strong argument for widening the front so that assault formations could go ashore side by side, each with their own front. To give Montgomery his due, he had made this point quite clearly in a memorandum to Churchill before he left Marrakech on 1 January. He had furthermore suggested even then that a British Army of at least three Corps should land side by side in one sector, and an American Army similarly in another sector.

Having agreed that the Normandy beaches should be the target area for the invasion and that the first strategic objective should be the establishment of a sufficient bridgehead to provide a firm base for the capture of Cherbourg and the Brittany ports, Montgomery and de Guingand then concluded that the area envisaged by the COSSAC plan should be considerably widened. For the outline initial plan it was recommended that the invasion should take place between the coast at the base of the Cotentin peninsula and the eastern end of the Normandy coast, at the mouth of the River Orne. This extended the front from the original twenty-five miles to a distance in excess of forty miles. The seaborne assault, though not as strong as Montgomery's original concept of three British corps alongside an American

Army, should be by five divisions (not the COSSAC three), with two more divisions already loaded and afloat for the immediate follow-up. There would be no difficulty with regard to manpower and equipment, but the problem arose with regard to the naval forces and landing craft. Minesweepers had to be in the van of the armada, clearing the way for all the hundreds and hundreds of ships to follow. Destroyers, frigates, corvettes, motor gunboats (MGB) and motor torpedo boats (MTB) would provide the escort and cover, whilst battleships and cruisers would be required for the heavy bombardment of the enemy defensive positions.

Admiral Ramsay had been allotted 467 warships and 150 minesweepers under the COSSAC plan, but he would need for this much enlarged invasion double the number of minesweepers and 240 more warships. With the typical confidence and determination of a first class Naval Commander, he was prepared to support Montgomery and to advise that the Royal Navy would do their part, as indeed they did. He did, however, enter the caveat that a target date of 1 May would be too early to commission the crews and train the seamen and officers for such a vast fleet, particularly for the huge number of landing craft that would be required. In the event, he was very nearly let down by the narrow-minded, tight-fisted American, Admiral King, who only agreed to a US Navy contribution as late as 15 April, and as Ramsay later recorded, his planning was always fraught with anxiety, and based upon speculation and hope.

The US Navy played a comparatively small part in the invasion of Europe, which may well be a matter of considerable surprise to many. More than three-quarters of the fleet of 200 major warships and 550 smaller vessels, and almost all of the 300 or so minesweepers were British. The problem with regard to landing craft was even greater, and the parsimonious attitude of Admiral King even more marked. Montgomery and Ramsay referred the calculations for the number of landing craft which would be required to the COSSAC staff to determine, as the additional requirement would be a matter for General Eisenhower to deal with. Appreciating that this would involve a struggle with the US Joint Chiefs of Staff, Montgomery sent a cable to Eisenhower whilst he was still in Washington, calling upon him to 'hurl himself into the contest and get what we want'. When the COSSAC plan was approved by the Combined Chiefs of Staff in May 1943, a total of 3,323 landing craft were allocated to the operation. Admiral King would agree to no more than 1,024 from the US Navy, although he had at his disposal more than 20,000 in all. Before his belated concession to a US Task Force on 15 April, 1944, King had a total of over 30,000 landing craft under his control. He was persuaded with reluctance to make 1,493 available for Operation 'Overlord'. Whenever he was challenged about this huge and ridiculous discrepancy, he said 'What operations are or are not conducted in the Pacific is no affair of the Combined Chiefs of Staff, since this theater is exclusively American.' — hardly the sort of observation one would expect to hear from a member of the Combined Chiefs of Staff, which was a body charged to prosecute the war in an alliance of two great nations.

It was pathetic of General Marshall to complain that there was a constant shortage of landing craft, when parts of the Pacific Ocean were almost awash with them. Lieutenant-General Bedell Smith and the COSSAC staff, knowing the form, came to the conclusion that some of the extra requirement would have to come from the Mediterranean, and that Operation 'Anvil' would have either to be abandoned or postponed, or reduced in size so as to provide landing craft for 'Overlord'. Eisenhower replied to Bedell Smith that he was most reluctant to interfere with 'Anvil'. The reason for his attitude was easy to find. While in Washington he was close to General Marshall, his mentor and chief, and was unwilling to upset Marshall in any way. So 'Anvil' at this time remained inviolate.

The only divergence of view between the three invasion Commanders-in-Chief arose over the use of airborne troops. As Montgomery was planning to put the equivalent of one division from the 1st US Army in at 'Omaha' beach, adjoining the three British beach sectors, and another equivalent division from US 1st Army in at 'Utah' beach at the side of the Cotentin peninsula, he and Bradley agreed that it was essential to assist both US forces and the 'Utah' forces in particular, by the use of airborne troops. There were two US and one British Airborne Divisions available for the invasion. Air Chief Marshal Leigh-Mallory saw no problem in the proposed use of British 6th Airborne Division in the furthest eastern part of the Normandy beaches to operate on the flank of the British forces, for the approach would be direct, avoiding strong anti-aircraft defences.

The original plan for the two American divisions was that one should be dropped in the area behind the 'Omaha' beach sector, and the other at the base of the Cotentin peninsula. This was objected to on the ground that it meant going in over assaulting warships, who might well be using anti-aircraft fire against the enemy, and also past the strong AA defences around Cherbourg. It appeared that Leigh-Mallory would reluctantly agree to this and accept high casualties, in view of the insistence on the part of Bradley and Montgomery that it was essential. So the planning went ahead.

However, further consideration of the American assault area led to a change in plan, which created a command crisis about the middle of May. At the base of the Cotentin peninsula there were large areas of inundations and water barriers, including a huge lagoon behind the 'Utah' beaches. If the causeways were not captured at their points furthest inland, the enemy would be able to use them and to deny their use by the assault forces, which would mean that the invaders would be unable to join up with the other American landings, or even to get off the beaches. So it was proposed that both US Airborne Divisions should be dropped behind the beaches at the base of the peninsula, so as to secure the causeways and the beach exits, and to prevent any enemy break-through aimed at dividing the two beach sectors.

This revived and intensified Leigh-Mallory's objections to this proposed use of airborne forces. It would mean an approach from the western side of the peninsula over and through the German air defences in the Channel Islands, and over territory known to be heavily defended against aircraft. He found himself resolutely opposed, and after fruitless discussions and argument the dispute was referred to Eisenhower for a Supreme Commander's ruling. Leigh-Mallory's staff estimated that casualties to men and machines would be as high as eighty per cent. De Guingand with his actual experience knew that anti-aircraft defences at night were slow to appreciate and identify an airborne attack and to direct AA gunfire. Eisenhower had no hesitation in overruling Leigh-Mallory's objections. Once the ruling was made, the Air Commander-in-Chief loyally accepted it. In the event the airborne attacks were partially successful, and the casualties to the US Airborne forces were no more than ten per cent. Moreover, after D-Day Leigh-

Mallory was the first to telephone Eisenhower and to admit that he was wrong.

This dispute came at the end of the planning period. Subject to initial anxiety expressed by Leigh-Mallory, the three Commanders-in-Chief and their senior staff officers were able within a few days of taking office under Eisenhower to evolve an outline plan for an assault with five divisions on a broader front. This was completed on 19 January, 1944, Eisenhower and Bedell Smith considered this plan at a meeting with the three Commanders at Norfolk House on 21 January, and, since it coincided with his own views, Eisenhower approved it and sent it off to the Combined Chiefs of Staff in Washington on 23 January. In addition, Eisenhower supported the advice of Montgomery and Ramsay that with the huge increase in the number of naval vessels and landing craft required for the enlarged invasion, and the consequent need for organizing and training the additional crews, it would be quite impossible to comply with a target date of 1 May, 1944. On 1 February the Combined Chiefs of Staff accepted the amended plan, and agreed to a postponement of D-Day from 1 to 31 May. The increased requirement of all types of ships, naval and landing, was noted, but nothing was done about this at that stage. This uncertainty was to bedevil the planning for months to come, and led to constant amendments of the nature and scope of the assault formations.

The outline plan having been approved, the three Commanders-in-Chief were able to submit an Initial Joint Plan, and Eisenhower accepted it on 1 February. Everything was now officially cleared for the detailed planning to proceed, but in fact the Commanders-in-Chief and their respective Chiefs of Staff had already set in motion the machinery for the staff organization, and much of the detail had been examined in the expectation that the Initial Joint Plan would receive approval. Even with the postponed target date, if would have been foolish if the last half of January had been spent in idly waiting for permission to proceed. The second phase of the planning for Operation 'Overlord' — revision and enlargement of the COSSAC plan and the creation of the whole of the command and planning structure — was now over. The final phase was now in being.

10

THE PLANNING FOR OPERATION 'OVERLORD' — FINAL PHASE

Whilst the three Commanders-in-Chief and their Chiefs of Staff and planning officers were busily engaged in the details of the approved plan for the invasion of Normandy, Eisenhower was faced with a problem over the strategic use of the Allied Air Forces. When he was Supreme Allied Force Commander at Algiers, the whole of the air forces were under command of Air Chief Marshal Tedder, who in turn was answerable for direction and control to Eisenhower. In the United Kingdom the position was different. There were three Royal Air Force Commands, namely Fighter, Bomber and Coastal, apart from Transport Command, whose offensive role was limited to operations with Airborne forces. The US Air Force was designated Strategic Air Force, and consisted of a huge fleet of Bomber aircraft and their protective long range fighters, all under command of General Spaatz. British Bomber Command was under Air Chief Marshal Arthur 'Bomber' Harris, who was directly responsible to Air Chief Marshal Portal, the British Chief of Air Staff. The combined British night bomber aircraft and US day bomber aircraft were controlled by Portal on behalf of the Combined Chiefs of Staff in a continuous bombing offensive, known as Operation 'Pointblank', with the objective of destroying German war industry and synthetic oil plants.

General Eisenhower had an Allied Air Force under command of Air Chief Marshal Leigh-Mallory, consisting of the British 2nd Tactical Air Force commanded by Air Marshal Coningham to operate with 21 Army Group, and US 9th Air Force commanded by Lieutenant-General Brereton to operate with

US 1st Army. However, as a result of his own experience in the Mediterranean, Eisenhower now wanted his Supreme Command to include the British and US Bomber Air Forces so that the whole of the pre-invasion air offensive could be made an integral part of Operation 'Overlord'.

Harris and Spaatz both strongly objected to any suggestion that their forces should be diverted from 'Pointblank', for each considered that, with their increased strength and improved technical equipment, they had reached the stage that they could, if left to their own devices without interruption, sufficiently destroy the German capacity to wage war without the need for any invasion on land. This was highly speculative in view of the heavy losses inflicted on the Allied Bomber fleets, and the recurring possibility that Portal might be compelled to order diversionary use of bomber aircraft for the neutralization of the German V1 and V2 construction and launching sites. Neither Harris nor Spaatz had much personal regard for Leigh-Mallory's credentials as a Commander-in-Chief involved in the strategic use of bomber aircraft, since his experience was entirely limited to the use of fighter aircraft, and Harris in particular was nearly as resentful of interference with his private war as was Admiral King in relation to the US Navy in the Pacific. Undoubtedly it was this unco-operative attitude, frequently brusquely and intemperately expressed, which led to the decision to leave Harris rewarded at the end of the war with a Knighthood, and not the peerage in the House of Lords which every other top British Commander achieved. Churchill would have given him that reward, but he had been succeeded by Clement Attlee as Prime Minister, who would no doubt have received advice from Portal.

In addition, Harris and Spaatz each had his own priority of objective, the former in favour of blanket bombing of industrial areas, the latter in favour of more pin-pointed attacks on oil refineries and storage installations, but these were complementary to each other: neither man was enamoured of Leigh-Mallory's preferred objective of rail communications, marshalling yards and maintenance and repair facilities, even though expert advice supported this policy. At the end of January, it was agreed that Air Chief Marshal Portal would, in consultation with Air Chief Marshal Tedder, take account of General Eisenhower's requirements for 'Overlord' in the direction of 'Pointblank'. This satisfied no-one. In the discussion which continued, Harris remained totally unco-operative, and maintained that the men of Bomber Command were not trained or experienced enough to carry out anything other than mass saturation attacks. It was not until 4 March, on Portal's direct orders, that RAF bomber crews successfully demonstrated that they had the skill to hit a precision target even by night. So Harris's opinion was proved false.

General Spaatz, on the other hand, was far more reasonable than Harris ever was. Nevertheless, he stuck to his belief that bombing of oil plants and storage installations would be a better way to assist 'Overlord' than attacks on the French transportation system. Tedder and Leigh-Mallory were just as convinced that transportation targets were preferable. Relying on his own Commanders' preference, Eisenhower was so irritated at the reluctance to use any 'Pointblank' bomber forces for the SHAEF strategy that he was on the brink of resigning his command. Fortunately at the meeting on 25 March under Portal's chairmanship between Eisenhower, Tedder and Leigh-Mallory on the one side and Spaatz and Harris on the other, with attendant advisers from the Ministry of Economic Warfare, the War Office and Joint Intelligence Staff, the advice was given and accepted that Spaatz's oil targets would have no impact in the immediate future, but would be profitable at a later stage. So it was agreed that for the immediate future the priority targets should be those involving transportation. At the beginning of April the Combined Chiefs of Staff issued an instruction that the Allied Bomber Forces were to operate under the direction of the Supreme Commander in conformity with agreement between him and the Chief of Air Staff (Portal). This meant that Eisenhower and Portal decided what Harris and Spaatz were required to do, but Tedder was the one who directed Eisenhower's requirements.

This strategic argument over the control and use of US Strategic Air Force and RAF Bomber Command was a complete justification for the necessity of a firm hand at the top, and the existence of a strong air element with Tedder as Deputy Supreme Commander at SHAEF. On the other hand, there was really nothing for the large military staff to do, although Eisenhower in his Report to the Combined Chiefs of Staff, which was largely written by the self-same military staff and contains quite a lot of inaccuracy and distortion, made out that the HQ 21 Army

Group's plans were subject to the supervision of the American Major-General H.R. Bull and the British Major-General J.M.F Whitely. At the most, this could only have been a cosmetic exercise to satisfy the *amour propre* of Eisenhower's 'top brass' by courtesy of Montgomery's Chief of Staff, de Guingand. Montgomery himself would have thrown a fit if anyone had tried to supervise his plans or his staff officers. At lower levels, the officers at HQ 21 Army Group were in practice completely disconnected from the staff at SHAEF, who, as far as appeared to be the case, were totally without significance.

The one useful thing which the SHAEF army staff did was to check the estimates of landing craft required for the enlarged plan, and then to brief Lieutenant-General Bedell Smith. Reference has already been made to the major error by the planners at Washington in calculating for the COSSAC plan the capacity of LST as the storage figure and not the operational figure. There was an even worse failure on the part of these gentlemen stuck away in the Pentagon. For the purpose of calculating the number of landing craft required to lift five divisions and preload a further two, they used the number of men in a standard US Army Infantry Division. They would have been much better advised to have used the 'divisional slice' figure first thought of by the British GHQ planners in the Spring of 1942. The assaulting formations had to bring with them a large number of supporting troops such as engineers and anti-aircraft and anti-tank artillery, in addition to the normal number of infantry personnel. Moreover, Montgomery decided to put the amphibious DD tanks and the specialist armour devised by Major-General Hobart in advance of the infantry, whereas the Washington planners gave their advice to the Combined Chiefs of Staff in terms of infantrymen only. Consequently, the number of craft required was considerably underestimated. As a result, there was no sense of urgency in response to Eisenhower's cry for more ships. It was only when he sent Bedell Smith in person to explain to the Combined Chiefs of Staff how hopelessly wrong was the advice that they were getting, that they woke up to realities. Nevertheless, the response of Admiral King was so niggardly that the Combined Chiefs of Staff were on 24 March forced into the postponement of Operation 'Anvil', first to July and then to mid-August, and to agree to the transfer of a quantity of landing craft intended for that operation for use in 'Overlord'.

All this uncertainty meant that the planning for the assault was constantly being amended, usually in a restricted manner. We scarcely knew from one day to another whether the landing tables would have to be altered yet again.

The American element at HQ 21 Army Group was established by the end of January. The officers, ranking mostly as Lieutenant-Colonels, were carefully selected, and were dedicated to the concept of joint planning and Allied endeavour. My counterpart was Lieutenant-Colonel Herbert Jordan, whose co-operation and friendship was a great privilege bestowed upon me. On the administrative (logistic) side, one of the biggest tasks was to work out skeleton landing tables in accordance with Montgomery's instructions as to the type of unit which had to be landed, and the order in which they were to be disembarked. He did not seek to impose any similar instruction on Lieutenant-General Bradley, leaving it to him and his staff to make the necessary decisions as to how the assault troops would be landed. Although dividing the whole assault area into five beach sectors, allocating the westerly two to the Americans and requiring each beach sector to be assaulted by a force equivalent to one division in strength with a clearly defined objective, he did not lay down the particular part of any beach which should be assaulted by any particular unit, whether American, British or Canadian. Nor did he insist that Bradley should use amphibious DD tanks and specialist armour as he did with Lieutenant-General Miles Dempsey, commanding British Second Army.

Dempsey and his staff were required to do the detailed operational planning for the British and Canadian assaulting formations within a very tight directive as to how the assault was to be carried out. With Montgomery's approval, Dempsey decided that 'Gold' Beach, next to the American 'Omaha' Beach, was to be assaulted by the 50th Infantry Division and 8th Armoured Brigade of British 30 Corps; 'Juno' Beach in the centre was allotted to 3rd Canadian Division and Canadian Armoured Brigade, and 'Sword', the furthest north-easterly beach, to 3rd Infantry Division and 27th Armoured Brigade, all part of British I Corps. The British 6th Airborne Division was to be put in to protect the eastern flank of the assaulting forces, and to capture bridges over the Caen canal and the River Orne. Behind the assault forces and the preloaded immediate follow-up, each of the two British Corps and the two US Corps was supported by a build-up of divisional strength, all preloaded.

Once Lieutenant-General Bradley had decided on the nature and the numbers of the assaulting troops on the two beaches allocated to the Americans, it was possible to make a fairly accurate assessment of the type and quantity of landing craft required, and the appropriate allotment to each of the Allied Armies. The Initial Joint Plan, which was based on an assault of five divisional strength, and an immediate follow-up equivalent to two further divisions and a build up of four more, all preloaded and afloat, all this to be supported by reinforcement at the rate of two to three divisions each day, now contained sufficient development in detail to enable the administrative (logistic) planning to proceed. This was done in the expectation that the necessary landing craft would be made available, which in the end they were , but HQ 21 Army Group was as much plagued by anxiety in this regard as was Admiral Ramsay over the delay in allocation of American Navy vessels.

On the assumption that enough landing craft would be made available to transport the assaulting forces and the immediate follow-up, the enormous logistic problem was how they, and later reinforcements were to be supplied and maintained. Even if Cherbourg was captured early, it was estimated that it would be several weeks before the port could be brought into use. There were no other ports to be considered, so therefore the supply and maintenance of both US and British Armies would have to be over the beaches, supplemented by a 'Mulberry' artificial harbour for each Army. These were unlikely to be in operation before a week or thereabouts had elapsed. Additional protection for landing craft and the barges and rafts used for transferring loads from ship to shore was to be provided by a line of sunken hulks, this breakwater being given the code name 'Gooseberry'. There were five or six of these altogether. A nice balance had to be struck between landing men and landing supplies and equipment. As the forces ashore increased, so the requirements for maintenance increased, and whereas in the assault the troops took their own ammunition and rations, as each day went by, and more troops required feeding and more ammunition was expended, the shipping allocated for maintenance increased in relation to that available for reinforcement of personnel.

The experience of most British commanders in the field was that the supply services tended to over-insure at base, but were sometimes caught short in the availability of transport if there was a breakthrough and rapid advance. It did not seem that this was likely to be the case in this operation. The problem would probably be that facilities for basic requirements would prove to be inadequate, particularly as the maintenance over beaches of such a large force for such a long time had never before been attempted. This would mean that priorities would have to be established and only essential transport, equipment and supplies put on board. The Americans were quite unused to selective supply, and just poured everything into the system, including vast quantities of cigarettes, chocolate and Coca-Cola. In the early planning stages for 'Overlord', the US G4 staff had to be firmly dealt with, and they soon saw the necessity for rigorous control and limitation of non-essentials. Each British and Canadian soldier landed with two twenty-four hour packs of 'hard' rations, and after forty-eight hours went on to what was called a 'Compo' pack. Operationally there was an equal control of the size of each unit to be landed, by imposing a limit of seventy-five per cent of the normal vehicle strength and the temporary exclusion of those personnel such as cooks and storemen who were not involved in the actual firing of weapons. Those left out were named as 'residues', and were called forward to join their units at a later stage.

Although maintenance and supply and reinforcement of personnel had to be meticulously planned, it did not have to be so rigid that the arrangements could not be varied and amended to cope with unforeseen or changing circumstances. In order to achieve flexibility so that alterations to the planned loading could be effected and different units or different types of equipment could be called forward out of turn, there was created an inter-Service organization designated Build-Up Control (BUCO). Apart from the Navy, Army and Air Force members, there were representatives from the War Office and ETOUSA, who were responsible for the actual movement of troops and equipment from all over the country. This outfit turned out to be a great success, and was invaluable in the smooth running of the build-up and in coping with the apparent disaster of the storms which lashed the sea about a fortnight after D-Day, 6 June.

The organization for the British beaches was devised by HQ 21 Army Group, although its actual creation in terms of manpower was delegated down to HQ 2nd Army and thence to HQs 1 Corps and 30 Corps. The system began with small establishments given the name of Beach Bricks: these were comprised of Naval as well as Army personnel. Then there were larger organizations called Beach Groups, and even larger ones called Beach Sub Area. There were three Beach Sub Areas, of which two were under command of 1 Corps and one under 30 Corps, and each corresponded with the target area allotted to each of the three assaulting divisions and were actually set up and controlled by Divisional HQ by the evening of D-Day. The plan was that the Beach Sub Areas would be expanded and to some extent amalgamated to form a Beach Maintenance Area. The successful setting-up of the various Beach Groups and three Beach Sub Areas is demonstrated by the fact that on the British sectors on D-Day alone, very nearly 60,000 personnel, 8,900 vehicles and 1,900 tons of stores were landed. The actual control on the ground was in the hands of Divisional HQ, as directed by Corps HQ. The intention was and in fact duly occurred for 2nd Army HQ to take over control from Corps HQ and then to hand over all responsibility for rear maintenance arrangements to HQ Lines of Communication, who in turn were to hand over responsibility to HQ 21 Army Group when they moved from England to Normandy.

As the advance proceeded and the Lines of Communication began to lengthen, it was planned to establish two Army Roadheads, one for British 2nd Army and one for Canadian 1st Army; once the forward troops had got far enough inland and were well clear of base, a Rear Maintenance Area was to be established to cope with the supply and maintenance of all the British and Canadian formations and later the European contingents as well. The organization devised by HQ 21 Army Group was a development from small units — the Beach Bricks — at water edge, thence to a broader-based set-up on the beaches and ultimately to a much larger outfit spreading inland.

The American system was not so closely and tightly organized. The whole approach was conditioned by an intrinsic belief in advance by size and weight. The United States possessed a vast reservoir of manpower and a huge capacity for manufacture, and therefore there was no need to pinch and scrape as the British were compelled to do. Moreover, the country was well away from any theatre of war, and the Americans never had to cope with the devastation and disorganization resulting from persistent bombing from the air or flying bombs or long-range rockets. The strategic plan as devised by Montgomery gave the US forces a much larger territory for rapid expansion, and in consequence they were able to plan their maintenance organization with much more room to develop, and to extend inland so as to avoid congestion on the beaches and the immediate exits there from. Nor were they obliged to create a system which depended solely upon maintenance over beaches supplemented only by one artificial harbour, for if all went well, they would have the use of a very large port, Cherbourg, and probably two or three more ports in Brittany well before the autumn storms set in. With all these advantages, it is not surprising that at times our American counterparts tended to be somewhat dismissive of our preoccupation with detail, and believed that the British could have done with a broader and looser system. When it came to the actual invasion, the staff officers of both nations were convinced that their way was right, but happily equally convinced that the other was also right for the particular situation in their case. So honour was saved and all was well!

Once the Initial Joint Plan was approved and became the official and final plan, Montgomery left de Guingand in charge of the planning and set off round the country to publicize the great Allied endeavour, and also himself. Of course he was a vain and conceited little man, but he was quite undeserving of the criticism and snide comments which were heaped upon him. As de Guingand himself, who knew his 'Monty' better than anyone, made quite clear, it was a deliberate, well-thought-out scheme to get not only all the invasion troops but also all the workers in the factories and shipyards thoroughly and totally involved in the preparations for a final assault against the Nazi tyranny. In his addresses to his officers and in his writings, Montgomery always put morale at the top of his list of factors essential to victory in war. He never deviated from this view, and time after time was proved to be entirely correct when he set out to create a high morale built upon a confidence in the high command, and a personal acquaintance with the self confidence of the commander. On his visits to the troops he would gather them round him and in simple terms impress upon them that they were going to win, and that he was the one to make sure that they did. It was a policy that came off. By the beginning of May there could hardly have been anyone in the country, man, woman and child, who was unaware of great things to come and final victory in the offing. Perhaps it was all a little bit overdone, because the people believed that once the invasion began, wherever and whenever it was to be, the war would be over in a few weeks. The reaction which set in during July 1944, when the more mercurial and timorous began to think that the invasion was bogged down, was totally unjustified, and the sniping of the 'anti-Monty' factions at SHAEF thoroughly unreasonable and unfair.

The general objectives and the manner in which the invasion was to be carried out was the subject of the first Presentation of Plans in the lecture hall of St Paul's School on 7 April, 1944. It was attended by the Allied Generals Commanding, from the Supreme Commander down to each Divisional Commander and their Chiefs of Staff or senior staff officers, and also their Naval and Air Force counterparts. Winston Churchill the Prime Minister and the British Chiefs of Staff also came. Montgomery took charge and opened the proceedings with a general outline of the plan, and the various force commanders gave a description of the role assigned to them. In this latter aspect, the American Major-General J. Lawton Collins ('Lightnin' Joe') was particularly impressive. Churchill himself contributed a stirring call to arms.

One or two of the Lieutenant-Colonels at HQ 21 Army Group were there to lend a hand with maps and models. The recollection of one of them, Lieutenant-Colonel C.P. ('Kit') Dawnay, must be at fault, or if accurate, indicates a strange failure on Montgomery's part to acquaint himself with what his staff officers had already done. Kit Dawnay has it that before the presentation began, there were no 'phase lines' other than one showing the Allied Armies reaching the line of the River Seine on D + 90, and that when as Military Assistant he raised the question with the Commander-in-Chief, he was told to draw some lines at equal parallel distances showing a methodical regular advance at appropriate dates. Maybe he did, but the 'phase line' map was already there on the wall along with other maps and diagrams. Copies of it have appeared in several of the histories and the books written about Operation 'Overlord'.

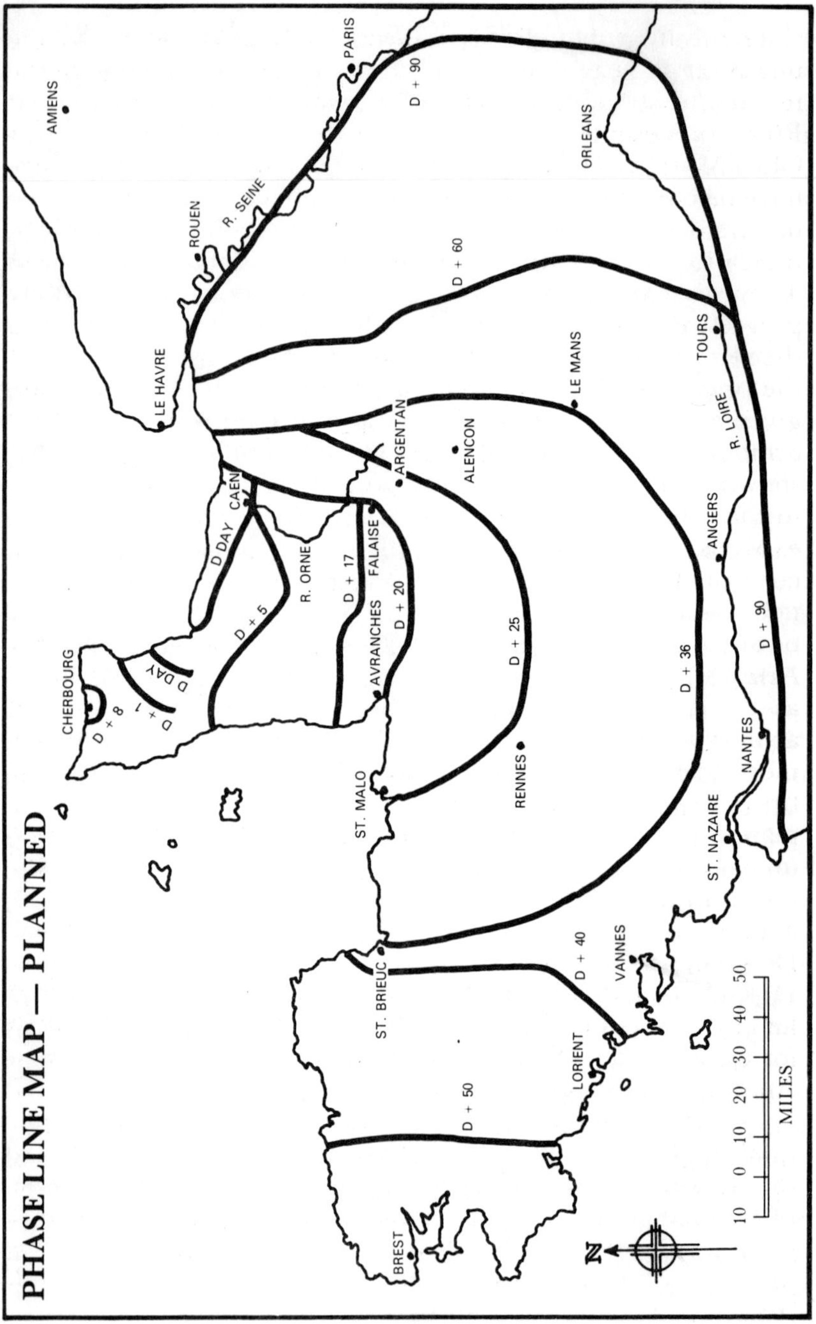
PHASE LINE MAP — PLANNED
AMIENS
PARIS
ROUEN
R. SEINE
LE HAVRE
ORLEANS
D + 90
D + 60
TOURS
LE MANS
R. LOIRE
ARGENTAN
ALENCON
CAEN
D DAY
R. ORNE
FALAISE
D + 17
D + 20
D + 5
AVRANCHES
D + 25
D + 36
ANGERS
D + 90
CHERBOURG
D DAY
D + 1
D + 8
RENNES
NANTES
ST. MALO
ST. NAZAIRE
VANNES
D + 40
ST. BRIEUC
LORIENT
D + 50
BREST
N
10 0 10 20 30 40 50
MILES

The subject of 'phase lines' gave rise to a lot of misunderstanding, and provided the basis at a later stage for much unreasonable criticism of Montgomery by the American Press correspondents and, regrettably it has to be said, by Air Chief Marshal Tedder, who was present on 7 April and cannot have paid attention to what was going on, or at least not to have understood. 'Phase lines' were not intended to be a firm indication of the state of progress made by the invasion forces. They were put in as an estimate of the most optimistic rate of progress for the assistance of the administrative staff in planning the sort of supply and maintenance organization required, and the provision of approximate quantities of this or that at any given stage. Thus, if there were nine divisions, three of them armoured, ashore by D + 14, and the foremost troops were shown as only ten miles inland on a broad front, this indicated to those of us who had to do the estimates that progress was expected to be slow and the fighting to be hard and intense; consequently, the prime requisite would be ammunition and not so much transport and petrol (gasoline). Nor would there be any necessity or even the possibility of setting up the planned Army Roadheads. The fact that the capture of Caen, shown as the British Second Army objective for D-Day, was not achieved until a month later made no real difference to us, any more than did the failure of the actual rate of advance in the first five days to match up to the phase line for D + 3. Our planning was done on the basis that the 'phase lines' were unlikely to be achieved on the day indicated. On the other hand, the administrative staff might easily have been caught out if we had relied on the phase line for the River Seine which was D + 90, whereas that river was crossed by the Americans on D + 75. Fortunately, the active co-operation between the British and US transport services meant that there was no hold-up even for one day, because of the startling rate of progress once the Americans got on the move.

Perhaps the most significant and important part of the 'phase line' map as drawn up before the presentation on 7 April was that it clearly showed the strategic as well as the tactical nature of Montgomery's operational planning. On the map, Caen was the furthermost easterly objective of the British and Canadian forces for the first twenty days of the invasion, whilst the American advance was shown as deep into France in a southerly and westerly direction. At a later date there was much ill-informed and biased criticism of Montgomery and the British contribution in the first three months of the campaign, which should never have been made and would not have been made if those persons who so indulged had heard the exposition of his plan on that day in early April. It so happens that the recollection of those who were there at the Presentation of Plans is confirmed by the notes which have been preserved, which Montgomery made for his opening speech on that occasion. It was repeated at the final Presentation of Plans in May, when his strategic plan was announced unaltered.

Montgomery gave out the task of the US 1st Army as the capture of Cherbourg as soon as possible, and then a development of operations, first southward to St Lo and thereafter a drive to capture Avranches and St Malo on the coast, and Rennes inland. The US 3rd Army under Patton was to take over the drive south and west and to isolate and overrun the whole of Brittany. The task of the British Second Army was to drive towards Caen, to capture it if possible, to capture suitable sites for airfields, to protect the eastern flank of the US 1st Army and subsequently to pivot on its left flank, and to offer a strong front against enemy movement towards the lodgement area. Knowing Rommel as he did, Montgomery was convinced that the German Panzer armoured divisions would be concentrated against the Allied eastern front to deny the capture of Caen and the open country behind and to the west of the city. This meant that the British and Canadian forces would have to bear the brunt of the German counter-attacks, whilst the Americans would have a comparatively easy ride.

The senior staff officers at SHAEF were either woefully ignorant of, or deliberately blind to the essential nature of Montgomery's plan. On the other hand, General Omar N. Bradley, who had no reason personally to like the man, was generous-minded enough to pay tribute to Montgomery's strategy. In his book *A Soldier's Story*, he referred to the role of the British and Canadian Armies as the sacrificial one of pinning down and engaging the enemy reserves in the area of Caen, while the US forces tramped around the outside flank to 'make our break on the long round-about road towards Paris'. This was an infinitely preferable and more accurate assessment made, as it was, by a fair-minded and highly competent commander who knew what he was talking about, than the superficial, petty judgement made second-hand by Ralph Ingersoll, a bigoted and biased American journalist, whose book infuriated the British and caused immense damage to the good relations between Britain and the United States.

There was one silly and unfortunate incident when Montgomery's brusque manner nearly caused a serious contretemps with some of the US top commanders. My recollection is that it occurred on the occasion of the Presentation of Plans, but on reflection this is unlikely, and it must have been the time early on in the year when Montgomery held a big conference at St Paul's School to explain his views on how to make war, and the principles on which he operated. All the General Officers in the forces under his command and senior staff officers were there. Whenever it was, it is certain that several of the top Americans were also there, and that two of us Lieutenant-Colonels were manning the entrance doors to the large lecture hall at St Paul's. It was Montgomery's practice to prohibit smoking when he was lecturing or addressing an assembly; moreover, he objected to interruption by coughing on the part of any of his audience. He always prefaced his address by an announcement that there was to be no smoking in the hall; that there would be a break of ten minutes to enable those who could not manage without a cigarette to go outside into the lobby and there indulge; that he was not to be distracted by anyone coughing, and that therefore all those who might be affected by a desire to cough must cough now and get it over with. At this there was a wholesale clearing of throats and precautionary coughing, somewhat similar to the variety of noises from an orchestra tuning up before the arrival of the conductor on platform! This happened on this occasion; no-one smoked, and no-one thereafter gave vent to the slightest cough. At the break we opened the doors, and several of the most senior American officers came out and lit up. It is pretty certain that General Omar Bradley was one. Promptly at the end of ten minutes, 'Monty' told us to close the doors. He knew perfectly well that the American generals were outside and had not finished their smokes. We tried to get them to stub out their cigarettes and go in, but they saw no reason why they should be treated as very junior officers, and ostentatiously went on puffing away. 'Close the doors, I said!' came the order which we dared not disobey. He resumed his address and, a moment or two later, the American officers marched in. He looked daggers at them, and they looked daggers at him. It was all very childish and very stupid, but it did not make for a happy relationship between Montgomery and the US 'top brass'.

Throughout February, March and April, the manifold preparations for invasion had been proceeding apace. Elsewhere, one of the preconditions laid down for a seaborne assault was achieved, albeit obliquely and not as part of the plan to assist Operation 'Overlord'. While Harris and RAF Bomber Command were every night methodically destroying German industry and in particular manufacturing capacity for fighter aircraft. Spaatz and the US Air Force attacked by day. In one week in February, he sent up hundreds and hundreds of Flying Fortress bombers on daylight raids, with the intention of forcing the Luftwaffe day fighters to engage in battle. In a strategic philosophy reminiscent of the Russian approach, he was prepared for near-sacrificial losses if the enemy could be heavily defeated. At the end of the week the American losses were grievous indeed, but the German day fighter force was almost wiped out, and the RAF bombers made sure that the building of replacement aircraft was made extremely difficult. The shortage of trained pilots proved to be an even greater handicap. Nevertheless, the Germans continued to produce a strong fighter force. By a strange irony, it was thereafter the RAF bombers who faced a far greater threat; despite their improved techniques for identifying and hitting a selected target; an attack in mass provided a much easier task for the numerous and experienced night fighter pilots. The result of this was that the British were to benefit from a partial switch of their air offensive by joining the Americans in unhampered daylight attacks on selected targets. Tedder was justified in persuading Portal that the RAF would not only contribute more, but would be better off by participating in the interdiction of transportation as planned by Leigh-Mallory and his staff, who were advised by civilian experts as to the French railway system.

The interdiction of the transportation system in France on which the Germans heavily relied built up to a crescendo as D-Day approached. It proved to be devastatingly successful, and the senior staff officers at HQ 21 Army Group and the military staff at SHAEF who had mockingly referred to this policy as 'pin pricking', were in the end made to look ridiculous. When it came to D-Day, the destruction of the railway repair and maintenance facilities and of the marshalling yards, and the cutting of bridges was of enormous significance. But of even more importance at the time of the assault was that there was hardly a German aircraft to be seen, and the fear that the invading troops would be heavily attacked from the air was never realized.

The absence of enemy aircraft over the beaches was partly due to the surprise achieved and partly to the bad weather conditions, but also to the fact that such day fighters as the Luftwaffe still possessed were for the most part based in the Pas de Calais area. This was understandable, because the German High Command was convinced that it was here that the main thrust of an invasion would be made. The original deception plan, code-named 'Starkey', was now brought into being and called 'Fortitude', and lent support to the German point of view. The application of the policy of attacking the rail system by the Strategic Air Forces of the Allies fitted naturally with the deception plan, for most of the repair and maintenance facilities and the main junctions and marshalling yards were north of the River Seine, and attacks on these were no pointer to an invasion in Normandy. The deception plan called for an even more intense attack on the wide range of targets in the whole area to the north of the river. For every ton of high explosive dropped in Normandy, two were dropped in the area around the Pas de Calais. For every reconnaissance flight over the Normandy beaches, there were two north of the River Seine.

Quite apart from the construction of dummy landing craft and their positioning on specially constructed 'hards' all round the Thames estuary and up the coast as far as the Wash, an elaborate system of signal and telephone control added to the deception. Towards the end of April, Montgomery moved his Main Headquarters from London to Portsmouth, where they were set up in the fields adjoining the grounds of Southwick House, which was Admiral Ramsay's Naval Headquarters. For the next six weeks before D-Day, all signals traffic by wireless (as radio used to be called in those days) was first transmitted by land live to a place in Kent and thence broadcast in code. The German direction-finding apparatus led them to assume that Montgomery's HQ was located south of London. The deception was taken a stage further by the impression which indicated to the Germans that Patton's 3rd US Army and the Canadian 1st Army were an assault force assembled in the South East of England and not, as they were in fact, follow-up forces. The assembly of such forces in this part of the country led naturally to the conclusion that the main thrust of an invasion would be in the direction of the Pas de Calais. Phantom armies were created and given names and commanders, and bogus signals and messages added to the illusion.

The deception plan was a complete success, for it confirmed the analysis made by Field Marshal von Runstedt, the German Commander-in-Chief West. He was the complete professional soldier, moulded to read an enemy's mind as if it were his own. It therefore seemed to him that any highly experienced military commander on the Allied side would reason, as he would, that an invasion should be launched across the shortest sea crossing, under the strongest air cover into a bridgehead and lodgement area from which lay the most direct route towards Germany. Moreover he had been advised by Admiral Krancke, the German Naval Commander West, that it was almost impossible for landings to be made on any large scale on the Normandy beaches because of the number of outcrops of rock in the shallow reaches of the Baie de la Seine. They were unaware that it was this characteristic on which the British scientists and the engineering experts were to rely for the positioning of 'Gooseberry' breakwaters and the 'Mulberry' artificial harbours. The Allies were able to harness the difficult conditions and to use them to their advantage. The Allies had an even greater advantage, in that the British had broken the German codes early on in the war, and it was kept a closely guarded secret, known only to a very few and unknown to the Germans, that all their coded commands were understood.

Field Marshal Rommel, who was made responsible for the defences of the Atlantic Wall and the command of the troops in the coastal defence regions, had vastly improved the number and quality of the concrete gun emplacements, particularly the underwater obstacles, mines and explosive devices in the shallow approaches to the beaches in Normandy. But although he was aware of experiments with amphibious tanks, he was not to know that the ingenuity of the British, to whom he gave little or no credit, had devised the means through 'Hobo's funnies' and specially-trained and equipped assault engineers, to overcome what he believed to be a devastating prohibition of any successful seaborne landings.

At the beginning of May, Allied Intelligence obtained indications of a considerable increase in the German reinforcements in the Normandy and Brittany area, and it was feared that the real intention of the Allied invasion forces had been discovered. If this was so, it was too late to change the plans, and Eisenhower and the three Commanders-in-Chief were forced to accept that they would be faced with much stronger opposition than they had expected when planning began in January and February, and that the operation would prove to be much more difficult. If the enemy really was fully prepared to meet an assault in Normandy rather than in the Pas de Calais, then all the work on deceiving him would have been of no avail. However, after the war was over it was learnt that there had been no discovery of Allied plans, but it was Hitler himself, who at times had an almost uncanny ability to make an intuitive guess as to what was likely to happen, decided that there would be a major assault across the Normandy beaches. So Rommel adjusted his defences to some extent. Fortunately for the Allies, von Runstedt was prepared only to accept the possibility of an attack in Normandy or Brittany as no more than a diversionary assault, whilst the real thrust would still be in the area of the Pas de Calais. In consequence, the German High Command remained deceived and, mercifully for the Allied cause, there was no shifting of any of the defending forces or the mobile reserves down south of the River Seine.

In the early stages of planning it had been decided that the relationship of tidal factors and degree of moonlight or pitch darkness, so that the convoys could approach under cover of the night and the assault troops could go ashore at first light in wading depth of water, all meant that there were only three or four suitable days for D-Day. The invasion must be either on 4, 5 or 6, or just possibly 7 June. Preparations were made with a target date of 5 June, and the choice of that date meant that the movement and loading and embarking of ships would in most areas have to commence hours or even a day or two before the evening of 4 June, when all the convoys had to concentrate on a vast assembly area in the Channel south of the Isle of Wight, which was known to the Navy as 'Piccadilly

Circus'. It was recognized that a lot of the troops would be aboard for many hours in cramped conditions even before the final assembly and departure across the Channel. The arrangements on the Navy side were as complicated as could conceivably be imagined, and, as has already been observed, the constant amendments and the uncertainty of whether or not the necessary shipping would be made available made it a planner's nightmare.

Some things could be decided well in advance of D-Day. The British Royal Navy Task Force (the Eastern Task Force) was under the command of Rear-Admiral Vian, famous for his courageous exploits with HMS *Cossack*, and was sub-divided into three assault forces, each responsible for landing the assaulting troops on one of the three beaches, code named 'Sword', 'Juno' and 'Gold', the initials of which designated each Naval Assault Force. The Western Task Force was under the command of Rear-Admiral Kirk of the US Navy, and again was sub-divided into two assault forces, O for the 'Omaha' beach and U for the 'Utah' beach. The British contingents were based at different small ports all round the coast from Felixstowe, Harwich and Tilbury for one assault force, deliberately leaving out Dover and Folkestone, which were involved in the deception plan, and, moving along the South coast, for another assault force at Shoreham, Newhaven and Portsmouth, which doubled for a third assault force also using the Solent. The US Navy assault force O was based at Weymouth and Portland, and force U at Plymouth, Brixham and Dartmouth. The preloaded follow-up division for the Americans was to embark at Plymouth and Falmouth, and the British in the area Nore at the mouth of the Thames Estuary.

Notwithstanding the use of every available berth from Harwich in East Anglia round to Milford Haven in South Wales, Admiral Ramsay and his staff had also to rely on berthing facilities as far away as the River Humber on the north-east coast, the River Clyde in West Scotland, and even in Belfast. One advantage of this wholesale dispersion of naval vessels and landing craft and supply and maintenance shipping, coupled with the positioning of dummies at various places, was that it would be quite impossible for German reconnaissance to draw any conclusions at all as to where the major thrust of an Allied invasion would be directed.

The organization of all this by the Admiralty in conjunction with Admiral Ramsay's staff was a fantastic achievement. So also was the cross-country movement of large bodies of troops, armoured vehicles and equipment to get the assaulting formations into position near the points at which they were to embark. This was the responsibility of the Q (Movements) branch at HQ 21 Army Group, working together with the War Office and HQ ETOUSA. Yet another remarkable feat of organization was the waterproofing of thousands of motor vehicles of all those types which were required to drive off down a ramp or off a ferry in two or three feet of sea water. Engines had to be sealed, and exhaust pipes lengthened and turned upwards so that no sea water could enter the exhaust system or block the escape of gas. This was supervised by the Q Staff at HQ 21 Army Group, and carried out by Army Ordnance and Engineering shops and civilian Ministry of Supply factories. Later arrivals of vehicles which could be driven off or lifted off from ship to berth without wading through water of course did not require this treatment. It was estimated that all vehicles would require waterproofing for the first six weeks.

From time to time, once the order of battle of the Allied assaulting forces had been decided, the formations involved practised assault landings at places where there were huge stretches of sandy beaches. Some of the troops were already well-trained, for there had been large scale exercises as long ago as May 1943 for the British, carried out under the auspices of HQ Combined Operations and HQ 21 Army Group in General Paget's day, and for the Americans in August 1943. It was now within six or seven weeks of D-Day, and the actual Naval assault forces and the actual army assaulting troops had to practise together. At the end of April 1944, the biggest American exercise, code named 'Tiger', ended in ghastly tragedy, due partly to misfortune and partly to incompetence. In Eisenhower's Report to the Combined Chiefs of Staff there is a disgracefully inadequate reference to this episode, which is dismissed in one sentence with the words — 'Owing to the fact that one of the escorting destroyers was damaged in a collision during the night of 26.27 April and was not on hand when the assault convoy was attacked by E-boats, there was an unfortunate loss of life in the sinking of two LSTs'.

This fateful exercise was a very large-scale attempt to practise the landings on 'Utah' beach, and the area chosen was Slapton Sands in South Devon, where not only was the size and configuration of the beach very similar to that at the side and base of the Cotentin peninsula, but there were small inland lakes behind the sand dunes, similar to those with which General Bradley's airborne plan was designed to contend. The US paratroops for one reason or another were unable to practise their drop and were driven to their destination by motor transport along the Devon lanes — a totally unrealistic and useless performance. US Navy assault force U was commanded by Rear-Admiral Moon, but thanks to the parsimony and procrastination of Admiral King, had not yet been put in possession of his warships. He had to rely on two spare destroyers from the British fleet, and whether or not one was damaged in a collision, as Eisenhower's report has it, or returned to port because of engine failure as other records suggest, there was only HMS *Azalea* left to look after the huge convoy of Landing Ships and Landing Craft, which had set out from Plymouth and Brixham fully loaded with raw untried troops, their equipment and armour. Admiral Ramsay's Naval Intelligence had noted a lot of activity on the part of the German E-boats for some days before this exercise, and it was known that there was a large flotilla of these deadly little ships based at Cherbourg on the other side of the Channel. Rear-Admiral Kirk, the US Navy Task Force Commander, must have known this, and it remains astonishing and inexplicable that the exercise went ahead with such inadequate naval cover. A squadron of E-boats from Cherbourg pounced on this huge lumbering convoy, easily evaded poor *Azalea* and sank two of the LSTs. 747 young American soldiers lost their lives, and a further 300 were wounded. Many of the dead were drowned, which was to be expected if their ship was sunk, but what about the number who died of wounds and those wounded who survived? There was a strongly-held view among the survivors that it was ill-directed fire from their own side which was largely responsible. As soon as Eisenhower learnt of this tragedy, he ordered an immediate wholesale security clampdown. He had to, otherwise US Army morale might have been badly affected. The ghastly secret was well kept. There now stands on the dunes a recovered submerged tank, put there by the local British inhabitants as a memorial to those who died. There is no American recognition, and there are no US records of where the dead were buried.

As 5 June loomed nearer, all was going according to plan, and the time was ripe for the sealing-off of the camps where the assaulting troops were accommodated, and for their briefing with maps and models of the actual task they were required to perform. Before this penultimate step was taken, there was a final Presentation of Plans at St Paul's School on 15 May. HM King George VI and Winston Churchill were both present. The planning was over and done with, and it could now be expounded in its final version and indeed the only major difference in the outline plan between this and the presentation on 7 April was the alteration of the American use of their airborne forces.

It had been decided quite early on that the best time for touchdown (H hour) would be three hours before high tide, that is halfway between low and high tide, but as the tidal flow varied between the beaches of the Cotentin peninsula and those at the mouth of the River Orne, there would have to be an adjustment in the actual timing for the western flank compared with that for the eastern flank. As far as the change from night to day was concerned, the time was the same for the whole front, and the ideal timing was forty minutes after nautical twilight, that is when there is the first perceptible change from darkness into light. The compromise, which took into account the difference in the time of high tide over the whole sectors, was that H hour for the Americans was 0630, compared with 0745 for the British 3rd Division. This gave a very short period for bombing and naval gunfire before the US forces were due to touch down, and an unnecessarily long period of daylight before the assaulting troops on 'Sword' beach were due to land. It was, however, the only practicable solution. Nevertheless, it required not only accurate navigation, but also accurate assessment of the distance from ship to shore for the naval assault forces to judge the moment when the assault landing craft were released from the 'mother' ship, and the amphibious (DD) tanks were put into the sea. The former manoeuvre was planned to be no more than eight miles out to sea and the latter no more than four miles, which was the largest distance that a DD tank was designed to 'swim'.

The 'fire' plan began with the use of RAF heavy bombers to attack the enemy coast defence batteries during the night preceding D-Day. This was to be followed by attacks on the other coast defence targets by medium bombers in the twilight before dawn, these to be supported by gun and rocket fire from naval assault craft. Once the light was strong enough, the heavy guns from the battleships, cruisers and gunboats were to take up the attack, as were also the bombers of the US Air Force. It was hoped that this buildup of devastating and relentless bombardment would render the coast defences useless. As it turned out, the plan only succeeded indirectly, for the concrete emplacements were so strongly constructed that they were not destroyed, but the crescendo of terrifying noise and blast did have the effect of stunning and demoralizing the enemy troops. In this respect, there was complete co-operation between the Navy, Army and Air Force. There was another interesting item of the careful and methodical way in which the British planned the seaborne aspect of the assault. It was decided to place two midget submarines on the sea bed a couple of miles offshore on the day before D-Day, ready to surface on call and to set up radar beacons as navigational aids for the approaching armada.

As the follow-up forces and the first build-up reinforcements were all embarked simultaneously with the assault forces, all ready to sail in after the assault forces had obtained their primary objectives, the landing tables and the allocation of assault craft and shipping had to be worked out on a basis of D-Day and D + 1. In all, the plan called for the landing on these first two days of 176,475 troops, 1,500 tanks, 5,000 tracked vehicles, 3,000 guns and 10,500 other vehicles of all types. For all this, 6,047 landing craft were required. The D-Day fleet consisted of about 4,000 landing craft and 1,600 ships, of which 230 were Landing Ships. There were four categories of specialist landing craft, namely Landing Ship Tank (LST), Landing Ship Infantry (LSI), Landing Craft Tank (LCT) and Landing Craft Vehicle and Personnel (LCVP). The LCT had several variants of different Mark, and were used for landing personnel as well as vehicles. The larger type were used for putting ashore the 'funnies' in the first wave; the type used for infantry in the assault were slung alongside the LSI and lowered overboard some way out to sea. The LCT were to be beached for discharge with either ramps let down or with ladders, so that the troops could begin wading ashore in two or three feet of water. The plan was for

LST to discharge tanks and vehicles on to 'Rhino' ferries, which were floating rafts made up of pontoons with an engine to propel the raft ashore. In the event, so many of the 'Rhino' ferries were damaged that a decision was taken to try and beach the LSTs. It succeeded, though at heavy cost in damage and repair work. For the follow-up and build-up, the plan included the use of merchant ships, some large enough to carry 2,000 men and others specially used for the conveyance of motor transport. The MT ships were to be loaded by derricks, and, to discharge their cargo using their own derricks on to another Mark of LCT for ferrying ashore.

All the landing tables were collated and collected at HQ 21 Army Group. There were hundreds and hundreds of sheets. Every single unit was included, and every single craft was shown with its complement of assaulting troops, whether specialist or infantry, and the little groups of anti-aircraft gunners, engineers, signals and members of the beach organizations. These detailed tables were not produced at the Presentation of Plans, but there was a summary of the guns, armoured vehicles and other vehicles broken down under various headings all due to be landed during D-Day and D + 1. This summary was even more open to the kind of criticism levelled at it by Winston Churchill than the form which has been recorded for history. The final 'official' version showed 10,500 vehicles set against only 1,500 tanks and 5,000 other tracked vehicles. Churchill's enquiring and, it has to be said, uninformed mind, could never appreciate why there had to be such a mass of administrative backup for the infantry and armour in the forefront of battle. The summary as we had prepared it was in accordance with War Office practice. This practice gave first a category of Armoured Fighting Vehicles (AFV), next artillery, for guns had to be moved about on wheels, and then First Line and Second Line transport. The two latter were referred to in general terms as administrative. These categories were not entirely satisfactory, and certainly were apt to give to the uninstructed a misleading picture of an excessive degree of support for a few 'teeth'. We had already run into difficulties when trying to produce a summary. Tanks were obviously to be included in the category of AFV, and so were self-propelled guns. It was the 'funnies' which caused problems. A flamethrower and a flail tank would qualify as a fighting vehicle, but what about the 'ramp' tank or the steel mat layer?

A Royal Engineers bridge carrier was not truly an administrative vehicle, yet there was no other suitable heading, for it certainly was not a fighting vehicle as the term was understood.

Once the King had left, Churchill stayed on and began one of his inquisitorial sessions. He became so involved that after a while he passed a message which reached me for execution. A telephone call had to be made to the War Cabinet Office, and as I was able to satisfy Leslie Rowan, the Assistant Secretary, of my credentials, and incidentally to remind him of Cambridge University days, the instruction was given that the PM was busy and would Mr Attlee please get on with the Cabinet Meeting. Churchill was indeed very busy: he asked Rear-Admiral Vian what weight of high explosive shelling could be fired from the British ships on to the enemy positions. There came back the bluff, honest sailor's answer that he had no idea. Rear-Admiral Kirk's aides were to be seen scribbling away on bits of paper and whispering into his ear. With typical American brashness, his confident reply was so many tons over so many yards in so many minutes. It was probably nonsense, but the Prime Minister seemed highly satisfied. He was not so pleased, indeed was very displeased, with the summarized figures of vehicle landings, and wanted to know why it was planned to land far more administrative vehicles than fighting vehicles, and made it very plain that it was unacceptable and would have to be altered. Montgomery was not bothered. He knew that his staff had prepared the details to carry out his operational designs, and as long as the required number of tanks and specialist armour were in the first wave, that was what really mattered, and he could rely on his staff not to overload the first two days of shipping with any unnecessary administrative vehicles.

Major-General de Guingand knew perfectly well that Montgomery could not simply ignore the Prime Minister's criticism. He also knew that it was quite impossible to make any substantial alterations to the loadings as planned for the first two days; nevertheless, perhaps something could be done to cope with this unfortunate situation. There then ensued a game of pass the parcel, or pass the buck as the Americans would have it. From de Guingand the buck went to Miles Graham, and from him to 'Gerry' Feilden, and from him to Val Duncan and me. We were told that as we were the only people who understood these things we must find the answer. Val Duncan found a good excuse to get out of it, and nominated Lieutenant-Colonel Donald Ross, his next in line, to take his place.

We began the operation of complying with the Prime Minister's expressed desire at seven o'clock in the evening. We finished at four am in the small hours of the next morning. The result was presented to 'Gerry' Feilden at nine o'clock. We were sensibly not asked what we had been up to, but merely if we could stand up to cross-examination if the solution was challenged. In fact the answer was simple, even though it involved hours of painstaking and tedious work. The obvious thing to do was to enlarge the category of fighting vehicles, because it was perfectly sensible to take the view that any vehicle landing in a small bridgehead was just as likely to be taking part in fighting as a tracked vehicle spouting gunfire. A track-laying tank was taking part in the fighting; the vehicles which carried the Number 19 wireless set, as it was called in those days, were as much an integral part of the fighting machine called an infantry company as the man with a rifle. There had to be constant communication between each company, and between a company and battalion headquarters. The Light Aid Detachment (LAD) provided by men of the Royal Electrical and Mechanical Engineers (REME) had to be on hand even under fierce bombardment to make urgent repairs to damaged tanks. They were fully involved in the fighting, even if they wielded a spanner and not a firearm. So we went through about a thousand sheets of paper, and altered and moved different entries in different columns. The end result was very impressive. There was no longer a heavy imbalance in favour of vehicles categorized as administrative. If ever there was a 'paper' solution this was it, but we never learnt whether the Prime Minister was gratified that his criticisms had been met, or indeed whether he was ever told!

Following this Presentation of Plans, the staff officers at HQ 21 Army Group were able to sit back and relax. The assault units had to be briefed and the various types of shipping assembled at their appointed places of embarkation, but this was not our concern. We had to wait until the Supreme Commander gave the word for Operation 'Overlord' to begin.

11

THE INVASION

The story of how the word was given to launch the great Allied endeavour across the Channel has been told over and over again, and there is nothing to be gained by repeating it in detail once more. D-Day was planned to be Monday 5 June, 1944. Those of us who were involved in the creation of the logistic machinery were well aware of the fact that if bad weather made it impossible for the assault to take place on that day, the implication of any postponement, even for a day, was serious. If the postponement were longer than a day then the whole operation was in jeopardy and months of planning and preparation would have been a complete waste of time. Cautious by temperament though he was, Montgomery was opposed to any postponement at all. Admiral Ramsay was prepared, with misgivings, to go along with Montgomery even though the weather conditions might be wholly unsatisfactory.

On the basis of 5 June as D-Day, the warships from Scapa Flow, at Belfast and in the Clyde had to set sail during the night of Friday 2nd/Saturday 3rd, in order to join up with the other assault forces in the area south of the Isle of Wight known as 'Piccadilly Circus' by the late evening of Sunday the 4th. The American forces starting from the harbours of South Wales and from South Devon had to set out, some earlier, some later, during the Saturday night, and the main body of the assault forces were under orders to start moving at about six thirty am on Sunday morning. Despite a forecast of worsening weather, the conditions were not too bad on Friday and Saturday, and the earlier starters had all moved off at the times planned. The weather began to worsen, and at a meeting of the Supreme

Commander and the three Allied Commanders-in-Chief in the library of Southwick House which was called for four fifteen am on the Sunday morning, Eisenhower, in spite of Montgomery's differing opinion, thought that conditions on Monday morning would be too difficult. He ordered a postponement of twenty-four hours, and a recall of those ships already at sea. The US assault forces had already found the going too rough, and had begun to put about. The conditions were so severe that ships which tried to make the shelter of Weymouth harbour could not get in. The weather on Monday 5 was nearly as bad, and established conclusively that the decision to postpone was undoubtedly correct.

In the planning stages it had been recognized that, as many of the troops would have to be embarked well before D-Day in very cramped conditions, they could not be expected to remain like that for any length of time. Temporary accommodation in special camps close by was arranged so that troops could be disembarked in the event of a short postponement. These camps were called into being and it was as well that they were, for many of those who had been at sea for many hours were badly seasick and rapidly losing morale.

At the meeting at four am on Monday morning the weather forecast was that there would be an improvement during the day, and that the conditions at H hour the next day would be just tolerable. So the order was given to go. There was really no alternative. It was now or never, and so the ships sailed across the Channel in strong, gusting winds and with waves running five or six feet high. When it came to H hour, many of the assaulting troops were wan and weak from sea sickness, and as they waded ashore were soaking wet and cold, and a number of the advancing craft had capsized in the rough seas. It seemed as if the weather had conspired against the Allies, but in truth it proved to be more of an ally than a foe. The enemy was taken completely by surprise, partly because of the deception plan which led them to expect an assault in another area altogether, but even more because of his reliance on the weather conditions, which were considered to be prohibitive of any invasion from the sea.

As Admiral Ramsay later described it, the passage of the vast armada had about it an air of unreality, for there was no enemy attack at sea, either by U-boats or E-boats. The German naval commanders never thought that any ships would put to sea in such conditions, and indeed had ordered the E-boats to remain in harbour. The Luftwaffe was deceived by the RAF scattering metal strips known as 'windows', and the ingenious towing of balloons, which wrecked the accuracy of the German radar and created the illusion of a huge bomber force heading for targets in northern France, whither the night fighter pilots were directed to fly. Over the approaches to the beaches of Normandy, there was no resistance from the air. On the ground, the German generals felt secure, and when reports of Allied activity began to trickle in, they were slow to react. The invasion was not challenged to the degree expected.

On each of the five sectors of the Normandy coast, things either went more or less as planned or went very differently indeed. The two US Airborne Divisions which Air Chief Marshal Leigh-Mallory had expected to be slaughtered suffered very few casualties, but the 101st Division were only saved by low cloud banks and the evasive tactics of the pilots, which on the debit side led to a substantial degree of failure in objective. The result of flying too high and too fast was that the paratroops were dropped all over the place in a huge spread extending for some twenty-five by fifteen miles. Only about one thousand out of a total of six and a half thousand men got to their rendezvous by dawn, and it took two days before their commanding general managed to gather up the whole of his division. More than half of their equipment was lost, and if they had run into any well-organized concentrated defence they would have been in deep trouble. As it was, this widespread dispersion confused the enemy as much as it did the attackers. The 82nd Division had mixed fortunes. One regiment was able to land with accuracy; the other two regiments were widely dispersed and had a difficult time, but fought with great gallantry to achieve a degree of success. Between them, the two Airborne divisions were able to acquire sufficient of their objectives and to succeed in enough of the tactical plan to prevent the Germans from sealing off the US infantry when they landed on 'Utah' beach.

In the River Orne sector, the British 6th Airborne Division was more successful. As General Eisenhower paid tribute in his Report, the troops were dropped precisely according to plan in the areas east of the river, and all the main military tasks were carried out. The various contingents were by midday on 6 June well established before meeting a fierce attack from units of the crack 21 Panzer Division which they were able to beat off, and to hold firmly to the objectives they had seized. Throughout the whole of the assault stages of the campaign, this Division never yielded and consistently maintained control of the Allied armies' eastern flank.

The American assault forces were in places unexpectedly successful and elsewhere subject to unexpected reverse, and neither conclusion reflected much credit on the commanding generals and their senior staff officers. Success was sometimes achieved because the landings were not in accordance with the plan; failure was encountered largely because of bad judgement in the planning stage and a measure of incompetence in some of the higher command. One of the mistakes was the failure to make full use of specialized armour. In the course of the detailed preparations following the acceptance of the Initial Joint Plan, General Montgomery made an inspection of the various types of specialized armour in the 79th Armoured Division under Major-General Hobart, and then tried to get General Eisenhower and General Bradley interested. Montgomery was most impressed, not only with the amphibious DD tanks which General Alan Brooke (by now Field Marshal) had already enthusiastically adopted and ordered in quantity, but also with most of the range of specialist armour. He was prepared to use almost all of the 'funnies' which were on offer. General Eisenhower was equally in favour of the DD tanks and, without the same critical assessment which led Montgomery to pick and choose, would have been prepared to take anything and everything. It was not however a matter for Eisenhower to decide, for the effective decision on the American side was that of General Omar Bradley. He was hesitant about all of them, and referred the question of the use of any of the specialized armour to his staff. This was a serious lapse of self-confidence on his part, very much out of character, and it was strange to find him taking a different view from an American Supreme Commander.

Bradley's senior staff officers and his Corps and Divisional commanders were all imbued with the attitude that nothing which the British came up with was to be relied on when set against the experience of the Americans in the Pacific war against the Japanese. They were unable to appreciate that the successful reliance on trained navy squads and assault engineers to breach the flimsy and inadequate beach defences of the Japanese in the various islands was an experience based on totally different conditions from those which existed in the well-designed and executed defences with which they would have to contend on the beaches of Normandy. They were reluctantly prepared to accept the amphibious DD tanks, and each assaulting US Division was allotted the support of some of these; not a single one of the other types of specially-designed assault tanks was called into service. The US VII Corps which had the task of assaulting the 'Utah' beach was commanded by Major-General J. Lawton Collins, and it is the only criticism which can be made against him from beginning to end of the campaign in Europe, that he allowed his highly successful experience at Guadalcanal to prejudice his opinion of the British-designed specialized armour. One of the reasons given against their use was there there would not be time to train the crews to operate these strange machines, but this hardly bears examination, for the flail tanks ('Crabs') were Shermans, the standard US Army equipment, and the driving and control of the British Churchill tank was not all that much different. Moreover the AVRE tanks were manned by men of the Royal Engineers, who were all trained in a totally new experience in the matter of a couple of months.

The bigoted denigration of the part which could have been played, and on the British beaches actually was, by the specialist armour, extended even to the official history of the 'Utah' beach landings. This account referred to the fact that the thirty-two DD tanks beached fifteen minutes after the first assault wave, and played little part in the assault. This was not only inaccurate, because four of these tanks never reached the shore and twelve actually beached in advance of the first troops to land, but was an absurd and ridiculous observation, quite contrary to the opinion of Colonel Van Fleet, Commander of the first regiment to land, and particularly to the reports of what the prisoners of war had to say, who spoke of being utterly surprised and quite terrified at the sight of these ironclad monsters arising out of the sea with their guns belching shellfire.

Fortunately for the invaders, a substantial error in navigation turned out to be a blessing in disguise. In the first place, the DD tanks which were supposed to have been launched overboard four miles out to sea were not so disposed until the carrying ships had moved in to within two miles off the coast. If there had been any effective coastal defence fire they would have been highly vulnerable, but in fact the result was that when they took to the water they were not only that much closer to the beaches but were considerably more sheltered from the winds and rough seas than they would otherwise have been. What turned out to be even more important was the mistake which carried the assaulting troops a mile beyond the intended area of disembarkation, to a stretch of beach where the defences were much weaker than those which would have faced the invaders if their plan had been followed correctly.

Here at 'Utah', and even more so at 'Omaha', the US top commanders and their staffs pursued in their planning the concept of a direct attack on the strong points in the enemy defences. This was typical of American military thinking, derived, so it is said, from the generally-held but mistaken belief that it was General Grant's tactics of head-on confrontation regardless of appalling casualties which were entirely responsible for the success of the Union forces in the Civil War, whereas in truth it was the long 'march to the sea' through Georgia by General Sherman and his men which divided the Confederate government from the Western states and was the most compelling factor in the defeat of the Confederate armies. Whether this was the basis of their training for war or not, the Americans were never disposed to listen to any suggestion of bypassing or encircling the enemy's strong points. It so happened that the error in navigation by US Navy Force U created the conditions for a successful bypassing of the heavily-defended intended objectives, and although it was never planned that way, the assaulting forces came up against much 'softer' targets and troops of lower quality. The Americans on 'Utah' beach were lucky that the plan went wrong.

The special squads of army engineers and naval demolition units were able to blast their way through the beach obstacles and minefields, and the absence of specialized armour was not felt. In war there are 'lucky' generals and 'unlucky' generals, and in view of what happened on 'Utah' contrary to plan, 'Lightnin' Joe' Collins must be considered one of the fortunate category. The VII Corps Commanding General's reliance on the tried system of the Pacific War paid off, for the engineers

Imperial War Museum

British landing on Juno Beach

Imperial War Museum

Coming ashore on Sword Beach

US troops on Utah Beach

Imperial War Museum

The breakout from Omaha Beach

Imperial War Museum

and demolition men were able to work scarcely disturbed by enemy fire. In due course, the assaulting troops successfully established themselves and moved northwards and inland, and joined up with some of the parachutists of the airborne force. At the end of the day, VII Corps was firmly in possession of a lodgement area and casualties were slight.

It was a very different story on 'Omaha' beach. The excuse given in Eisenhower's Report and in some of the official war history, that the terrible shambles of that assault was due to the arrival in the area of the German 352 Infantry Division, and that consequently there was an unexpected strong defence simply will not do. The senior staff officers and commanding generals of US V Corps (Major-General L.T. Gerow), 1st Division (Major-General Huebner) and 29 Division (Major-General Gerhardt) had between them produced a plan for the assault which bore all the hallmarks of American 'bull at a gate' philosophy, and ignored all the commonsense which had been dinned into the British by the ghastly failure of the Dieppe attack two years earlier.

The beach code named 'Ohama' presented problems. From the beach there were four natural exits created by water-courses, which led down to sand and shingle three hundred yards in depth and four miles in length, concave in configuration with high cliffs at each end. The Germans had created a very strong system of defences which were in no way dependent upon or affected by an additional infantry division, which merely happened to be in the vicinity because it was involved in a training exercise, and from which only one regiment or battalion was close enough to play any part in resisting the landings. On the beach itself there were underwater obstacles, mines and barbed wire. Each of the four water-courses was blocked by mines, anti-tank ditches and concrete obstructions. There were strong points with trenches and concrete bunkers, and pill boxes from which the fire of machine guns and anti-tank guns could be directed, and which were placed at the mouth of each of the four water-courses and on top of the cliffs. The 'soft' areas were those between the heavily-defended natural exits. With the lessons of Dieppe firmly in mind, a British force commander would have concentrated his assault attacks on those sectors which were comparatively lightly defended, and bypassed the strong points. But not so the Americans. A British force commander would have enlisted the whole gamut of specialist armour, flail tanks to deal with the beach obstacles and minefields; searchlight tanks to blind the defending troops; flame-throwing tanks to burn them out of their bunkers, and ramp tanks to get armoured vehicles over the sea wall. But not so the Americans. The young men in the US assaulting divisions had to pay a fearful price for this narrow-minded attitude.

The story of the assault on the 'Omaha' beach begins with stupidity in high places during the planning, incompetence in high places during the early part of the assault, failure on the part of the air and ship-to-shore bombardment, and ends with the gallantry of the fighting men, restored to manhood after preliminary disaster and defeat, by the heroism and inspiring leadership of the officers who led the cowed and demoralized troops away from the deathtrap of the shell- and bullet-raked sands. With the utmost difficulty they made their way through the minefields, and the shattered remnants regrouped and went on to the attack. But casualties were staggeringly high.

It was not merely the Army 'top brass' which pigheadedly began the pattern of disaster. The US Navy O Force Commander, Rear-Admiral Hall, no doubt supported by Rear-Admiral Kirk, the US Western Task Force Commander, ignored Admiral Ramsay's advice about the manner in which transfers should be made for landing ships to assault craft. With their great experience, the British Commander-in-Chief and Rear-Admiral Creasy, his Chief of Staff, decided that the change from ship to landing craft should not be so close to shore that the transfer presented a sitting target for enemy coast defence guns, nor too far out where high wind and boisterous seas would make the transfer difficult, and the distance in bad conditions make accurate navigation almost impossible. The most appropriate distance for a lowering area was estimated to be not more than eight miles out. Even that would impose great hardship on the assault troops, and would require superb seamanship on the part of the crews of the landing craft to make an accurate touch down. Any further distance added immeasurably to the difficulties.

Unnecessarily perturbed at the prospect of being fired on by the German coastal batteries, and ignoring British Naval opinion, the US Navy chiefs ordered the lowering areas to be twelve miles out and the transfer to be made under cover of darkness. This was bad enough for the crews of the landing ships, but was terribly unfair on the assault troops who were tossed about in rough seas for three hours in prolonged anxiety, fearful of what lay ahead, and it presented a task beyond the powers of the young Navy officers who had to navigate the landing craft. In the event, more than half the companies in the leading battalions were landed over half a mile from the places where they expected to wade ashore. The conditions were so bad in the lowering area that several of the landing craft were swamped almost at once as they touched water. Those that were not capsized were kept afloat by men baling out the sea water with their steel helmets. When it came to the use of DD tanks, the launching was ordered to take place too far out in the rough sea, and the decision was taken to abandon the plan altogether with regard to the thirty-two tanks allotted to one of the assaulting battalions; of the other thirty-two only two reached the shore, some having sunk when they began to 'swim', and others while on their way. For this, the weather conditions were not entirely responsible. The training of the tank crews had been inadequate, and the crews were not able to cope. The unfortunate infantry were in consequence left entirely without support of any kind of armour, and the engineer and demolition squads were under intense fire and quite unable to perform the tasks of clearing and making safe the beaches and the exits therefrom which the specialist tanks were able to carry out on the British sectors of the invasion front.

Instead of landing on beaches where the enemy had been stunned and demoralized and the defences broken and shattered by intense bombardment from sea and air, the assaulting troops had to face the full fury of an unhampered defence. The warships, far from pulverizing the German positions, as Rear-Admiral Kirk had boasted to Churchill that the US Navy force would do, found that they could not identify the planned targets, still less hit any. They did succeed in creating vast clouds of dust and smoke, which prevented the Air Force navigators and bomb aimers from seeing anything at all. To avoid hitting their own troops who, for all the airmen knew, might already be esconced on the beach, their bombs were released well behind the enemy defences, where their assistance to the assaulting forces was negligible. Two companies of the 1st Battalion of the 116th Regiment and two companies of the 2nd Rangers were put ashore as planned opposite the strong point of Vierville. Some of the landing craft were hit; some had grounded on a sandbank, and the men had to try and wade ashore in water up to the armpits. Many were drowned; many were killed by enemy fire, and those that got on to dry land were mown down as they tried to run across the sand and shingle to the comparative safety of the sea wall. The leading company was virtually wiped out; less than half of the full strength of men got there and those that did were pinned down and could not move.

By contrast the 5th Rangers went ashore not according to plan, but in an area between two strong points. Only five or six out of four hundred and fifty men were lost. In their case it was a mercy that the plan had miscarried. Elsewhere on the sector the assaulting troops met with mixed fortunes. Two small groups of men, carried to the east beyond the deathtrap, landed in a pall of smoke which gave them cover, made their way through a little gap, and got half a mile inland. Another infantry company went ashore even further away from the Vierville water-course, and they too were able to join the other two groups. Between them they managed to get into Vierville itself and to hold the village against a German counter-attack. The other two battalions of 116th Regiment got ashore all right, but because they were well away from the intended touchdown, all was confusion to begin with; however, after an hour or so, throughout which they were under fire, a gap was found and the men were able slowly to move in single file through the minefields which the engineer and demolition squads had not been able to clear. Then enemy gunfire sealed the gap, and those troops and vehicles who followed on to the beach were bottled up and presented an easy target for the Germans. At the eastern end of the beach, two battalions of the 16th Regiment were due to land at 0630. They did, but not where they were supposed to do, and some three companies found themselves opposite the strong point at the mouth of the water-course that led to Collville, and they were subject to murderous fire. Those that survived were pinned down and dug foxholes for shelter. The other battalion sustained severe losses in landing craft; one company was landed in comparative safety well away from the intended touchdown; another was an hour and a half behind schedule.

Shortly before ten am, Major-General Huebner,

Commanding General of US 1st Division, received a signal on his command ship to the effect that thirty LCTs were offshore and could not beach because of enemy shelling, and the beaches were cluttered up with vehicles which were not required; the troops ashore who were still alive were dug in, and more combat troops were badly wanted. He responded to this message by getting the Navy to shell the enemy strong points, even though his own men might be at risk. He then ordered the 18th Regiment to go ashore. One company managed to get into landing craft and succeeded in landing; the other three companies for some reason or other took four hours before they too managed to land. Partly as a result of successful support fire from the Navy, here and there the officers with great bravery were able to get their men on their feet and slowly, dangerously, and with many casualties began to filter through the minefields, and by midday the enemy defences were beginning to disintegrate. The battle began at long last to move in favour of the assault, but it was not until the evening of D-Day that a foothold had been obtained. If the Germans had launched a concerted and determined counter-attack this flimsy foothold would have been lost. Mercifully, a large scale counter-attack never happened, for the Germans were satisfied that they had the local situation under control, and concentrated their resources against the British and Canadians who were attacking in the much more sensitive and important area in the vicinity of Caen. So the Americans on 'Omaha' beach sector were not thrown back into the sea and were there to stay. But the casualties were enormous, and for most of the day it looked as if the assault would end in ghastly failure.

This tragic tale of ineptitude and disaster has been described more dramatically, but fearlessly, frankly and in devastating detail in the account entitled *Omaha Beachhead* by the US War Department Historical Division. The authors do not seek to apportion blame, but they do make it clear that the men who emerged from this holocaust with credit and indeed with everlasting glory were the redoubtable Colonel G.A. Taylor and other gallant officers, whose courage and inspired leadership brought the cowering survivors to their feet and slowly, painfully, led them out of disaster through a veritable hell into the hinterland, where they could fight on equal terms and create a little bridgehead for others to develop. It was yet another instance in American wartime experience of how the colonels, the majors, the captains, the lieutenants and the sergeants of the infantry and Rangers units came to the rescue and, despite sacrificial loss of life, salvaged some degree of success out of the failure of those at the top to provide the men who had to do the fighting with a reasonable chance of succeeding in an operation which could and should have been devised without such obvious exposure to the risk of death and disaster. The twin alibis of the extra German forces and the bad weather were no excuse for stupidity and bad planning.

Bad though the conditions were on 'Omaha' beach, they were no worse than those which faced the British and the Canadians. On the three beaches, 'Gold', 'Juno' and 'Sword', the preliminary bombardment, although accurate enough, had not succeeded in neutralizing the enemy strong points as much as had been expected. However, this and the supporting fire from assault craft did succeed in blasting the field works and barbed wire entanglements behind the beaches, and also detonated some of the minefields, all of which made the task of the assault troops that much easier. Nevertheless, without the specialized armour the assaulting troops might well have been in as bad case as the Americans were on 'Omaha'.

Because of the weather conditions it was only on 'Sword', the furthest to the east of the three beaches, that the amphibious DD tanks were able to swim ashore and land, as planned, ahead of the infantry. Elsewhere on the British and Canadian sectors, the weather was so bad that the original plan for their use was abandoned and they came in after the infantry. Nearly all the DD tanks did get ashore in the end. Once landed, they played an important part in the immediate aftermath of the first touch down, giving actual and moral support to the attacking troops, but the vital role was played by the various types of specialized armour, which, except on 'Juno' beach, did land ahead of and with the infantry. On the extreme western flank of the British 50th Division attack on 'Gold' beach there was a very strong defensive point in the village of Le Hamel, where guns were sited to fire in enfilade across the point of high tide, preventing any advance beyond the first two or three hundred yards of exposed sand. Here the flail tanks (Crabs) had landed first and battered a way through the minefields before all but one were knocked out, and that one burst through into the strong point of Le Hamel and drew the fire of the defenders long enough to enable two companies to get off the beach and get behind the line of fire, but it took three or four hours of fierce engagement before the defences were overcome. On the other part of the 50th Division front, the specialist armour did all that was required of it. The mat-laying tanks covered the patches of clay on the beach, the flail tanks beat a path through the minefields and the AVRE demolition tanks did their job on the concrete obstructions. At one point two AVRE tanks knocked out the pillbox defences and a third charged the sea wall and cleared it like a steeplechaser. In the evening the British destroyers and small craft put down a barrage in front of the advancing armour and infantry as they wheeled westward, and the important objective of the little port of Arromanches where the 'Mulberry' artificial harbour was to be constructed fell to the invaders before nightfall. On a sector six miles wide the forces of 30 Corps had penetrated to a depth of five miles, and were not far short of the objective for D-Day which Montgomery had given them with deliberate and intended optimism. The biggest shortfall was the failure on the flank to reach Port en Bessin, where it was planned for the British beachhead to link up with the US V Corps, but as they were not there either, there remained a gap between the British and American assault forces which mercifully the Germans failed to exploit at the time, being content to leave the garrison in control, not realizing that the Royal Marine Commandos were poised to attack at first light next day, which they successfully did, although there were as yet no Americans from 'Omaha' beach with whom to link up. US patrols arrived later that day.

Pursuant to his strategic design of holding the main strength of the German defences in and around Caen while the Americans were to move deep inland and to wheel towards Cherbourg, Montgomery had given to Lieutenant-General Dempsey, the Commander of British 2nd Army, as his objectives, one, to land on the right flank with 30 Corps to gain a lodgement and aim for Bayeux, and two, on the left with 1 Corps under Lieutenant-General J.T. Crocker, to capture the airfield at Carpiquet, eleven miles from the shore, and to capture the important nodal point of Caen itself. The 3rd Canadian Division and the 2nd Canadian Armoured Brigade were to land on 'Juno' beach and to strike out for the airfield, and the 3rd British Division and

27 Armoured Brigade on 'Sword' beach were to try and get into Caen before the Germans consolidated their hold.

At the Presentation of Plans, the 'phase line' for D-Day extended just beyond Caen, and included the Carpiquet airfield which Air Chief Marshal Tedder and the Royal Air Force commanders had been pressing for. They and some of the senior officers at SHAEF seem to have thought that it was a serious failure of the plan, because at the end of the day the British and Canadian forces were two or three miles short of their stated objectives. But Montgomery deliberately pitched his objective orders higher than could reasonably be expected. He knew perfectly well that the German 21 Panzer Division was in the country adjoining Caen, and the 12 SS Panzer Division was not all that far away. The three Generals, Montgomery, Dempsey and Crocker, were well aware that it would be a miracle if the objective could be achieved, but it was even more important that British 1 Corps should not stretch itself too much, so as to be caught off balance when the German armoured divisions mounted a strong and concerted counter-attack. If the Generals had known that the four motorized infantry battalions of 21 Panzer Division were actually stationed in the outskirts of the town, their private conclusion would have been that the best that could be hoped for was to get an adequate lodgement with sufficient force of infantry and armour to pose a threat, and then draw the German armour into conflict.

On 'Juno' beach the weather was worse than anywhere else. The Canadian 7th Brigade on the right flank did have support from DD tanks which had been launched close in, but the other specialized armour for breaching the defences was late, and the infantry and the DD tanks were able to manage without them to some extent. The strong points were overcome and one or two beach exits were made, but the late arrival of the AVRE tanks meant that these exits were too few and far between, and the beach soon became badly congested with guns and vehicles, and the armour and the reserve battalion found it very slow going trying to get off the beach to catch up with the leading infantry units, who had made excellent progress. In the result, the impetus of the attack was lost and the objective not reached. The Canadians did, however, have a legitimate excuse, for the plan was all right but was disrupted by the weather and nothing else. The 8th Brigade had to land without the DD tanks, for the seas were too rough for them to 'swim' ashore, and they were beached just behind the leading infantry. With their aid and that of the specialized assault armour, the men got off the beach after a short skirmish in which a lot of casualties were suffered as a result of the fire from a strong point, until the guns of an anti-aircraft vessel were brought close in to shore and it was knocked out. Here again the delay in getting off the beach resulted in serious congestion, which in turn slowed down the pace of the advance. Nevertheless, by nightfall the Canadians had made the deepest penetration of any of the assaulting forces, and in places had advanced more than seven miles inland. The worst casualties were in the landing craft, dozens of which were grounded or sunk.

On 'Sword' beach, the preliminary bombardment from sea and air was stupendous — the heaviest concentration anywhere on all the fifty miles of coast, and following the barrage the DD tanks and specialized armour led the landings of the infantry companies. The initial breakthrough was quickly achieved, but as the advance troops approached their objective they came up against strongly-held defensive points. As was expected, the enemy had made the withstanding of an assault in this area a primary concern. The three battalions of 8th Infantry Brigade had been trained to expect a fury of fire immediately the landing craft approached the beach, and knew that they must get ashore at any cost, but they were not trained to exploit an unexpectedly easy landing. Rather than rush some of the inland defences, they dug in, and in places waited for the tanks of 27th Armoured Brigade to come up and join a planned attack. But the armour was badly delayed, this time because the whole area behind the beaches was being fed with men, guns, vehicles and tanks. It was a situation which called for bolder action in order to make more room for manoeuvre, or, if this was not possible, for a holding back of some of the follow-up vehicles. These were, however, comparatively minor criticisms, for although they were quite a distance away from the town of Caen, the British forces were well established and firmly in control of a more than adequate lodgement area.

As Montgomery himself expressed his own conclusions of the first day of invasion, the situation everywhere except on 'Omaha' beach was satisfactory; a foothold had been gained, and every one of the assault and immediate follow-up divisions had been

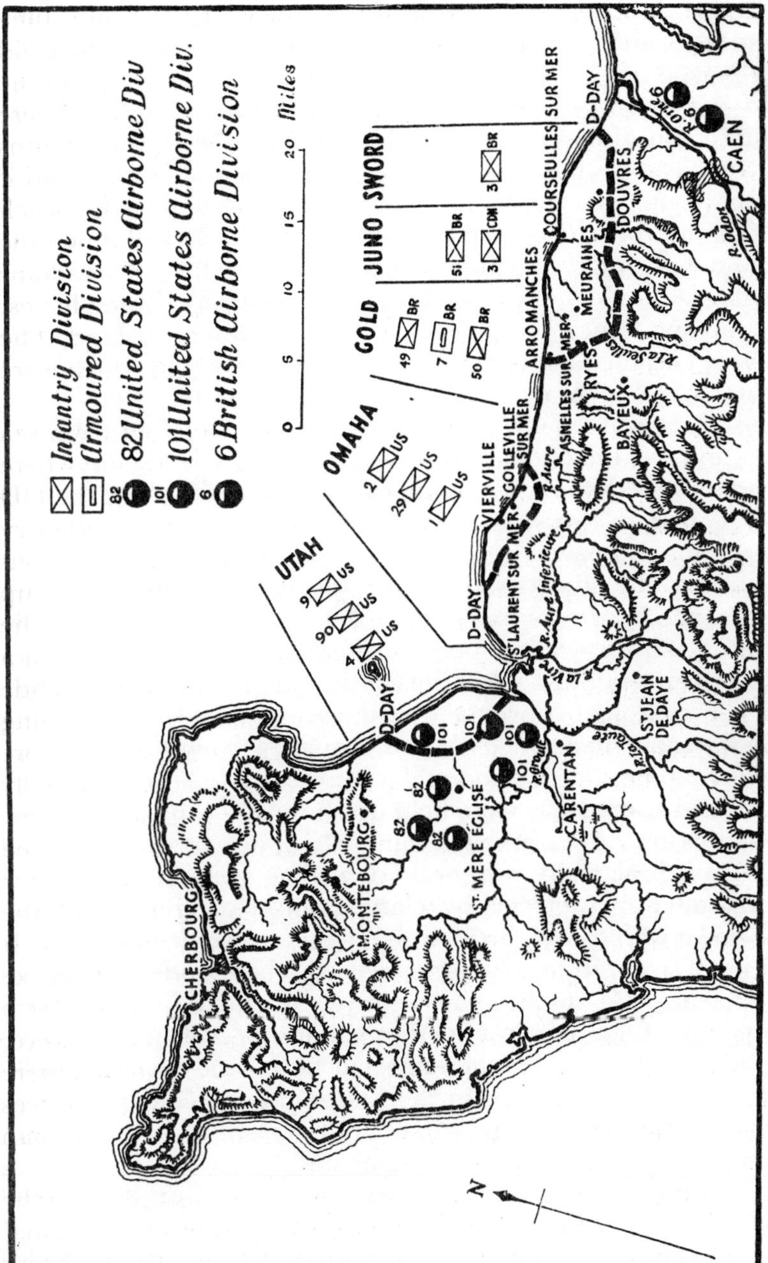
Infantry Division
Armoured Division
82 United States Airborne Div
101 United States Airborne Div.
6 British Airborne Division
0 5 10 15 20 Miles
UTAH
OMAHA
GOLD
JUNO
SWORD
D-DAY
CHERBOURG
MONTEBOURG
ST. MÈRE EGLISE
CARENTAN
ST. JEAN DE DAYE
ST. LAURENT SUR MER
VIERVILLE
COLLEVILLE SUR MER
ARROMANCHES
ASNELLES SUR MER
RYES
BAYEUX
MEURAINES
COURSEULLES SUR MER
DOUVRES
CAEN
R. Aure
R. Aure Inferieure
R. la Vire
R. la Taute
R. la Seulles
R. Odon
R. Orne
N

THE ASSAULT

landed. In landing and getting a few units off the shore and inland at 'Omaha' beach, the Americans suffered more than 4,500 casualties. Elsewhere and in total, the number of men killed and wounded was but a fraction of those which had been expected. But the weather played havoc with the logistic plans, and for days the build up of supplies fell behind schedule.

After an anxious night and a worrying next day, the US forces on 'Omaha' beach survived to hold on to the flimsy foothold and to put an end to the immediate anxieties of the Allied High Command. Once the troops had been inspired by their officers to get up and fight, they did so with great gallantry and dogged courage, and the men of US 1st Division, already heroes of the Mediterranean campaign, well deserved the praise extended to them by General Eisenhower and General Montgomery. From the second day onwards, it was the British 3rd Division and the Canadian 3rd Division who had the hardest task. They had to stand against the thrusts of the two German armoured divisions. These, though heavy, were not as concentrated as they might have been. The attacks were spasmodic and piecemeal, and it was learned afterwards that the interdiction of rail communications by aerial bombardment had had a devastating effect on petrol supply, while the continuing air attacks resulting from the complete supremacy of the Allied air forces by day made the movement of German armoured formations possible only during the short period of darkness at night. Although the British and Canadians were held up short of Caen, there were no worries on the extreme left flank when, just before nightfall on D-Day, practically every one of a huge armada of gliders, 256 in total, fully protected by a large number of fighter aircraft, came down with troops, artillery and light tanks to lend immense additional strength to the paratroops who had landed eighteen hours earlier. Montgomery was entirely justified in saying that except on 'Omaha' beach the situation everywhere was satisfactory. As none of the expected fierce and concentrated counter-attacks developed in the first two or three days of the invasion, there was growing confidence in the Allied commanders' minds that the invasion had succeeded, and it was now the time to set about the destruction of the German forces and to develop a firm base for offensive operations.

On D-Day more than 130,000 men had come ashore and, if the three Airborne Divisions were added, the total force in enemy territory amounted to 155,000 men. The oft-quoted 'official' total of vehicles which were landed on that first day over the whole front was 6,000, including 1,200 tanks. Where this figure came from it is impossible to find out. It probably emanated from senior officers at SHAEF, who from time to time displayed considerable ability in getting things hopelessly wrong. A truly accurate number cannot be ascertained, because in the shambles of 'Ohama' beach there was no one to make a tally; but it is possible to use some authenticated figures to get an approximately correct total. On 'Utah' beach, 23,250 men and 1,700 vehicles were landed. On 'Omaha', 34,350 men were put ashore, and, from the signals sent to Major-General Huebner, the complaint was that there were too many vehicles and not enough men; so, making every allowance for this and doubling the ratio of personnel to vehicles, there must have been at least 1,000 vehicles on that beach. If the 6,000 figure was correct, that would leave no more than 3,300 vehicles to be apportioned over the whole of the three beaches on the British.Canadian sector. This is patently absurd. It is known that on 'Juno' beach 21,400 men and 3,200 vehicles were landed. On the other two beaches the total number of men was 53,800, and therefore, by applying the same ratio of about 7 to 1, a further 7,800 vehicles would be an appropriate number, making 11,000 in all for beaches 'Gold', 'Juno' and 'Sword'. This sort of exercise can be a dangerous one, for in actuality the proportion of vehicles landed on 'Juno' beach was out of pattern and much higher than on other beaches. The true figure for the three beaches was known to HQ 21 Army Group, and was 8,900. Taking this accurate and correct total on its own, and ignoring the two American beaches, demonstrates that the 'official' count of 6,000 was ridiculously low. The true figure, taking all five beaches into account, was nearly double that, and must have been at least 11,500 vehicles altogether. It was a stupendous performance and far, far better than the records suggest.

The figure of 1,200 tanks is about right. It was planned to land 1,500 in all, and there were probably about 300 which never made it from ship to shore. The biggest shortfall against planned performance was in tonnage of stores. Instead of an anticipated 5,000 to 6,000 tons, the total weight of stores discharged on to the beaches was 4,000 tons, but this was just about enough to keep the invading forces fully maintained and supplied. This colossal total of men, machines and supplies represented a fantastic achievement in terms of logistics. The planners worked in theory and had the easier task. All that was required of us was to ensure that there were enough ships at the right places and the appropriate number of men, tanks, guns, vehicles and stores and equipment to be put on board when the time came. The real credit for this stupendous performance was shared by the crews of the landing craft, those who manoeuvred the ferries and the DUKW amphibious vehicles, and particularly the members of the beach units on shore who marshalled the men and got the vehicles off, and manhandled stores and equipment. All this to begin with was carried on while under continuous enemy fire.

Just as the assaulting troops, though sick and miserably wet and cold, had, because of German misjudgement in relying upon the conditions, on balance gained more from the bad weather than they had lost, so on the logistic side the Allies lost more than they gained. The shortfall in equipment and stores was not really serious at first. It was the continuing and increasing amount of backlog which became the big worry. For this the weather was almost entirely responsible. The beaches and the approach waters were cluttered up with wrecked or damaged landing craft. This slowed down movement and passage of transport, supplies and equipment, and as the bad weather persisted for a few days, the planned logistic build up fell substantially behind schedule. The actual loss of craft did not matter so much, because allowance had been made for a high figure of damage by enemy action. Montgomery had good reason to complain about the elements, but he had no complaints about the planning, and indeed made the generous concession that the only over-insurance and unnecessary congestion of unwanted material was due to his operational staff insisting upon an excessive quantity of anti-aircraft artillery in the early touch down. But even this was forgivable, because no-one could have assumed that enemy reaction in the air would be negligible. The German Air Force was strangely quiet and appeared to be avoiding contest in the air, the explanation for which could only be that the Luftwaffe High Command was husbanding its resources to meet what was believed to be the threat of a major invasion in the Pas de Calais. The greatest activity was the laying of mines by night, which meant that the Royal Navy minesweepers were fully occupied for days to come.

There is a curious passage in Eisenhower's Report where, referring to the continuing problems of the Americans on 'Omaha' beach on 7 June, it reads, 'I decided to alter the immediate tactical plan to the extent of having both V and VII Corps concentrate upon effecting a link-up through Carentan.' The Supreme Commander, having given the decision to launch the invasion, had a right to intervene on a question of strategy, but not the power of control of the tactical plan. This control on the American sector would have been vested in General Omar Bradley as commanding General of US 1st Army, just as it was in General Dempsey on the British sector. In between them and the Supreme Commander there was General Montgomery, the overall Commander-in-Chief of the assaulting army forces. If anyone had a right to intervene and change the objectives given to a Corps it would have been Montgomery, and if this happened, as Eisenhower put it, this would have been an improper interference with the chain of command, and would have entitled Montgomery to ask Eisenhower to keep out of it. The decision was no doubt a correct one and made no difference to Montgomery's general scheme of things, but if Supreme Commanders start interfering on matters of tactics they lend themselves wide open to the sort of criticism which the German generals made of Hitler's involvement in the affairs of his top commanders.

It has to be assumed that it is a correct statement, as Eisenhower lent his name and signature to the Report. If so, it does him no credit, but in his favour it is more likely that it is yet another inaccuracy by the writers of the Report which Eisenhower failed to pick up and correct when he came to sign it. It may well be that it was in fact Bradley who made the decision, and that it was made after discussion with Eisenhower, a course which they were entitled to adopt; and as Montgomery, who was rather touchy about these things, made no reference to this tactical change, the obvious inference was that he thought it was a perfectly proper decision by the US 1st Army Commanding General. If it had actually been an interference by Eisenhower, and Montgomery got to know about it, he would certainly have had something to say!

There is yet another inaccuracy in the Report where it deals with the counter-attack against the Canadians by the German 21st and 12th SS Panzer Divisions on 7 June. The passage in question reads 'This counter-attack penetrated nearly to the coast and drove a wedge between the two Allied divisions . . . .' In fact, on 7 June the Canadians had made a substantial advance and penetration inland, and the Germans drove them back from their forward positions, but never as far back as the position which had been reached on D-Day. The gap between the 3rd British and 3rd Canadian Divisions was there on D-Day, and an attempt in the evening by the Germans to turn this into a wedge petered out. By the time the German Panzer Divisions launched their attack on the 7th, there was no gap and no wedge. There remained a German salient with its apex at Douvres, but the enemy never got nearer than three miles from the coast. Except for this slight indentation of the line, the British and Canadian forces by the evening of 7 June firmly held a bridgehead which was twenty-two miles wide and varied in depth from five to ten miles.

Montgomery moved his Tactical Headquarters — a couple of caravans and a few tents — to Normandy on 8 June. This meant that within three days all of the top Army commanders actually involved in planning and executing the assault phase of the invasion left their Navy Command vessels and were physically on shore. Headquarters 21 Army Group remained in England for several weeks under the charge of Major-General de Guingand, Chief of Staff, who was in daily touch with the Commander-in-Chief at TAC HQ. While the fighting formations were battling away to enlarge the bridgehead, the administrative staff back in England were kept pretty busy endeavouring to ensure that the requirements of the troops in Normandy were always met. It was our task to pass on the demands from HQ 2nd Army. The main adjustment to the planned landing of supplies which resulted from the shortfall was the creation of top priority for ammunition, which was being expended more than anticipated, in place of petrol (gasoline) and engineer stores which were not so urgently required. We were buoyed up and encouraged by the knowledge that the invasion had succeeded, if not quite to the full extent of the more optimistic forecasts, nevertheless at a fraction of the cost in human lives which the pessimists had feared. The stage was set for the defeat of the German armies in France and an advance towards the Fatherland of the foe. But many weeks of desperately hard fighting were to follow.

12

THE CAMPAIGN IN SUMMER

Within two or three days of the first landings it became clear that Montgomery's strategy was succeeding beyond measure. The British and Canadian forces had drawn on to the sector around Caen the whole of the enemy armoured formations, and the town and its environs was the focal point of enemy resistance. The Americans were able to begin their advance against Cherbourg, and the nature of the opposition was variable; they had to overcome some tough and well-disciplined units and some of poor quality. Compared with the opposition with which the US V and VII Corps had to contend, the British 2nd Army was faced by the middle of June with four Panzer divisions. The US forces had to contend with none. Even a month later, the Americans had to cope with only two armoured divisions while the British and Canadians had six Panzer divisions fighting against them. It was very tough going right from the start, and it became apparent that Caen could only be taken after a carefully planned and organized assault which would take several days to prepare and mount.

A week after D-Day, there began a deal of criticism about Montgomery's generalship and the slowness of the British performance. Air Chief Marshal Tedder, although personally on quite good terms with Montgomery, had a natural antipathy to British Army commanders, something which he frankly admitted in his memoirs, aptly named *With Prejudice*, and Lieutenant-General Frederick Morgan, who was regarded at SHAEF as the real architect of 'Overlord', could see nothing good in Montgomery ever since the day when his COSSAC plan had been so rudely and cavalierly rejected. Complaints about the failure to capture Caen and in particular the airfield at Carpiquet, on which the RAF commanders had set such store, were fuelled by a biased and exaggerated report on 14 June from Air Marshal Coningham, the Commander of the British Tactical Air Force. He said that the 7th Armoured Division had suffered a severe reverse and that the situation on that part of the front was critical. In fact it was nothing of the kind, although the 7th Armoured had been worsted in battle. Coningham had joined the 'anti Monty' club because he was jealous of Montgomery's publicity and resented the lack of praise and attention bestowed upon him and his 2nd Tactical Air Force. It was all very petty and childish, but Montgomery has to bear much of the blame for a persistent failure on his part to give due credit to other commanders, and his tendency to hog the limelight. The situation might have become very serious, but fortunately for Montgomery and the Allied endeavour there was at this time an admirable relationship between de Guingand and Bedell Smith. De Guingand had all along kept his friend and opposite number fully in the picture, and interpreted many of his Commander-in-Chief's brusque utterances and closely guarded intentions into language which could be understood by the US Chief of Staff and the American 'Top Brass'.

If slowness to capture Caen is a matter for criticism, what about the estimate of the senior staff officers at SHAEF that Cherbourg would fall to the Americans on D + 8 (14 June)? The US forces did not enter the town until 26 June, and the harbour did not surrender until the 28, that is, three weeks after D-Day and fourteen days later than the projected planning date. General Omar Bradley was more realistic, and his opinion always was that it would take at least fifteen days after landing. Moreover, as has previously been observed, he was the one senior American officer who, after the end of the war, readily acknowledged that Montgomery's plan was for the British to take the weight of the German defensive reaction around Caen while the Americans went on a wide and deep semi-circular manoeuvre. On the other hand, if Eisenhower and Bedell Smith had paid any attention to what Montgomery had said at the Presentation of Plans, it would have been perfectly clear what the strategy was, which makes it quite astonishing that both of them referred after the war to an enforced change of tactics when the British failed to break through Caen, and make for the River

Seine. The statement in the Report can be explained away as yet another of the many mistakes and inaccuracies for which the writers at SHAEF were responsible, and to which Eisenhower carelessly or with shortness of memory put his name and signature. But Bedell Smith's observation in a newspaper article is quite inexplicable, particularly as he and de Guingand were so close and must have discussed regularly the success of the plan for the British to hold the nub while the Americans went on a rampage. Perhaps the poison which Tedder and Frederick Morgan first spread in early June ultimately ate into the minds of two otherwise generous and fair-minded men.

Although it was nonsense for Coningham to talk about a serious reverse and a critical situation, it has to be admitted that the performance of 7th Armoured Division, the famous 'Desert Rats', was extremely disappointing. They failed to adapt themselves to the conditions imposed by the *bocage* country, which were so different from the wide open desert where they had won their reputation. The *bocage*, with small fields divided and separated by thick hedges on high banks, was inhibitive of sweeping deployment of tanks, and ideal for the defenders who were able to take toll with hidden anti-tank guns, and whose snipers were able to pick off the tank commanders riding with head and shoulders exposed.

In this regard, the Americans were much quicker to adapt to the conditions. Whereas in the assault they had failed to make use of specialized armour and suffered badly in consequence, now they applied their ingenuity by creating a new form of specialized armour. A contraption, for the most part made of steel salvaged from the German beach obstacles, was attached to the front of the tanks with a sharp edge to cut through the hedges and bulldoze through the banks. In the Cotentin peninsula itself, Lieutenant-General Collins commanding US VII Corps was now able to build on his experience in operating in close country and thick undergrowth at Guadalcanal. He dispensed with the use of armour in the *bocage*, and pushed his infantry in a series of short thrusts, regularly relieving the leading battalions with fresh troops and made rapid progress. It was a first-class performance by a first-class commander in the field.

'Freddie' de Guingand had always been most impressed by 'Lightnin' Joe' Collins, and was quick to give full credit where credit was due. On the other hand, there was a section of

Lieut. General
J. Lawton Collins

Imperial War Museum

Ingersoll's infamous book which intensely annoyed the normally courteous and kindly disposed British staff officer. It was suggested that the difficulties and dangers of operating with tanks in the *bocage* country had never been appreciated by Montgomery and his staff, who had ignored the advice of Colonel Bonesteel, one of the US officers attached to HQ 21 Army Group. Nor, it was said, had they taken into account the devastating use by the Germans of the 88 mm anti-aircraft gun as an anti-tank weapon. In fact, the staff at HQ 21 Army Group were fully aware of the difficulties of deploying armour in the *bocage*, but tank support for the infantry was deemed essential, and the difficulties had to be accepted. Moreover, the suggestion that they were unprepared for the use of the 'eighty-eights' was positively laughable when it is remembered that the British Eighth Army had suffered from these for over two years in the desert war, in Sicily and in Italy. De Guingand was probably also deeply hurt that Colonel Bonesteel would appear to have behaved in an underhand fashion in providing Ingersoll with false material for unfair criticism when, for his part, de Guingand had gone out of his way to make Bonesteel one of the family at HQ 21 Army Group.

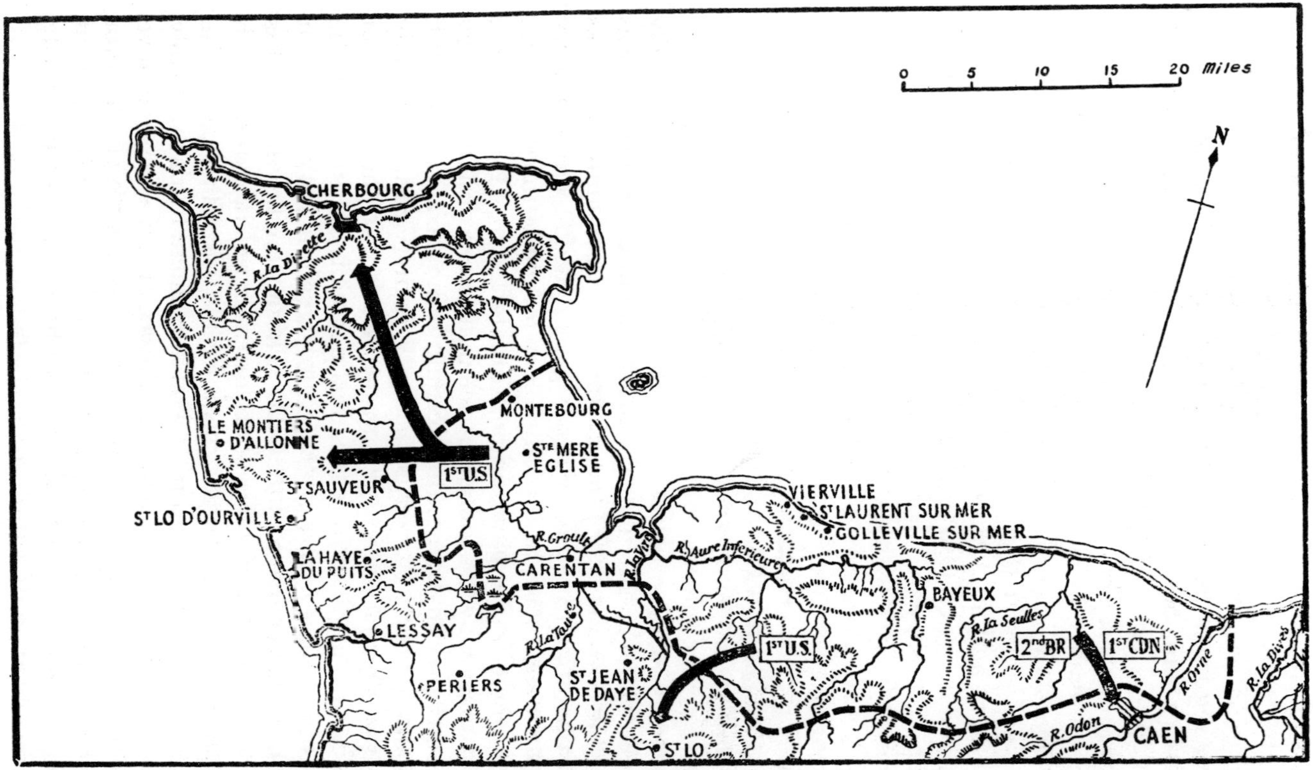

ESTABLISHMENT OF THE LODGEMENT AREA

Montgomery's intention was that British 2nd Army should mount a fully prepared attack on Caen which involved an enveloping movement by armoured and infantry divisions advancing from the west to threaten the city in the area to the south east. He had hoped that this operation could be launched on 18 June, but owing to the delays in unloading imposed by the bad weather, essential types of ammunition and special units were not available. He ordered a postponement until 22 June, but a ferocious gale which blew up on the 19 and did not abate until the 22 interfered so much with the planned arrival of troops, equipment and ammunition that he was compelled further to postpone the operation until 25 June. The enemy made good use of the three days' delay, so that once the attack began the British were faced with much stronger and co-ordinated defence as well as a serious shortfall in the forces required for the operation. There were good reasons for the initial delay, for it would have been extremely risky to have tried to rush an attack prematurely against a strongly-entrenched enemy. It was only the ill-informed and ignorant men at SHAEF who thought otherwise. The subsequent postponement and the consequential increase in enemy power to resist was entirely due to the intervention of persistent bad weather, culminating in the savage gale which began on 19 June. Ultimately, the preliminary stage of the operation to capture Caen began on the 25, with the main attack the next day, which led to some of the bitterest fighting in the whole of the Normandy campaign.

Whatever may be said about the indifferent quality of some of the infantry divisions, the German armoured divisions and particularly the SS Panzer Divisions were first-class. They were well-trained, well-equipped with the formidable 'Tiger' tanks, well-led and inspired by a fanatical devotion to 'Fuhrer, Volk und Reich'. They were prepared to carry out Hitler's orders to fight to the death, and they did. These were the troops who fought desperately and were only defeated because of the total disruption of their full organized strength by the Allied air attacks on the transportation system and on movement by day. It really was preposterous of the American Press Corps to stir up trouble and endanger the Alliance by querulously asking why the British were not doing any fighting.

The first stage of the operation was the enveloping movement with the objective of getting across the barrier of the River Odon to take up a position threatening Caen, and then later to co-ordinate with two British and Canadian divisions in a direct attack on the city. By the evening of the 28th, the 11th Armoured Division had established a bridgehead on the other side of the river, but the real significance of this part of the battle was not ground won, which was not extensive, but in the resounding defeat inflicted on the 1st and 2nd SS Panzer Corps when their fierce counter-attack was launched.

British 2nd Army regrouped and prepared for the assault on Caen. This took place successfully on 8 July, when the British 3rd and Canadian 3rd Divisions entered the city, although the Germans held on to the suburb of Vaucelles on the other side of the River Orne. The attack had been preceded the evening before by a huge naval bombardment from three British battleships and an even bigger aerial bombardment by aircraft of British Bomber Command, which was impressive in the devastation it wrought and the stunning demoralization of the defenders, but of considerable disadvantage in that the craters and demolished buildings made it impossible for tanks to get through and exploit the entry of the infantry. On the whole, this use of heavy bombers to precede an attack on the ground was not of much benefit. The really useful part of the Allied air force support was the damage to the railway system and the extensive and persistent harassing of enemy armoured and troop movement by day.

The fact that Montgomery and the British were on the receiving end of American Press criticism is a good example of blatant selective reporting, based on the proposition that the US forces were good and the British were not. The war correspondents had skated over the shambles of the American assault on 'Omaha' beach, and had written it up as a triumph of courage over adversity. The allegation that Montgomery was not using the British 2nd Army enough, but was relying on the gallant Americans, was not only a distortion of the truth about the battle for Caen, but also ignored the failure of Bradley's 1st US Army to break out southwards and capture the vitally important road junction of St Lo. This was more of a disappointment than the slowness in capturing Caen. The US 1st Army by the beginning of July consisted of four corps and fourteen divisions, and out-numbered the Germans who faced them by more than two to one, and they were expected to do much better than they did. Montgomery did not criticize Bradley any more than did Bradley criticize Montgomery. Each man was there on the spot, and each knew of the appalling problems posed by the nature of the country, the persistent rain and cloud and the fanatical defence of the best German units. The US offensive petered out on 10 July, and Bradley had pretty well exhausted his supplies of ammunition. He had to call a halt.

The American supply system at this time was overstretched and unable to keep pace. In the first two weeks of the invasion, men were pouring in by the thousand, but the landing of stores and vehicles fell badly behind schedule. The biggest bottleneck was caused by the failure of the 'Rhino' ferries to cope in the bad weather and rough seas with the unloading of LSTs, and as a result these craft had to be beached ashore at high tide so that tanks and vehicles could be driven straight on to the sand. The LSTs could not be floated off until the next high tide. This slowed down the turnround and caused substantial delay. It was therefore doubly important for the 'Mulberry' harbour piers to be completed to the extent of providing facilities for ships to be discharged alongside. The first blockships for the 'Gooseberry' breakwaters were sunk in position on 7 June, and the first of the component parts of the harbour set off on D-Day and the tow of these across the channel was completed forty-eight hours later. The 'Gooseberry' breakwaters provided a sheltered anchorage for ships and landing craft, and there were five of these — one for each beach and two of the five formed part of the 'Mulberry' harbours. These consisted of, first, the sunken breakwater, then huge concrete caissons which were also sunk, enclosing an area of sheltered water two miles long and one mile wide. Within this area were floating piers which rested on the rocky foreshore at low tide. There were seven miles of piers and fifteen pierheads. The total of units to be towed across the Channel numbered four hundred, and altogether weighed a million and a half tons.

The US Navy and Engineers were less careful and methodical than the slower British, and rushed through the construction of the American 'Mulberry' artificial harbour leaving it inadequately planted to withstand the gale of 19 June, which wrecked it beyond repair. Such portions which could be salvaged were towed across to the British 'Mulberry' off Arromanches, and used to rebuild that one, which also had received a savage battering from the high seas. The storm was so bad that the convoys setting off for France were forced back into port. Dozens of ships and landing craft dragged anchor and were blown and tossed ashore, and when he saw what had happened, General Bradley spoke eloquently of the dreadful sight of wrecked and damaged vessels littering the beaches. The whole of the supply on all the beaches was thrown out of gear, and it was this unforeseen and unfortunate interruption which compelled the postponement of the attack on Caen until 25 June. It was nothing to do with Montgomery's alleged slowness.

After the gale died down, the anchorages within the shelter of the 'Gooseberry' breakwaters were filled with ships and craft trying to catch up with the backlog. On the American beaches the ferrying was almost entirely dependent on DUKW amphibious vehicles, but big and heavy equipment presented a problem for which a bold decision to beach large coasters and to offload direct on to lorries proved markedly successful. Although the tonnage discharged on 'Omaha' beach alone was much greater than the maximum achieved through the British 'Mulberry' harbour at Arromanches, this use of beached coasters was so very expensive in wrecked and badly damaged ships that it could never have been included as a realistic possibility during the planning stage, when shortage of shipping was prohibitive of anything which might exaggerate this disability. The practice became unnecessary after 20 July, when the port of Cherbourg was opened after clearing the mines and dealing to some extent with the wreckage and demolition created by the departing Germans. The US logistic difficulties became steadily eased; by the end of August the port was dealing with 10,000 tons a day, and a month later it was fully operational.

By a prodigious effort the British 'Mulberry' harbour was quickly repaired after the ravages of the great storm, and it was in partial use within a day or two of the onset of calmer weather. As the beaching of landing craft for the discharge of vehicles came to an end it was no longer necessary for vehicles to be accompanied by drivers, and once they were offloaded by derricks on to the piers anyone who was available was pressed into service to drive them away, even though it was the first time some had ever sat behind a steering wheel! Once this practice became known, several of the more cunning units, possessed of experienced Quartermaster-Sergeants, sent drivers down to the unloading points who presented themselves as skilled volunteers, and once in the driving cab set off for their own unit headquarters and not the vehicle park. The middle-rank staff officers at HQ 21 Army Group and probably at HQ 2nd Army were always prepared to give full marks for ingenuity, and it is highly unlikely that this unauthorized poaching was even made known to anyone above the rank of Lieutenant-Colonel.

It so happened that, although technically described as an advance liaison officer, the position of trouble-shooter and resident spy came my way after the gale died down. There appeared to be no trouble that required shooting, and the spying had to be carried out with extreme benevolence, so it was a very pleasant interlude. The crossing of the Channel was an experience deeply etched in memory. It was a fine sunny morning, about the only one for the best part of a month. In Portsmouth harbour, seeking, with the authority of the Chief of Staff, some mode of conveyance, there came into view a Motor Gun Boat moored alongside, with the skipper, a very young RNVR Lieutenant sitting in his shirt sleeves reading a paperback novel. He was delighted to have the opportunity of a trip across, and agreed to take also a Brigadier from the Canadian Army who was standing by looking lost and forlorn. We shot out of the harbour and into open sea, and to our starboard a good nautical mile away there was a fantastic sight of the convoy which seemed to stretch unendingly all the way from the Isle of Wight to Normandy. The Canadian Brigadier seemed a little uneasy, and asked if we were in a mine-swept lane. In his deep Cornish brogue the young man said 'No, zur, but if you're worried, get up to the sharp end — we're doing forty knots, so if we do hit one, it'll only blow the backside off us.' Somewhat put out, the Brigadier stayed where he was. We did not hit a mine, so the Lieutenant's judgement was never tested.

In the early stages of the invasion, administration planning and control was exercised by British 2nd Army and US 1st Army under the general direction of HQ 21 Army Group. Headquarters Lines of Communication (HQ L OF C) landed on 24 June (D + 18) and took over the actual command and control of all base installations on the British side, and Headquarters Communications Zone (Com Z) correspondingly did so on the American side. Administrative control passed from 2nd Army to HQ 21 Army Group on that day, and a small advance section of the headquarters moved over with HQ L of C so that the exercise of control could be effectively transmitted from London, where the bulk of the headquarters was still established. On the operational side, HQ 21 Army Group assumed control of both the British 2nd Army and the Canadian 1st Army on 23 July, and the Army Group was now fully effective, but Rear HQ remained in London until it was set up in the fields around Vaucelles on 11 August. There they remained until the move to Brussels on 23 September. Throughout the whole period while fighting was going on in Normandy, Montgomery operated from his Tactical Headquarters (Tac H), and de Guingand, his Chief of Staff, used to make a visit every day, generally in the evening. This one man, person-to-person link was really his only contact with his huge headquarters. It was his practice to plan and control the battle and issue orders to the commanders serving under him, while his headquarters had to see that the machinery worked to carry out his designs.

Lieutenant-General George Patton had been appointed to the command of US 3rd Army in the early Spring of the year, but there was no 3rd Army to command. In fact the 'ghost' army to which he had been appointed played a most important part in the deception plan code-named 'Fortitude'. His headquarters were supposed to be in Kent where he and his Chief of Staff and other senior officers were stationed. The Germans believed that there was a huge force to be led by him, poised to invade in the Pas de Calais area. At first Patton, who was by far the senior American in terms of service, had been bitterly disappointed when he learnt that Omar Bradley was to lead the US 1st Army into the invasion, but he was much happier when Montgomery explained at the Presentation of Plans that the US 3rd Army would have the task of bursting through the enemy into Brittany.

At the earliest opportunity, which was 6 July, Patton flew over with his senior staff officers and established a Command Post at Nelou, near Bricquebec in the middle of the Cotentin peninsula. It was a trying time for such an impetuous go-getter, and from all accounts he was continually harping at Bradley's slowness (which he blamed on Montgomery!) and made it very plain how much better he could have done the job (particularly because he would pay no attention to Montgomery's strategic design!). Regrettably he was never known to have praised the British soldier; it was the American solider who was the best in the world — a judgement which would be disputed by the Germans as well as the British.

When General Bradley called a halt to US 1st Army attack against St Lo, he advised Montgomery that he was not in a position to mount another large-scale operation for about ten days. A breakthrough offensive was therefore planned for 20 July and was named Operation 'Cobra'. In the meantime, US 1st Army was steadily plugging away and gaining ground all the time, and St Lo was captured on 18 July. The American forces were now well placed and poised for the breakout.

Intelligence sources indicated that the German Command was beginning to move armoured formations to the west, which if proceeded with, would make Bradley's proposed breakthrough much more difficult and hazardous. Something had to be done, and Montgomery and Dempsey therefore planned Operation 'Goodwood' to take the pressure off Bradley and to reverse any transfer of enemy armour to the American sector. This operation was to be a powerful thrust by three armoured divisions, followed by two infantry divisions with a third coming up behind on the right flank, aiming to strike out from the small bridgehead on the eastern side of the River Orne and to make for the high ground five miles south of Caen. The offensive was to begin with a massive aerial bombardment, this time the use of high explosive bombs by British Bomber Command being limited to the flanks, well clear of the armoured thrust, so that cratering and demolition would not impede the tanks. In front of the three armoured divisions, the US heavy and medium bomber aircraft were to plaster the Germans with anti-personnel and fragmentation bombs, and the fighter bombers of British 2nd TAF were to strafe the enemy assembly areas. Montgomery's intention was always made clear to those under his command, but was seriously misunderstood by senior officers at SHAEF, including Eisenhower himself. Once again, his Report got it wrong and introduced a complete fairy tale about a plan for the British and Canadians to break out and exploit an advance in the direction of Paris and the middle reaches of the River Seine. It was apparently believed that the British 'Goodwood' and the US 'Cobra' were the two prongs of an all-out assault on all of the German defensive formations, aiming for a complete breakthrough on the whole front. The misunderstanding may have arisen from a 2nd Army Operational Instruction which included Falaise as a possible ultimate objective. To make the position clear, Montgomery had sent a personal memorandum to Lieutenant-General O'Connor, the British 8th Corps Commander. He set out that the operation was to engage the German armour, and to 'write it down' so that it ceased to be of any value; nevertheless the eastern flank remained a bastion on which the whole future campaign in Normandy depended, and 8th Corps must on no account be overstretched and lose the initiative, for the prime task was to ensure that there was a firm base east of Caen. It can be seen that Montgomery's prime objective was limited in scope, but he nevertheless realized that if the Americans made a breakthrough as planned, then it would be necessary a week or so later for British 2nd Army to make a concentrated and powerful effort against Falaise. But for this the time was not yet ripe.

Operation 'Goodwood' began with a feint in a southwards direction two days before the main offensive was due to begin on 18 July, and this succeeded in drawing some of the enemy armour away from the point of the main attack. The aerial bombardment was colossal, again more effective in its demoralizing and stunning effect, and the British armoured divisions made satisfactory progress until they came up against the hard core of the German defensive system. The defences were ten miles in depth, and once the battle was fully joined progress was slow and hard-fought every yard of the way; the British armoured units were faced with a strong anti-tank screen which held up the advance to the high ground. Then on 20 July down came the rain again, and the whole battle area was turned into a sea of mud. The tanks had to be halted, and the infantry moved in and took up a holding role.

The end was a disappointment; nevertheless, Montgomery regarded the operation as a success. An advance of some five or six miles had been achieved against fierce opposition, and the bridgehead beyond the River Orne widened to a distance of twelve miles. Three SS Panzer Divisions and two other Panzer Divisions had been committed to battle, and if not completely 'written down' and rendered of no value, had been severely mauled. There were no Germans left in the suburbs of Caen or in the greatly extended area to the east and south east of the

River Orne. The base had been considerably enlarged, and provided a bastion which was firmer than it had ever been.

At the end of the first day of Operation 'Goodwood', Montgomery, with his mind conditioned by the limited scope of the orders he had given to 8th Corps, issued a communiqué which referred to the fact that 'early this morning British and Canadian troops of the 2nd Army attacked and broke through into the area east of the Orne and south east of Caen.' This was strictly correct, but the term 'broke through' gave the Press correspondents the impression that the long-awaited breakout from the Allied lodgement had at last come about. It also added to the misconceived opinion held by Eisenhower, Tedder and senior officers at SHAEF, that Montgomery intended to make for Falaise and even threaten Paris.

The day before the British 2nd Army offensive ground to a halt in a sea of mud, there was an outburst of another kind of stormy weather at SHAEF, at the heart of which was the frustrated Deputy Supreme Commander, Air Chief Marshal Tedder. Neither Eisenhower nor his Deputy emerge with much credit from the sorry tale. Dealing at a much later stage with the critical comments which were being spread about at this time, Major-General de Guingand, always a straight-forward and honest gentleman, put on record that Eisenhower never criticized Montgomery's tactics, and that being in close contact almost daily with the Supreme Commander and his Deputy he was never shown 'any attitude except one of understanding of Montgomery's difficulties and a great willingness to help him by every means . . . '. If they gave such an impression to de Guingand, whose truthfulness has never been questioned by anybody, they must have been two-faced masters in the art of duplicity. The other side of the picture comes from the account given by Captain Harry Butcher, Eisenhower's aide, that 'They were completely disgusted with the lack of progress', and that when in the evening of 19 July Tedder called Eisenhower to say that Monty had stopped his armour from going further, 'Ike was mad'. Moreover Tedder told the Supreme Commander that 'the British Chiefs of Staff would support any recommendation that Ike might care to make with respect to Monty'. If Tedder got any such notion, it could only have come from Air Chief Marshal Portal, for the airmen tended to get together, whereas the Chief of the Imperial General Staff and Chairman of the

Chiefs of Staff Committee, Field Marshal Viscount Alanbrooke as he had now become, knew and trusted his Monty, and would have stoutly resisted any suggestion that Montgomery should be relieved of his command. Neither would he have been impressed by any criticism alleging that Montgomery was falling down on the job. It may be that Tedder had in mind that Eisenhower should take over the actual command in the field. Whatever he intended it was a mean performance, which was largely brought about by the failure, as the RAF top commander would have it, to meet their demand for the capture of more open ground for airfields. From the start of the 'Overlord' planning, Leigh-Mallory and Coningham, stoutly supported by Tedder, had pressed for the early capture of Carpiquet airfield, south west of Caen, and as the Minutes of the Senior Staff Officers' meetings clearly indicate, de Guingand constantly repeated that Montgomery's plan involved no promises at all in this regard. Moreover by this time it seemed to the Army commanders that there was enough territory to make fifteen airfields, and that was good enough!

Somebody must have dropped a hint of dissatisfaction to Winston Churchill himself, for he spoke to Montgomery about it when he visited him in Normandy on 20 July. It was never an easy task to satisfy the Prime Minister when he was on the rampage calling for speedy action, but to his credit he had on several occasions already acknowledged that Montgomery's apparent slowness and delays had ended in great victories, and in consequence he readily accepted the explanation of what had happened and what were the expectations for the future, and was fully prepared to let Montgomery carry on with his proposed design for the Allied Armies. There was no further attempt to dislodge Montgomery from the overall command, and Eisenhower was content to leave him in that position until the end of August. Montgomery and Bradley agreed on the general nature of operations, and they never fell out at this stage of the campaign.

The heavy rain of 20 July put paid to General Bradley's original intention to start Operation 'Cobra' on that day. His forces were in position on the 19, with the forward troops in their foxholes waiting for the aerial bombardment which was to be the prelude to the attack. They stayed like that for six days while the rain poured down almost incessantly. On 24 July, there was a false start. The order for attack on that day had been postponed because thick mist and heavy cloud would have made it extremely difficult for the men in the air to navigate or to identify the targets. The men on the ground got the message that the whole thing was off for yet another day, but unfortunately the order for postponement did not reach the US Air Force who came over, found that they could not see, and most of the aircraft returned to base without releasing any bombs. Those that did, unhappily dropped them on their own troops who were taking cover in their foxholes, but mercifully the casualties were not extensive, although this unhappy performance could not have done much to help the fighting spirit of the sodden men. Montgomery was considerably worried that this false start may well have alerted the enemy, who would in consequence strengthen his defences against the Americans, but his hope that the German Command might regard it as less important than holding the British 2nd Army was justified, and there was no substantial reaction to this piece of bungling ineptitude. Most of the German armour remained facing the British and Canadian formations.

On 25 July, the conditions improved and the aircraft were unleashed. Nearly 1,500 heavy bombers of US 8th Air Force and almost 400 from AEAF saturated an area five miles by one in extent, and medium bombers and fighter bombers attacked enemy artillery and troops in areas behind the American front and in the area to the south-east of Caen. For this aerial bombardment, General Bradley was prepared to shorten the distance between the bomb line and the forward troops to 1,500 yards. He did this on the understanding that the American bomber aircraft would fly in from the west, following the line of the road between Periers and St Lo, which ran parallel to the US front. If they had done that there would have been no problem, but they flew in from the north at right angles to the road. This brought the aircraft in over the heads of the troops. Many of the bombs were released a mile short of the bomb line, and for the second day in succession fell among the wretched soldiers huddled in their foxholes. This time heavy casualties were suffered, including the death of Lieutenant-General Lesley McNair, who thought he was safe enough watching the intended attack from a slit trench a short way back from the front line. Two decimated battalions had to be withdrawn and their places taken by two from the reserve, all of which created a delay of several hours on this part of the front. McNair was a personal friend of both Eisenhower and Omar Bradley, who was so deeply concerned and upset by the whole tragic occurrence that his subsequent Report not only stressed that he would never have agreed to the close support bombing if he had known that the US Air Force were going to try what he called 'a perpendicular approach', but led him to take an unduly pessimistic view of the first day's fighting and to wonder whether the attack had failed.

Bradley, though properly sensitive to the untimely death and wounding of so many fine and splendid men, need not have been so worried about the success of the first day's operations, for on the whole the bomber offensive was stupendously successful. Bayerlein, the Commander of Panzer Lehr Division which took the main weight of the aerial assault, said later that at least seventy per cent of his troops were out of action — dead, wounded, crazed or numbed. The ground action involved a concentrated thrust, which Montgomery persuaded Bradley was more likely to lead to a breakthrough than the usual type of American offensive on a broad front. US VII Corps under Lieutenant-General J. Lawton Collins was given the major task to force a breach to the west of St Lo, and for this he had four infantry divisions and two armoured divisions under his command. General Bradley may well have been somewhat despondent at the apparent slowness of progress by the three infantry divisions on the first day, but they had fought well and took on most of the enemy resistance, so that the next day Collins' reserve infantry division and the two armoured divisions were able to make excellent progress. The American use of the cutting spade attachment on the front of the tanks (nicknamed 'Rhinoceros') for bulldozing a way through the *bocage* and bypassing the strong points on the roads was particularly effective. The three weeks of manufacture and training devised by Bradley and the tactical operation by Collins paid handsome dividends. In twenty-four hours the US 2nd Armoured Division made a breach seven miles in depth. On 27 July the two armoured divisions of US VII Corps advanced rapidly against the vitally important centre of Coutances on the far western side of the Cotentin peninsula. Meanwhile US VIII Corps from their station in the heart of the peninsula charged down the thinly-defended territory on the extreme right flank of the American advance. By 28 July, Operation 'Cobra' was virtually over, and the breakthrough out of the Allied lodgement area had been achieved. Montgomery's plan had succeeded as he always believed it would.

Bradley's tactical design had been for a period of consolidation and then a resumed attack on a broad front in the usual American style, but he was now in a position to follow Montgomery's original directive that in the event of a breakthrough, US 1st Army should drive on southwards and then make 'a wide sweep south of the *bocage* country'. Eisenhower had intended that Lieutenant-General Patton's 3rd Army should become operational on 1 August, taking over VIII Corps with two armoured and three infantry divisions in place of the original four infantry, and one armoured division and XV Corps were to be added to the strength of US 3rd Army.

As VIII Corps was about to be transformed from US 1st Army to 3rd Army and was already in action, Lieutenant-General Omar Bradley invited Lieutenant-General George Patton, unofficially, on 28 July, to assume command of VIII Corps, whose task and opportunity had already been marked out. In consequence, when Patton took over as Commanding General of US 3rd Army on 1 August, he not only took over the troops and armour but also a tactical plan which had been decided, and in which he was not originally involved. Patton's charge into Brittany was made possible by the leadership of others, by the gallantry of soldiers over whom he had not exercised command and by the almost total absence of German resistance, which Eisenhower's Report (correct for once) described as negligible. The success of the breakthrough by the Americans was due, first, to Montgomery's strategy and the attritional battles between the British 2nd Army and the cream of German armour in and around Caen; second, to the preliminary bombing by the Allied Air Forces; third, to Lieutenant-General Bradley's careful planning and sound leadership, and fourth, to the fighting prowess of the US 1st Army and particularly VII Corps, commanded by 'Lightnin' Joe' Lawton Collins. Patton's assumption of credit for the US 3rd Army, which did not even exist when the battle was at its fiercest, and his bland assertion of the success of his 'go-getting' approach was positively nauseating to anyone who was there and knew the true position.

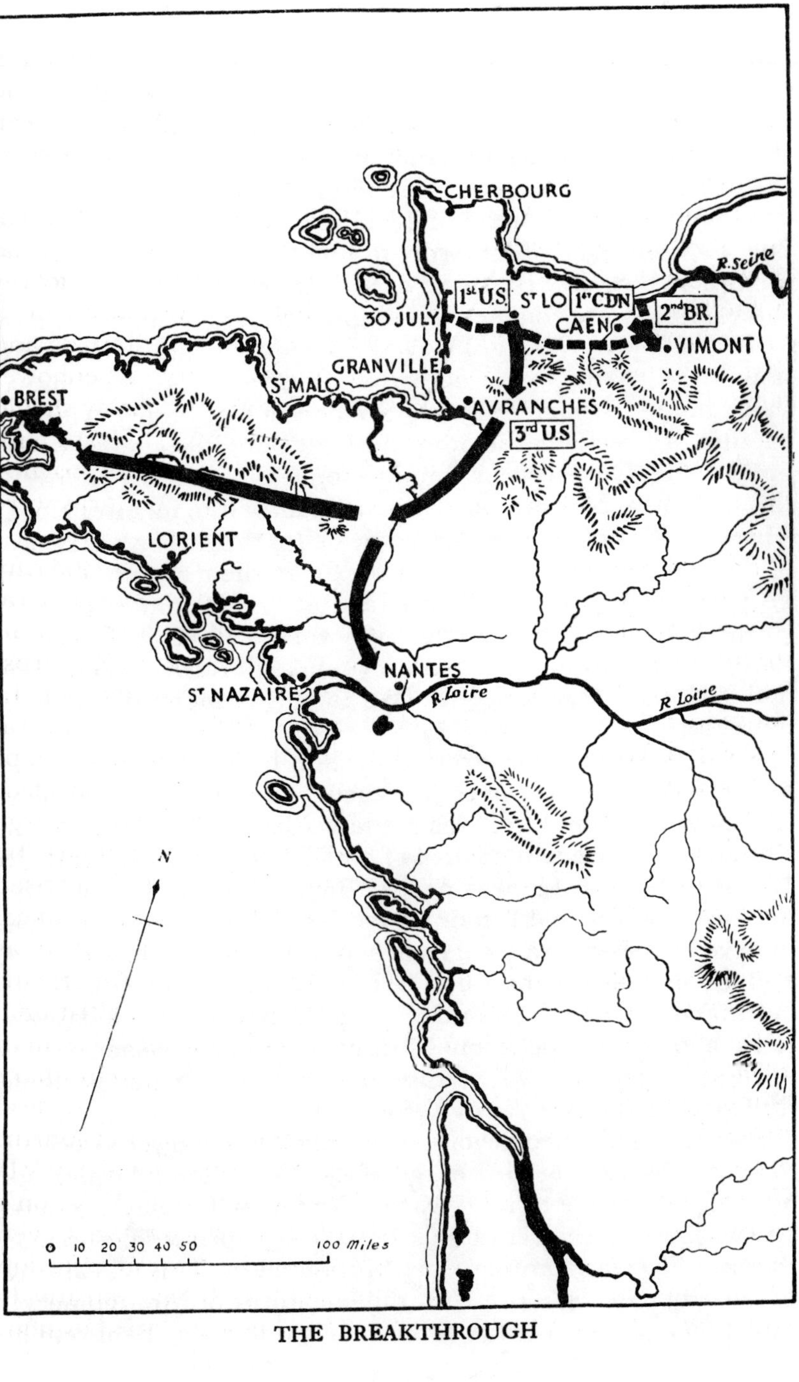

THE BREAKTHROUGH

Superficially to those who did not know the truth, Patton's lightning advance into Brittany seemed to be dramatic and magnificent, whereas in reality he was given an easy ride by the courageous efforts of Bradley's 1st Army.

On 1 August, Lieutenant-General Omar Bradley took over as Commanding General of 12 US Army Group and handed over the command of 1st Army to Lieutenant-General Hodges, an army which now consisted of V, VII and XIX Corps. These three Corps were engaged in holding off any German counter-attacks and progressing slowly and steadily, while VIII Corps, now in 3rd Army, went careering all over Brittany as fast as they could. Ultimately it was decided not to bother with the capture of Brest and the other ports, leaving the control of the area to VIII Corps whose composition was once more changed, this time from part-armoured, part-infantry into infantry alone. This switching of divisions from one Corps to another was typical of the way the Americans worked, for in their system a Corps HQ was really no more than a tactical operational command. In the logistic context, Army HQ worked direct to Division. Patton then moved the divisions round still further, so that he had XII, XV and XX Corps all largely armoured and fully mobile.

Despite the pressure exerted on him by Tedder and others at SHAEF to take over the active exercise of Supreme Command, Eisenhower was content to leave Montgomery in overall command and control of both 21 Army Group and US 12 Army Group. He was never a man who could operate on his own at a Tactical Headquarters like Montgomery. He had to have all the apparatus of hs headquarters available with him, and the huge caravanserai of SHAEF began moving across to Normandy during the month of August; it was not in a position to function as an operational supreme command headquarters until 1 September, when Eisenhower assumed the personal direction of the two Army Groups.

Patton was irritated beyond measure by Eisenhower's decision to leave Montgomery in charge of the Allied Land Armies, for he realized that he himself was under Omar Bradley's orders, and whenever he had criticisms to make he expressed the opinion that Bradley was dominated by Montgomery. This was absurd because one of the more admirable features of Montgomery's direction and control of Allied forces was the very light rein he used for the Americans, whom he rarely, if ever, presumed to order about. He had the good sense to realize that the tight rein and detailed exercise of tactical control which was a feature of the British system of command would not do for the Americans, who were accustomed to doing their own thing in their own way once an objective had been set. When Montgomery relinquished all control of US forces on 31 August, a grateful Prime Minister agreed with Alanbrooke, the Chief of the Imperial General Staff, that he should be rewarded with promotion to Field Marshal.

Pursuing his predetermined strategy, Montgomery had ordered British 2nd Army and Canadian 1st Army to continue to 'operate intensively' before and during the early stages of the American Operation 'Cobra'. On 25 July, the Canadian 2nd Corps made an attack in the direction of Falaise, with the limited objective of gaining the high ground at Bourquebus, but the shattered German armoured divisions had regrouped and been reinforced, and in hard fighting compelled the Canadians to come to a halt two days later. The next move was up to British 2nd Army, who were ordered to concentrate in the Caumont sector to the west of Caen and the River Orne, in order to launch a powerful thrust against the strong enemy forces who were dug in and positioned in depth on the slopes and hills of the Mont Pinçon range, and fully protected by extensive minefields. The attack, timed to begin on 30 July, was entrusted to 8th Corps and 30 Corps with three infantry divisions and the equivalent of four armoured divisions at their disposal, and was preceded yet again by an enormous aerial bombardment. In spite of this, the German positions were so strong and well-organized, and the protective cover of minefields so extensive that the formations in 30 Corps found the task of capturing Mont Pinçon and its hills extremely difficult. In particular, the 7th Armoured Division, the 'Desert Rats', made such poor progress that the Divisional Commander, two of his senior staff officers and one of the Brigade Commanders were all summarily dismissed. The unfortunate Corps Commander, Lieutenant-General Bucknall, also caught the backlash, and he too lost his job. In his place there was appointed Lieutenant-General Brian Horrocks, who turned out to be one of the ablest and most successful of all the British top command, and his appointment revitalized all the formations in the Corps. After a fierce struggle lasting several days, Mont Pinçon finally fell on 6 August when elements of

43rd Infantry Division reached the top by a roundabout route.

On the right flank, 8th Corps had an early success. On 1 August, 11th Armoured Division advanced due south from Caumont, threatened Vire and drove a wedge between the German VII Army, which was holding up US 1st Army, and V Panzer Army, which was containing British 30 Corps around Mont Pinçon. Some patrols actually got into Vire but withdrew, partly because this advance was a trespass upon US 1st Army territory, and so British 2nd Army had to start to wheel and to swing round facing east, aiming for Falaise, which was about to be threatened by Canadian 1st Army coming down from the north. Some fifteen miles to the south of Falaise lay the small town of Argentan, and in all the operations which followed the Germans were determined to prevent any closure of this gap.

While the Germans were grimly holding on in the Mont Pinçon sector, they mounted a fierce attack against the American forces, aiming for Avranches on the far western side of the Cotentin peninsula with the object of cutting Patton's 3rd Army supply lifeline. For this purpose, no less than five armoured divisions were assembled. Bradley had anticipated a move of this kind, and concentrated five divisions in the area around Mortain under Lieutenant-General Hodges of 1st Army and Collins's famous VII Corps who were braced to meet the onslaught. The German attack was something of a gamble; if it came off, Patton's drive might be checked altogether and his forces isolated; if it did not, then the Germans were committed to a head-on clash with US 1st Army, with the British 2nd Army and part of US 3rd Army closing in on each flank. The day before the main offensive on 7 August the Germans had lost control of Vire, which meant that any advance in that area was denied to them. Their main thrust was in the area north of Mortain, and at one stage the German armour got within ten miles of Avranches, but their advance was checked by two US infantry divisions and by the havoc caused by British rocket-firing aircraft of 2nd TAF among the enemy tanks and vehicles.

8 August was an historic day. Here the German offensive was checked; to the north, the Canadian Army began its advance towards Falaise; to the south, Patton's 3rd Army had begun the investing of the Brittany ports using his VIII Corps, and after the liberation of Rennes, the provincial capital, four days earlier, some of his forces had now got into Le Mans, while

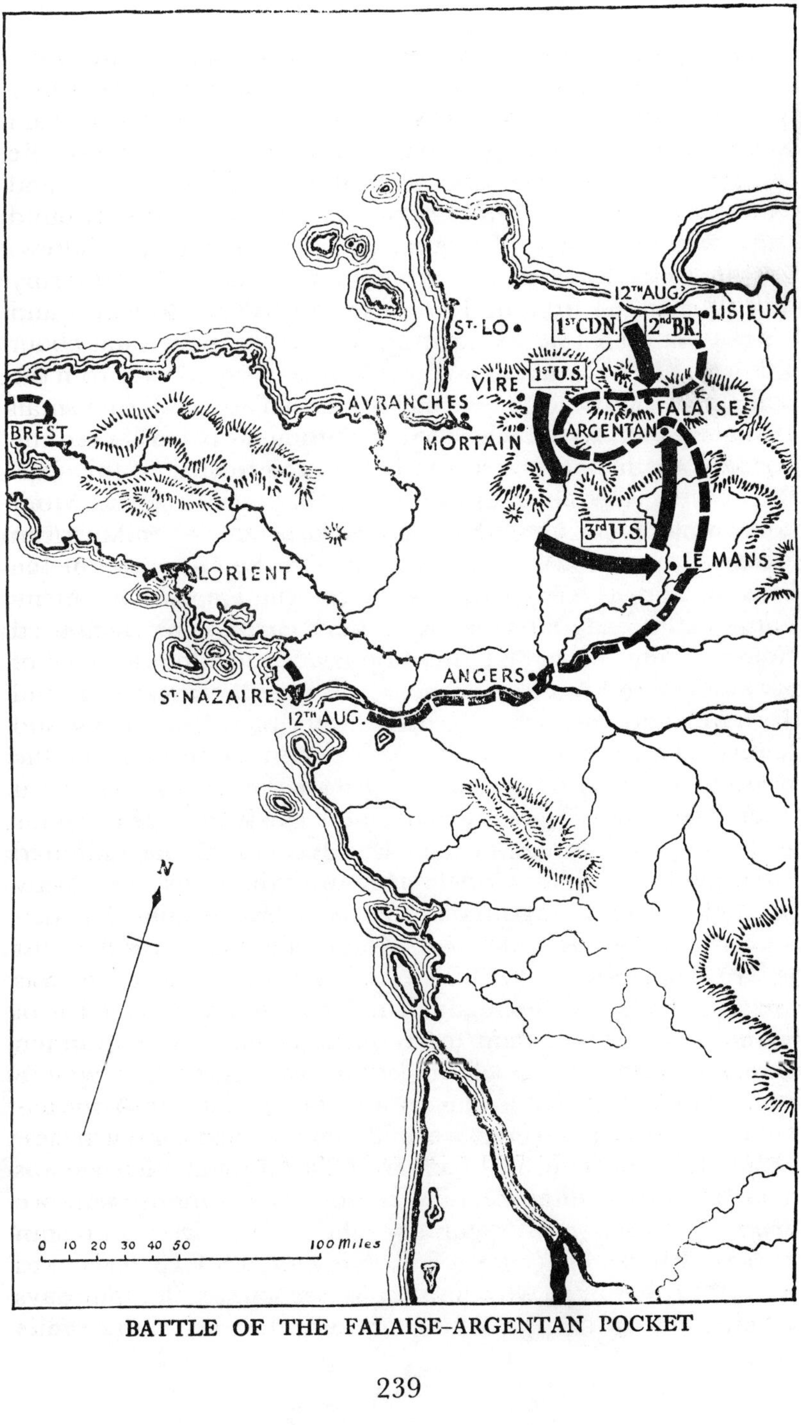

BATTLE OF THE FALAISE-ARGENTAN POCKET

others captured Angers and had reached the banks of the River Loire. While Patton was switching his divisions about and bringing into operation his XII Corps to join VIII, XV and XX Corps with the objective of swinging his Army, less VIII Corps, south and east, and while the Canadians were on the way to the capture of Falaise, the US 1st Army was locked in battle with the German VII Army. For four days there was bitter fighting round Mortain, which was the furthest indentation made in the American front line by the enemy salient. The Germans fought on desperately, carrying out Hitler's personal orders although his generals knew it was hopeless. By 12 August it was plain that the drive to Avranches had failed, and the writing was on the wall for the whole of the German forces in Normandy.

The Canadians found it hard going against what Eisenhower's Report described as 'the strongest defences yet encountered in the campaign'. Even with the aid of stupendous bombing from the air, it was not until 14 August that the German line was broken, and it was 16 August before the Canadians entered Falaise and a day later before it was cleared. The British 2nd Army, facing the same kind of opposition, had earlier pushed slowly forward from Mont Pinçon and forced a salient in support of the Canadians. The German forces had no option but to withdraw, and had on 13 August begun to do so in orderly fashion. Holding firmly to the tip of the salient and using armoured formations to keep open the gap between Falaise and Argentan, the Germans began a withdrawal of all their surviving forces, giving priority to the armoured divisions and leaving the majority of the infantry to their fate. Meanwhile it had been agreed between Eisenhower, Montgomery and Bradley that Patton should direct most of XV Corps from his general advance towards the River Seine and put 5th Armoured, 2nd French Armoured and 90 Infantry Divisions followed by 79 Infantry Divisions into a sharp left wheel northwards, making first for Alençon and then for Argentan. On 12 August, 5th Armoured Division reached the outskirts of Argentan, and Patton ordered Major-General Haislip to advance towards Falaise. When he heard of this, Omar Bradley personally countermanded the order. It was not Montgomery who did so. Many accounts criticize Montgomery for a failure to close the gap earlier, but it is difficult to see why he should be blamed, for there was nothing wrong with the plan which he had agreed with Bradley.

There are occasions in military history when criticism should be muted and credit given for the skill and courage of an enemy whose conduct of operations prevented any quicker advance.

General Patton must have been so conditioned by the ease with which his Army had rampaged virtually unopposed through Brittany that his judgement became severely clouded. Thus, for instance he later said in his account of those days that he had considered talk of a German offensive towards Avranches as a rumour and bluff. He would hardly have thought this if, instead of gallivanting all over Brittany, he had been in General Hodges' shoes trying to control a face to face onslaught by five first class Panzer divisions. His instruction to Haislip, if carried out, would have led to disaster. He was furious when Bradley ordered Haislip to halt, and the nature of his attitude to a jointly-agreed Allied strategy was demonstrated by his plea to Bradley to let him go on to Falaise, and 'we'll drive the British back into the sea for another Dunkirk', which, even if it was a cheap joke, took no account of the fact that it was not the British he would be colliding with, but the Canadians, who were advancing on Falaise. According to his recollection, the reason for halting him was that the British had sown a large number of time bombs in the area. How, when, and with what must forever remain a mystery. It can only be a fairy tale. The foolishness of his request is however demonstrated by the fact that the Germans were still in Argentan, and would have fought with every power in their command; for this, there were four Panzer divisions to take on two American armoured divisions. It is of course possible that the other two Corps in 3rd Army could have been brought up to give the necessary punch to get to Falaise, but if this had been done, it would have delayed and possibly prevented altogether the far more important role which Montgomery and Bradley had devised for the US 3rd Army. That was to advance towards the River Seine and to threaten Paris from the south-east.

With Falaise lost and the Allied forces closing in on three sides and squeezing the gap from the north, by 17 August the orderly withdrawal became a rout. The encircling formations were in danger of getting themselves not only entangled with the fleeing enemy, but with themselves. On 17 August, the French armoured divisions and the two US infantry divisions from XV Corps of the US 3rd Army who had been halted outside

Argentan were transferred to V Corps of 1st Army, and by the evening of the 19 they had moved sideways and along a line from Argentan to Chambois, where they linked up with the Polish Armoured Division from the Canadian Army. The gap was closed. The bolt was stiffened by British 30 Corps who had got into Argentan, and by British 12 Corps who were moving in from the west. For the next two days the Germans made desperate attempts with three Panzer divisions from the outside of the ring to reopen a gap. They failed, and by 22 August it was all over.

There had been the best part of ten Panzer divisions and eight infantry divisions all within the salient at one time, and as they struggled to escape, being unceasingly hammered from the air and drenched with artillery gunfire, the devastation was horrific. Eight of the more mobile armoured divisions managed to get away, and then only with most of their equipment destroyed or abandoned; two armoured divisions and all the infantry were either wiped out or taken prisoner. It really was churlish to complain, as some did, that the shattered armoured divisions managed to escape. Two whole Armies, which Hitler had ordered to throw the invaders back into the sea were utterly destroyed, and the Allies were poised to recover the whole of France.

On 15 August, American and French forces landed on the French Riviera. The operation, formerly known as 'Anvil', was now code-named 'Dragoon', and although Churchill and the British Chiefs had still endeavoured to have it cancelled and priority given to the campaign in Italy, Eisenhower had personally insisted that it go on to form part of his concept of an Allied advance on a broad front. The US 7th Army to begin with operated independently, and came under Eisenhower's command a month later. After the landings the Franco-American forces were engaged by the German 19th Army, who were so resolute and skilful in defence that the advance was much slower than Eisenhower expected.

While the battle for Falaise and the destruction of the enemy forces in the Falaise/Argentan pocket was proceeding apace, Patton was unleashing his armoured formations in the great sweep eastwards. On 16 August, US XII Corps reached Orleans and XX Corps got to Chartres; a day later, the remaining two divisions of XV Corps entered Dreux and began an advance to the River Seine. On the 19th, the day when the Poles and Americans had joined up at Chambois, XV Corps reached the river at Mantes-Gassicourt, and some elements of 79th Infantry Division made a crossing the next day. The main body of the Corps wheeled left and advanced along the western bank right across the front of the British 30 Corps, whose objective was Vernon on the river. With Montgomery's agreement, US XIX Corps also moved up the left bank to Elbeuf in front of both British 30 Corps and British 12 Corps, with the Canadian Army coming up to the Seine on the left flank. In order to tidy up the advance, 30 Corps were ordered to hold back to avoid getting entangled with the Americans, who began to withdraw to within the boundaries of 12th US Army Group front, and then all the Allied forces were lined up, each Army on an axis facing the river. By 25 August the Allied forces were in position, ready to cross the lower reaches of the Seine. They had reached the planned 'phase line' fifteen days ahead of schedule. Where were they who feared that Montgomery's direction of the war was leading to stagnation?

Away to the right flank of the American front, US XX Corps pushed on from Chartres to Melun, thirty miles to the south-east of Paris, where they were due to cross the river, which they successfully did on 23 August and having done so, began to encircle Paris and got to Chateau Thierry, sixty miles to the north-east. On the 28th Lieutenant-General Collins' VII Corps from US 1st Army followed across the river by the same crossing point, and then wheeled left and struck out due north to get behind Paris. Patton's XII Corps crossed the Seine at Sens, and by the 26th had captured Troyes, way out to the east. In order to try and avoid fighting in Paris itself, Bradley had intended to invest the city and cut it off, but his hand was forced by a rising of the Resistance forces of the FFI, who, when in danger of being ruthlessly put down by the German garrison in fighting all over the capital, managed to get through a cry for help to the Americans. Bradley therefore ordered US V Corps, consisting of 2nd French Armoured Division and 4th Infantry Division, to enter the city. After two days of skirmishing, Paris was liberated on 25th August.

The great distances covered by US 3rd Army in a little more than three weeks put a tremendous strain on the administrative service, for the consumption of petrol (gasoline) was enormous.

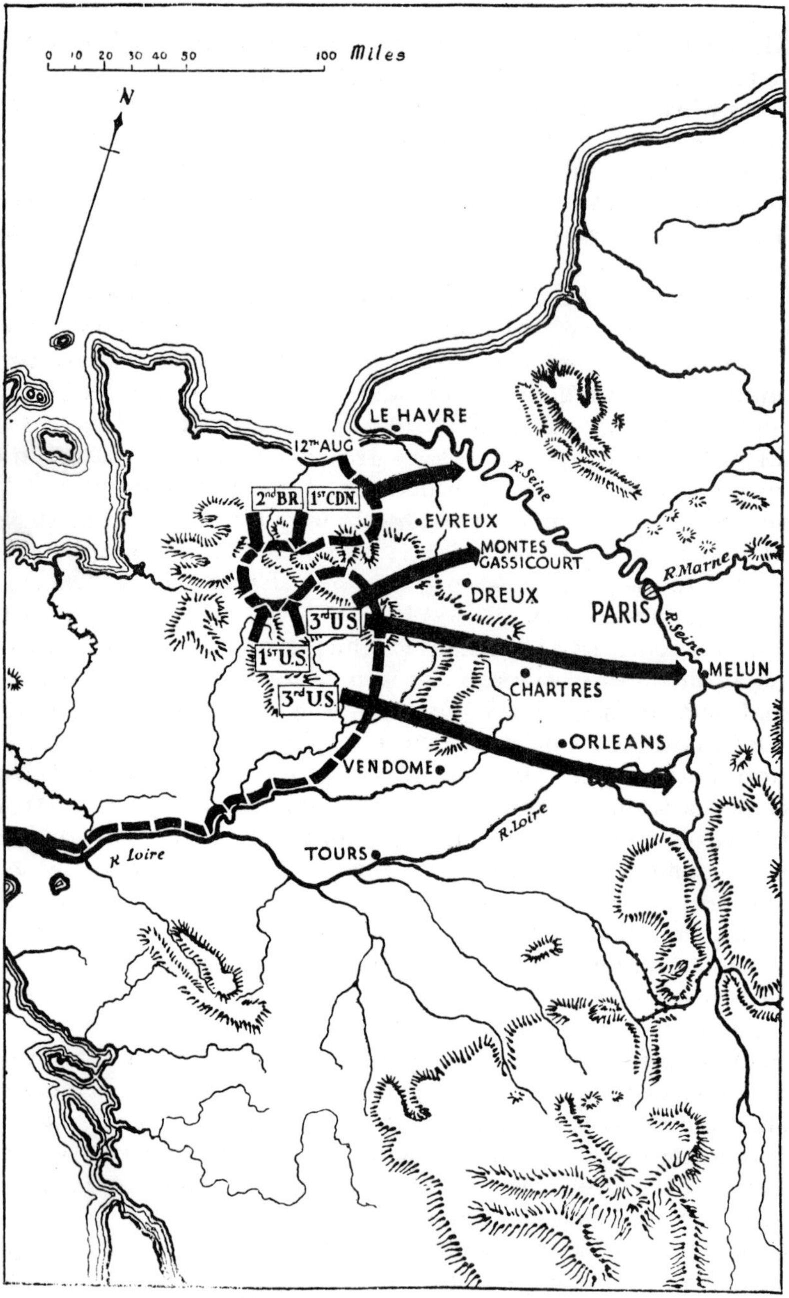

ADVANCE TO THE SEINE

Moreover, the stocks were either at Cherbourg or near the 'Utah' and 'Omaha' beaches, miles and miles away from the areas where the advancing tanks were operating, and the supply lines were not only continually stretched more and more, but to make things worse, had to change axis when Patton swung his army eastwards towards the River Seine. As they neared the river it became obvious that transportation by trucks was quite inadequate, and in order to keep the armoured formations on the move it was arranged for a daily lift by air to 3rd Army forward bases first of 1,000 tons, then increased to 2,000 tons.

That his tanks were never halted was not due to any administrative skill on Patton's part or on the part of 3rd Army supply services. All that he had to do was to urge his men forward; it was up to others to provide the means to keep his formations moving, and in his view it was only his Army that anyone need bother about. Although undoubtedly a dashing and inspiring leader who achieved spectacular successes, Patton tended to adopt a blinkered and narrow-minded attitude; he was incapable of visualizing the campaign as a whole and was totally uninterested in the needs of any army other than his own. As an illustration, there was the celebrated incident when he told one of his Corps' commanders who, for fear of running out of gas, had halted his troops, to 'continue until the tanks stop, and then get out and walk'. He knew perfectly well that General Bradley would then have to transfer gasoline from the US 1st Army to get the 3rd Army on the move again. Nor was he prepared to admit any obligation to others or to acknowledge the help he received elsewhere. In fact, his columns would undoubtedly have ground to a halt if it had not been for some sensible co-operation between two Lieutenant-Colonels, one British and one American; without it, Patton would have been made to look extremely foolish.

One hot sunny afternoon two or three days before Eisenhower arranged the airlift, an officer from US 12 Army Group came charging in his jeep up to the fields where 21 Army Group Rear Headquarters was located, and asked for Lieutenant-Colonel Brown by name, who was, as it happened, the senior officer available. Presumably someone, and it was probably Lieutenant-Colonel Herbert W. Jordan, had said that this officer was sufficiently soft-hearted to listen to a tale of woe. In highly disrespectful terms it was explained that this guy Patton was just blinding on regardless of whether or not there was any gas to keep going, and 12th Army Group and Com Z just had not got the trucks to get it up to him. Now at that time 21 Army Group had one hundred six ton lorries in reserve, waiting to cope with the supply for a rapid advance once the River Seine was crossed, a situation which could not possibly arise for five or six days, and so it occurred to me, the officer concerned, that to help an Ally in distress, these lorries and their drivers might be lent for a day or two. So a promise was given, and off went a much-relieved American officer. When Major-General 'Gerry' Feilden arrived back he was really rather cross, but would not renege on a promise given. Nevertheless it had to be a private arrangement, and was never reported to Major-General Graham, the Chief Administrative Officer, nor officially recorded. Neither of us would have given or honoured the promise if we had realized that our Allies were unable to keep their word.

These one hundred lorries and their drivers were loaned for a maximum of forty-eight hours to provide a double lift of 600 tons a day, enough to boost the existing supply of gasoline for another three or four days. At this time there was already an official loan of three British transport companies, made on 6 August for a period of eight days. Although, strictly speaking, they were due back at the time when this extra assistance was given, no-one would have insisted on holding the Americans to the terms of that loan, but the actual delay in return until 4 September was an unforgiveable breach of agreement. On the third day, when there was no trace of these 100 lorries, a message was received to the effect that the drivers were being turned away when they tried to get back. One of our majors — probably Paul Wright — was sent to investigate, and on his return gave a dramatic description of what had been going on. Whenever a column of British vehicles attempted to get back they were faced by General Patton himself standing at the crossroads shouting 'Git on! Git on!', and brandishing a pearl-handled revolver. Obviously the gallant old soldier could not be bothered to consider whether they were unloaded, and assumed that they were Com Z trucks carrying gasoline for his tanks. Equally gallant, the British Major drove a few miles towards the front and, using his authority as the representative of HQ 21 Army Group, diverted the lorries on to a side road by way of escape from any confrontation with the US Commanding General.

A day and a half behind schedule, the exhausted drivers got back to base and earned a day or two of well-deserved rest. Apart from our feeling of intense annoyance, we were very grieved that there was never a word of thanks from anyone. In Patton's favour, it may well be that no one dared tell him that it was the British who had come to the rescue and pulled his chestnuts out of the fire. That left him free to blame Montgomery as the evil genius behind every attempt by Eisenhower and Bradley to hold him in check while some other Army, including the US 1st Army, was given the opportunity and the petrol to make an advance.

Whilst all this was going on and the British 2nd Army was advancing towards the River Seine, the left flank of the British and Canadian Armies ran into considerable difficulty in pushing the Germans back over the river. There was no way the enemy troops could escape except by moving east up river to where the ferries were carrying the retreating forces to the other side. Locally near to the coast, those that did not get that far stood their ground and fought desperately. Along the actual coastline, the Belgian Brigade operated under the command of British 6th Airborne Division, as did the Royal Netherlands Brigade, a mile or so further inland. On 24 August the Belgians reached Deauville, and by the next day troops of the 6th Airborne and the Dutch Brigade had cleared Pont l'Eveque. Although operating tactically for the time being under the command of 6th Airborne Division, these Allied Independent Brigades were the direct responsibility of 21 Army Group, and I was sent over on a jeep driven by one of our majors to find out how they were getting on, and to see if they wanted any help.

All was plain sailing until we got into Deauville and found the Brigade Headquarters in one of the large hotels on the sea front. Suddenly, all hell was let loose. Artillery fire, probably from the coastal gun battery at Honfleur, and mortar fire, which could only have come from an overlooked pocket of resistance, descended upon us in considerable volume. Expecting every moment to be our last, we huddled down with the Brigade Commander and his staff behind the shelter of an outside wall, whilst the room was filled with dust and smoke, and bits of metal and debris flew all around. Having escaped death and injury from innumerable bombs in numerous places, this was an experience I could well have done without, and neither of us was inclined to stay any longer than necessary, so taking our leave during a slight lull, we ran for our jeep and set off for safety — as we thought. Largely due to poor navigation, but again no doubt because of a determined counter-attack by the enemy, our journey was not as safe as it should have been. Driving along a bumpy little track and then on to open ground, the unmistakable sharp crack of small arms fire assailed our ears, and there to our right were without any doubt British troops dodging and weaving and firing from the hip as they moved forward. In a very nasty moment, as bullets pinged off the metal of our jeep, we realized that we were on a course right between the advancing British and the defending enemy, and into a stream of crossfire! Never was a motor vehicle so quickly reversed and turned away. The two occupants, undeservedly unscathed but severely shaken, made the rest of the journey without incident.

By way of postscript to this cautionary tale, it is perhaps worthy of note that the next time an unexpected explosion in a most unlikely place brought down a shower of debris but did no other harm was thirty years later, when an IRA bomb was exploded outside the Central Criminal Court at the Old Bailey, where as a High Court Judge I was presiding over a trial for murder.

13

THE CAMPAIGN — FROM THE SEINE TO VICTORY

General Eisenhower took over the operational direction of all the Allied Armies on 1 September, 1944, but he had stamped his authority on the future strategy at a meeting on 23 August with Montgomery and Bradley. Patton recorded that in conversation with Bradley before the meeting, Bradley told him that he feared that Montgomery would persuade the Supreme Commander to send all or part of US Armies up northwards, and subsequent to the meeting Patton observed that 'Monty had won again'. This was nonsense. In fact, Eisenhower had decided even before D-Day that after crossing the Seine he would push forward on a broad front, with priority on the left in order to neutralize the bases for the V weapons, to open up Antwerp and the Channel ports, and to threaten the Ruhr. He also intended to send the US 3rd Army eastwards, aiming for the Saar and linking up with the Franco-American forces coming up from the south. This was the 'broad front' policy which dominated Eisenhower's thinking throughout the whole campaign.

Before Montgomery handed over the control of the American forces, the decision about how and where the Seine should be crossed was one of agreement between the three men in accordance with Eisenhower's strategic design, which was not to the liking of either Montgomery or Patton. Each wanted a concentrated powerful thrust, the one northwards in the direction of the Ruhr, and the other eastwards in the direction of the Saar; and of course each desired to be in command of sufficient forces for the purpose, even if it meant that others had to be deprived of logistic support and remain on the defensive. Patton was at a disadvantage in that he was not a member of the triumvirate and had to leave his case to be argued by Bradley, who, if Patton's version of events is correct, must have presented a totally distorted view of the discussions which took place then and on subsequent occasions, by repeatedly giving the impression that Eisenhower always gave way to Montgomery which only served to fuel Patton's pathological dislike of Montgomery and all his works, and his contemptuous dismissal of British achievement. Most regrettably, it has to be said that in this context Bradley fell far short of his own high standards of honesty and fairmindedness, for he must have known that it was Eisenhower's 'broad front' policy which put paid to both subordinate commanders' belief in a single concentrated thrust. Moreover, Bradley had an equal obligation to US 1st Army which meant it may have disappointed Patton who was incurable. He described 29th August as one of the critical days of the war because he was prevented, through the diversion to US 1st Army of 140,000 gallons of gas which he wanted, from carrying out his wishes to drive towards Verdun. Again, he blamed Montgomery for a change of plan; again, he got it all wrong. There never was a change of plan, and Montgomery was in no way responsible for the decision to give priority to 1st Army.

The agreed plan for the crossing of the River Seine was that, leaving Patton's 3rd Army to exploit towards Verdun and Nancy, 1st Army was to cross at Mantes Gassicourt and Melun and strike northwards. British 21 Army Group would cross at points below Paris, and then aim to clear the Pas de Calais and to capture Antwerp. After these tasks had been performed, Montgomery's main objective was, in his own words, to 'bounce' a crossing of the Rhine, which was a formidable barrier in the way of an entry into the Ruhr. Two or three days were spent in forcing crossings to get the various formations established in bridgeheads ready to move forward. The great advance began on 29th August when US 1st Army moved away from the Seine, and in a remarkable drive arrived at the Belgian frontier on 2nd September. Lieutenant-General Collins' VII Corps swung eastwards and reached the German frontier defences nine days later. There they were halted. On the Allied left flank, the Canadian 1st Army left their river base on 30th

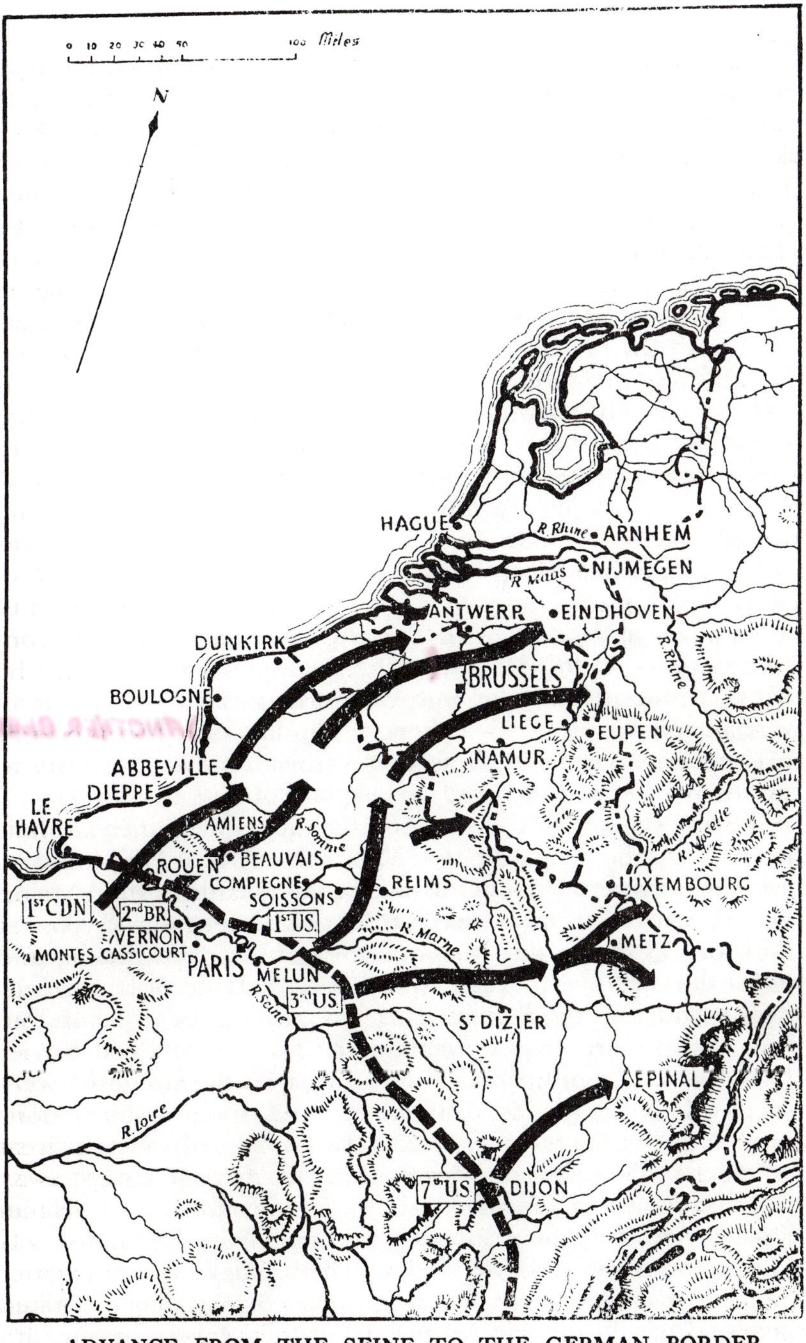

ADVANCE FROM THE SEINE TO THE GERMAN BORDER

August and, by-passing Le Havre, had within three days captured first Rouen and then Dieppe — an objective thoughtfully allotted to them by the British Commander-in-Chief as sweet revenge for their disastrous experience two years earlier. They swept on, and in less than two weeks had cleared the whole of the Pas de Calais and advanced through Belgium into Holland. On the right of the Canadians, 12 Corps, with 7th Armoured Division and 4th Armoured Brigade in the van and 53rd Infantry Division following up, were directed towards Ghent, which lay in Belgium to the south-west of Antwerp. These forces met with considerable resistance, having to cope with three newly-arrived enemy divisions, and entry into Ghent was a day behind the timetable achieved on the British right flank. Here the most spectacular performance of all was credited to 30 Corps, who having established themselves in the bridgehead over the Seine on 29th August, next day began an advance spearheaded by the 11th Armoured Division and the Guards Armoured Division. They crossed into Belgium on 2nd September, and on the 3rd the Guards Armoured liberated Brussels and on the 4th the 11th Armoured took the port of Antwerp and then went on into Holland, and a week afterwards were halted a mile or two short of Eindhoven.

The performance of these two British armoured divisions surpassed even the much-vaunted exploits of Patton's 3rd Army. In the first six days of the advance, the tanks covered 250 miles. So much for the allegation that Montgomery could never move fast! Patton boasted that in the fourteen days ended 14th August, his 3rd Army had 'advanced farther and faster than any army in history'. On that day he may have been correct, if one adds up all the distances covered in careering about Brittany, but these manoeuvres did nothing to further a direct attack in the direction of Germany. It was his drive to the east which was of comparable significance. If one measures the circumference of the wheel, the longest distance covered would be about 200 miles and the time taken was ten days, so the daily average was far less than that which the despised British managed to achieve. Whereas Montgomery paid tribute to the achievements of the US 3rd Army in their advance into and from Brittany and, rightly, to the support provided by the administrative machine, the performance of the British forces never earned even a passing mention from the disgruntled and self-centred American general.

It was about this time that the names of two very young Armoured Brigade Commanders, both under thirty, were ringing around HQ 21 Army Group. One ended his career as Field Marshal the Lord Carver, Chief of Defence Staff.

The speedy advance of the two Armies in 21 Army Group required huge fleets of vehicles to keep them supported in petrol (gasoline) in particular, and also ammunition and other supplies. The tremendous devastation of the railway system by the Allied air forces now proved a severe handicap, and movement by road supplemented by a degree of air lift was the only method by which administrative support could be maintained. In 21 Army Group, 8 Corps was ordered to remain behind and, except for essential vehicles, all its transport was used to help to maintain the momentum of the advance.

The haul of supplies from the Rear Maintenance Area near the beaches in Normandy up to the formations in Belgium and Holland was along a supply line which extended for 400 miles. In anticipation of some sort of breakthrough, it had been decided at the beginning of August that the shipping of some supplies should be curtailed, and several transport companies were brought forward from reserve in England. Indeed it was from this pool that the loan of one hundred six ton lorries had been made, which saved US 3rd Army from grinding to an ignominious halt. Unhappily, a large batch of the smaller three ton lorries had engine faults and could not be used. This time, the Americans came to the help of the British. On 12 September, Lieutenant-General Bedell Smith promised Montgomery a lift of 500 tons a day by US ten ton trucks using an extension of what was known as the 'Red Ball Route', a one-way system on selected highways from which all other traffic was excluded, and also a daily air lift of some 400 to 500 tons of supplies. Most of this was flown into Brussels Evere airport.

This friendly assistance required friendly co-operation and it fell to me to do all that was possible in this regard. This portion of the 'Red Ball Express' was detailed to start on 16 September. Autumn had set in; the nights were cold, and the early mornings raw and foggy. At about five am the flap of my tent was opened, and the night duty sergeant announced a Colonel someone or other. Groping for a torch to give some light in the pitch darkness and putting on a great coat to keep out the cold, I was confronted by an enormously tall and rangy Lieutenant-Colonel of the US

Army. 'Say, Colonel, I got my boys all loaded up with gas and raring to go, but where the hell no one knows' was his greeting in an unmistakable Texas drawl. That was something I could help about, but it would have been a serious lapse not in accordance with the high standards of hospitality customary in the Deep South to send him on his way unfortified. There was no Bourbon, nor Scotch to offer, but the rum ration for the whole headquarters was in a stone jar entrusted to my keeping, of which the unauthorized issue of even a mere thimbleful was a Court Martial offence. Nevertheless this was an exceptional occasion when a generous helping hand required a reciprocal gesture of allied friendship, and into an enamel mug went the equivalent of ten men's rations of this immensely powerful and concentrated brew. Down it went in a couple of gulps, to be followed by a refill of equivalent quantity and a heartfelt 'Say, Colonel, that was fine, mighty fine', by way of genuine appreciation. Then into the darkness we plunged and made our way to where his jeep was parked at the head of a column, presumably of fifty ten ton trucks, but it was too dark to see. On getting into his vehicle, where his driver was patiently waiting, he stood up to his full height and raised his arm upwards and brought it down in front of him, with the old US Cavalry command of 'Forrrward!' He should have been in blue, wearing a wide hat and white doeskin gauntlets and mounted on a horse, but it was magnificent just the same. The trucks went roaring after him, but as they went past in the gloom, all that could be seen in each cab, for the drivers were coloured men, was a pair of white eyeballs and a row of white teeth.

Having sped them on their way, it then became possible to concentrate on the next task, which was to lead a small group of officers to Amiens where we were to set up a transport control centre (TRANCO). As the Lines of Communication stretched for 400 miles from the Rear Maintenance Area in the vicinity of Bayeux by the Normandy beaches right into Holland, and as HQ 2nd Army was now forward of Brussels, it was quite impossible for that headquarters to execute any control over supply by road. In those days the maximum distance that two-way communication by wireless (radio) could be carried on was about 200 miles, and the only telephone wires were those laid by the Signals Corps, and these did not function from one end of the supply line to the other, so Amiens were chosen because it was roughly halfway along the Lines of Communication. It was also a big rail centre, and a skeleton railway service had already begun to operate north and south of the River Seine, although this was severed by the absence of any railway bridge across the river.

TRANCO had to co-ordinate all means of transport from the Rear Maintenance Area to the two Army Roadheads, one south-west of Brussels for 2nd Army and one at Bethune in Flanders for the Canadian Army. All transport vehicles, other than those required for onward transmission from the Army Roadheads, were withdrawn and put under 21 Army Group, and operated in accordance with the instructions issued by the small staff at TRANCO. HQ 2nd Army and HQ 1st Canadian Army submitted estimates of daily maintenance requirements for five-day periods five days in advance, and we then issued an outline rail and road programme and made up lists in order of priority of what had to be supplied, varying these every five days to fit any changes in priorities. It worked, and we had no complaints about any shortfall up to Army Roadheads, although there were occasional shortages between 2nd Army and forward troops, something over which we had no control. Whereas Major Paul Wright and a couple of Staff Captains aided me in the exercise of the operational control, Colonel Val Duncan and Lieutenant-Colonel Donald Ross, as the Q (Movements) specialists concentrated on trying to get the railway system working. This was a mammoth task, because not only was there the devastation caused by repeated Allied Air Force bombing, but the engine drivers, signalmen and others were not at all well-disposed to the British, and were doggedly unco-operative. This was understandable, as they had been kept employed and left alone in four years of German occupation, and it was the Allies who had destroyed the locomotives, the marshalling yards and repair facilities, and put them out of work. Their attitude was consistent with the general pattern of events. Despite the descriptions of the joy with which the French were supposed to have welcomed the invasion of Normandy by the Allies, in truth they were for the most part quite sullen, and the farmers distinctly hostile. Here again they had enjoyed prosperity under German rule, and it was the Allies who had shelled and bombed their homes into ruins, and who had killed their cattle and destroyed their crops. It was not until the British entered Brussels and other

Belgian towns that a really genuine welcome and heartfelt gratitude became evident. In fact the damage to the railway system throughout northern France was such that before any trains could operate satisfactorily, some 900 locomotives were shipped across from England as well as a vast quantity of rolling stock. How fortunate it was that the same gauge of railway line was used in Europe as in Britain.

In the meantime, the successful advance into Belgium and Holland by the British and Canadians had prompted Montgomery to bombard Eisenhower with requests that he should be allowed to make a powerful thrust towards and across the lower reaches of the River Rhine, which would need the support of not only two or three divisions of the remainder of 1st Army and a portion from 3rd US Army as well. At Q Branch 21 Army Group, we had no doubt that the logistic difficulties could be overcome if there was a wholesale switch of US transport and allocation of gasoline. Some of us privately, with our experience of General Patton's attitude towards the British, thought that this could never come about, and of course we were right to be pessimistic, as subsequent events demonstrated.

General Eisenhower flew up from his headquarters at Granville in the Cotentin peninsula, and a meeting took place on 10 September in the aircraft at Brussels Evere airport. This was the occasion when Montgomery, wrongly believing that Humfrey Gale, Eisenhower's Chief Administrative Officer, was blocking the 21 Army Group proposals, impudently insisted on Graham being present, to the exclusion of Humfrey Gale. This much was agreed, but Eisenhower had politely but firmly to remind Montgomery that he was the boss when the British general ranted on about the failure of the Supreme Commander and his staff to give due consideration to his requests. Eisenhower was not prepared to agree to Montgomery's plan, but did compromise a little on his 'broad front' policy, to the extent of issuing a directive on 15 September that operations on the left would take priority in all forms of logistical support, that US 1st Army should use all possible resources to seize bridgeheads near Cologne and assist the British in the capture of the Ruhr, that after the US 3rd Army was established across the River Moselle they would receive supplies sufficient for security, reconnaissance and the opening of ports. The opening of ports was interpreted by Bradley and Patton as permission to capture Brest, which, because the port was useless and was never used, was a time-wasting and utterly pointless exercise which tied down some 80,000 troops and a number of truck companies, which could much more usefully have been employed in the drive against the German frontier. Bradley was either incapable of or unwilling to curb Patton, who totally disregarded the spirit of Eisenhower's orders by interpreting reconnaissance into attack, and went charging on until they came up with a bump against strong, well-organized enemy resistance. Once faced with firm opposition, his famous 3rd Army was no better than any other. Although Patton attempted to shrug it off as a mere nuisance, the fact remains that it was five weeks before Metz was captured in his attempts to breach the Siegfried Line, and the occasional success like the brilliant victory of the US 4th Armored Division over two Panzer brigades at Luneville has to be seen as a repulse of an enemy counter-attack, rather than a penetration of the enemy defensive system.

The serious effect of Patton's disregard of orders was that he continued to receive the same amount of gasoline as Hodges' 1st Army, although Eisenhower had directed that 1st Army was to have priority. Nor was Patton averse to underhand conduct in his blinkered desire to push on. He never disclosed that his troops had captured a stock of 110,000 gallons of gasoline, which a fair-minded Allied commander would have recognized ought to be reckoned as part of an Allied shareout, and he privately, though, of course, not officially, approved of some of his Ordnance officers dressing up and masquerading as 1st US Army officers in order to steal from their stocks gasoline that belonged to Hodges' forces. Worse, Patton's attempts on the Siegfried Line were dragging the impetus of the Allied advance southwards, to the detriment of the central thrust and thereby in turn to the detriment of the northern thrust. The weakness of the 'broad front' policy was exposed; it led to a failure to make a decisive breakthrough anywhere, and it gave the enemy a breathing space in which to recover and time to reorganize and consolidate his defences. In this the Germans were well-served by the very able and successful Field Marshal Model, the new Commander-in-Chief of Army Group B, and among the Army Commanders, General Student, the creator of the German Airborne forces, and General Manteuffel, one of the best Panzer army commanders.

Montgomery did at least win approval for the use of part of the newly-created First Allied Airborne Army in an operation to capture bridgeheads over the River Waal and Lower Rhine (Neder Rijn) at Nijmegen and Arnhem. This Army was commanded by the American Lieutenant-General Lewis H. Brererton, and consisted of 82nd, 101st and 17th US Airborne Divisions, the 1st and 6th British Airborne Divisions, the US IX Troop Carrier Command, and 38 and 46 Groups of the RAF. Montgomery's plan for the operation, code-named 'Market Garden' and timed to begin on 17 September, was for a combined offensive from the air ('Market') and on land ('Garden'). It was bold and imaginative, and even Bradley, whose personal dislike of Montgomery and critical opinion of his strategy in the later stages of the Normandy campaign tended to sour his judgement, was compelled to admit that he was astonished that Montgomery should be capable of devising an operation which he described as one of the most imaginative of the war. The airborne attack also took Field Marshal Model and General Student by surprise, as their assessment of Montgomery was that he was a very cautious general who would never indulge in a highly risky enterprise. Montgomery himself described the operation as 'laying a carpet of airborne troops' across the five main water obstacles — three rivers, Maas, Waal and Neder Rijn, and two canals — and for troops of 30 Corps to use the 'carpet' and advance northwards to Arnhem, there to form a bridgehead from which further advance could be made to the Zuider Zee. He believed that if the operation succeeded the way would be open to the Ruhr. It is interesting to note that after the war Eisenhower tended to belittle all of Montgomery's ideas of making a thrust at this time towards the north-west of Germany, arguing that they would not have succeeded, but all of the top German commanders were unanimous in their opinion that they would have been quite unable to have withstood a thrust mounted with as few as fifteen divisions. This Eisenhower could easily have provided, if he had not been fixed in his desire for a broad front. As it was, Operation 'Market Garden' was launched without any logistic support from the Americans. It was entirely British in the administrative context.

The task of capturing Arnhem and its two bridges was entrusted to British 1st Airborne Division. The 82nd US

Airborne Division was to take the crossing of the Maas at Grave and the important bridge over the Waal at Nijmegen, while the 101st was directed to the area north of Eindhoven. There were insufficient aircraft for the full force to be brought in at once, but the main parties were successfully landed with few casualties in fine weather on the morning on 17 September. The only tactical error in the actual operation was the decision to land the British 1st Airborne Division eight miles to the west of Arnhem on the northern side of the river, because it was believed that the area close to Arnhem was unsuitable and this was, as it turned out, a mistake of very serious import. The eight miles gave the Germans the time to take steps to intervene before the northern end of the bridge could be reached in strength, and also gave them the space into which a blocking force could be moved. By sheer misfortune, not only was the 9th SS Panzer Division close at hand, but both Model and Student happened to be in the vicinity and, after the initial surprise, had time enough to take charge and direct the German forces. The 2nd Parachute Battalion in due course reached the northern end of the bridge and seized it, but the Germans had brought up SS troops to block the southern end, thereby to cut off any attempt to create a bridgehead. Worse still, the remainder of the Division was isolated in its landing area by a move of enemy tanks and troops into the gap between that area and the town. The story of how the 2nd Parachute Battalion gallantly held the northern end of the bridge for eight days in spite of worsening and fearful casualties, and how the remainder of the Division fought on within a small perimeter round the Dropping Zone, until finally the remnants still alive were evacuated at dead of night on 25 September by boats ferrying them across the river, is one of immense courage and gallant failure.

The primary objective of Operation 'Market Garden', the creation of a bridgehead and a firm base north of Arnhem was never realized. This failure might have been avoided if the weather, so fine to begin with, had not turned and remained bad, and prevented the dispatch of planned follow-up and other supporting troops, and disrupted the whole programme. After the operation came to an end, Montgomery claimed that, because the two American Airborne Divisions were successful in their tasks, and British 30 Corps occupied the territory between the Maas and the Waal, and eight of the nine bridges were secured, it had been ninety per cent successful. This cannot be right when the main objective was not attained, but he was correct in saying that it was the weather which led to the failure at Arnhem, and in this he was supported by no less a person than General Student, who was there and who knew more about airborne operations than anyone else on either side.

The 101st US Airborne Division captured Eindhoven on the first day; the next day the Guards Armoured Division linked up with them and then pushed on to Grave, which had been taken by 82nd US Division who, according to plan, then occupied the ground between Grave and Nijmegen. The Guards, when they came up, tried to break through the defences south of the large and important bridge over the Waal at Nijmegen, but the bridge was only taken when a Regiment of the 82nd crossed by boat upstream and captured the northern end. British forces advanced up to the Lower Rhine and shelled the enemy investing the beleaguered remnants of British 1st Airborne Division, but were unable to break the enemy ring, and so the Arnhem offensive came to an end. The performance of the 2nd Parachute Battalion at Arnhem bridge earned from Major-General Gavin, Commanding General of US 82nd Airborne Division, the accolade of having conducted the outstanding parachute battalion action of the war. In the best traditions of Allied comradeship on the field of battle, Gavin, in turn was met by General Dempsey, the Commander of British 2nd Army, with the words that he was proud to meet 'the commander of the greatest division in the world today'. Once again the Alliance of Britain and America was seen at its best when the soldiers of the two nations fought side by side: what a contrast with the bickering and backbiting which went on between the 'top brass'.

On 22 September, while the battle for Arnhem was reaching its climax, there was a large conference of senior officers of the Allied nations at Versailles. In addition to the Supreme Commander and his Deputy, all the Commanders-in-Chief of all the Forces, with the sole exception of Field Marshal Montgomery, and all the chief staff officers took part. HQ 21 Army Group was represented by Major-General de Guingand, Chief of Staff, and Major-General Graham, Chief Administrative Officer. Montgomery's absence was strongly resented, and many regarded it as an insult to Eisenhower and to the other Commanders-in-Chief, who were all there. It was extremely unfortunate that he decided not to attend, and psychologically it was a bad mistake, for it gave strength to his critics and did no good to the Anglo-American Alliance. Those who were closest to him at that time, and this included the young Lieutenant-Colonels who were his military assistants, detected a mood almost of depression. He was convinced that Eisenhower was wrong; his own Chief of Staff was siding against him; he had been denied additional resources which he knew the Americans could provide if the 'broad front' was curtailed; he felt that the weather was cheating him of ultimate success at Arnhem, which, if it had been achieved, would have been a complete justification of his design, and would have forced Eisenhower to recognize that it was his grave strategic error which had prejudiced an early victory.

Whatever the other Allied Commanders and their staff officers may have thought, those who knew Montgomery well enough would have laughed at the suggestion that he was deliberately intending to snub the Supreme Commander, or that he realized that his absence would be regarded as discourteous. Although he had tried desperately over and over again to reverse Eisenhower's decision in late August that he was not to be given the extra resources to enable him to make a powerful thrust over the Rhine and towards the Ruhr, yet once the decision had been made he had loyally tried to do the best he could to carry out the directives of the Supreme Commander. True, he had behaved outrageously to begin with when he met Eisenhower in his aircraft at Brussels on 10 September, but was quick to apologize when his boss had to pull him up. The one person who was not offended by his absence was Eisenhower himself. The personal relationship between the two was friendly, and Eisenhower understood Montgomery better than any other American did. The two of them used to exchange letters on strategic plans during all this dispute, and Montgomery's strong feelings were appreciated even though they had to be overruled.

Montgomery entrusted his Chief of Staff with the task of putting his case with regard to future strategy and the next stages of the Allied Campaign. In this he was wise, for de Guingand was listened to with respect, whereas Montgomery made it obvious that he regarded conferences as a waste of time, and if he had attended he would very probably have offended a lot of equally senior officers by his attitude. At the conclusion of the conference, de Guingand sent a message to his Commander-in-Chief that his plan had been entirely accepted. The proposal was that British 2nd Army should, in Montgomery's words, 'develop a strong left hook against the Ruhr', which would be done by advancing along the west bank of the Rhine river towards the Ruhr, and that simultaneously US 1st Army should develop a right hook so that in due course the Northern Group of Armies, as they were now called, could launch a massive offensive to cross the Rhine. It followed that 1st Army should transfer its impetus northwards and co-ordinate operations with British 2nd Army, and that priority in supply should be theirs at the expense of Patton and US 3rd Army. The minutes of the conference stated that 'the envelopment of the Ruhr from the north by 21st Army Group supported by 1st Army, is the main effort of the present phase of operations.' The minutes went on to record that two US divisions were to support British 2nd Army, and the bulk of US 1st Army was to attack the Ruhr from the south. The rest of 12th Army Group, that is US 3rd Army and US 9th Army, were to take no more aggressive action. This general statement was in full accord with Montgomery's plan of a left hook and a right hook, with the Ruhr as the objective.

Neither Montgomery nor de Guingand seem to have given sufficient attention to the most important proviso which Eisenhower put in as a first priority even before any offensive action, and that was the opening up of the port of Antwerp. In this respect, Eisenhower and his senior staff at SHAEF were quite right to stress that for both the British and the American forces it was an 'indispensable prerequisite for the final drive deep into Germany'. Montgomery cannot have realized that this was going to be the major problem that it turned out to be. The administrative staff at HQ 21 Army Group were undoubtedly misled, for no-one queried our basic assumption in all our logistic planning that the port could be reopened within a week or two of its capture, unharmed and undamaged, on 4th September. That it was not opened until twelve precious weeks had elapsed was not the fault of the engineers or the labourers. There was a serious failure of appreciation to which the General Staffs, both Operations and Intelligence at the headquarters of 21 Army Group, British 2nd Army and Canadian 1st Army all contributed.

From Antwerp to the sea there was a channel seventy miles long formed by the estuary of the River Scheldt. The Germans had established coastal barriers at the mouth of the estuary on the mainland to the south and on the island of Walcheren to the north, and these prevented the entry of any ships, large or small. Even if they were not stopped by gunfire, they would have had the task of trying to navigate through hundreds of mines laid throughout the whole length of the channel. The dock area itself was subject to incessant artillery attack from positions to the north of the town, and to sporadic bombing by VI pilotless aircraft and V2 long-range rockets. Once it was appreciated that the strength of the enemy defences and resources necessitated a large-scale well-planned assault to clear all the area, the preparations took a whole month before the Canadian Army was ready to start on the task. It took six weeks of ferocious fighting before the defences were all finally overcome, and even then it was only with the help of a very gallant seaborne attack by Royal Marine Commandos supported by 52 (Lowland) Division.

Once the minesweepers were able to come in on 4th November, it took one hundred of these vessels three weeks making sixteen sweeps of the whole length of the channel before it was safe for merchant shipping to use the port. The first ships came in on 26th November. In addition to the use of a large number of installations for the reception of petrol (gasoline) in bulk, the port quickly developed into an intake of 40,000 tons a day, of which a good deal more than a half was allotted to US forces. This generous sharing of the capacity of a major port, in the capture of which there had been no American participation, was a good example of the way the British element of the Allied forces co-operated fully in a joint alliance, and was in marked contrast to the attitude we had come to expect from General Patton and also, it was regrettable to record, from General Omar Bradley as well. The arrangements for sharing the port and the setting-up of a dual control was the last occasion when the administrative staffs of HQ 21 Army Group, HQ 12 US Army Group and SHAEF worked together. Thereafter in this context, except for a short interlude during the battle in the Ardennes, we all went our several different ways under the general direction of the Supreme Commander.

After the Versailles conference, with the British 2nd Army

consolidating its position and occupying south-west Holland up to the River Maas, and with the Canadian Army preparing for the clearance of the Scheldt estuary, Montgomery was working on the plans for his 'left hook'. He now had the recently created US 9th Army on his right flank, and the attacks by British 2nd Army and the US 9th Army were to be co-ordinated. If all went well, the 9th Army was in due course to come under command of 21 Army Group and swell the strength of the Northern Group of Armies.

In the centre and to the south the other American forces were heavily engaged with German resistance, which was always dogged and courageous, and which varied in strength at different points in the long frontier. The 1st US Army breached the Siegfried Line at the beginning of October, but the garrison at Aachen resisted so strongly that it was three weeks before the town was fully captured. The *coup de grace* was delivered by Lieutenant-General Lawton Collins's VII Corps, who yet again demonstrated that they were probably the pick of all the American forces, notwithstanding Lieutenant-General Patton's constant refrain that his troops had no equals. On the 3rd Army front, Nancy had been captured, but the attack on Metz had been repulsed and there then followed a very slow advance towards the Saar. Further to the south there was now an additional Army Group, the 6th, commanded by General Devers, consisting of US 7th Army and French 1st Army, who had come up from the landings on the Riviera coast, and these two Armies lined up alongside Patton's forces. Eisenhower's 'broad front' along the German frontier was now complete, from Holland in the north down to the Vosges mountains in the south.

The big offensive began on 15 November. In view of the delay in clearing the Scheldt, the waterlogged condition of the ground and the unexpected strength of enemy resistance, Montgomery's plans had to be altered, and once 2nd Army had cleared the whole of the Nijmegen area and the west bank of the River Maas and were in position for an advance across the Rhine, they were held back from proceeding any further. The main thrust of Eisenhower's plan was to be carried out by 1st and 9th US Armies advancing from Aachen in the direction of Cologne. The attack was preceded by a barrage of artillery fire and a huge bombing raid by US and British aircraft; a total of seventeen

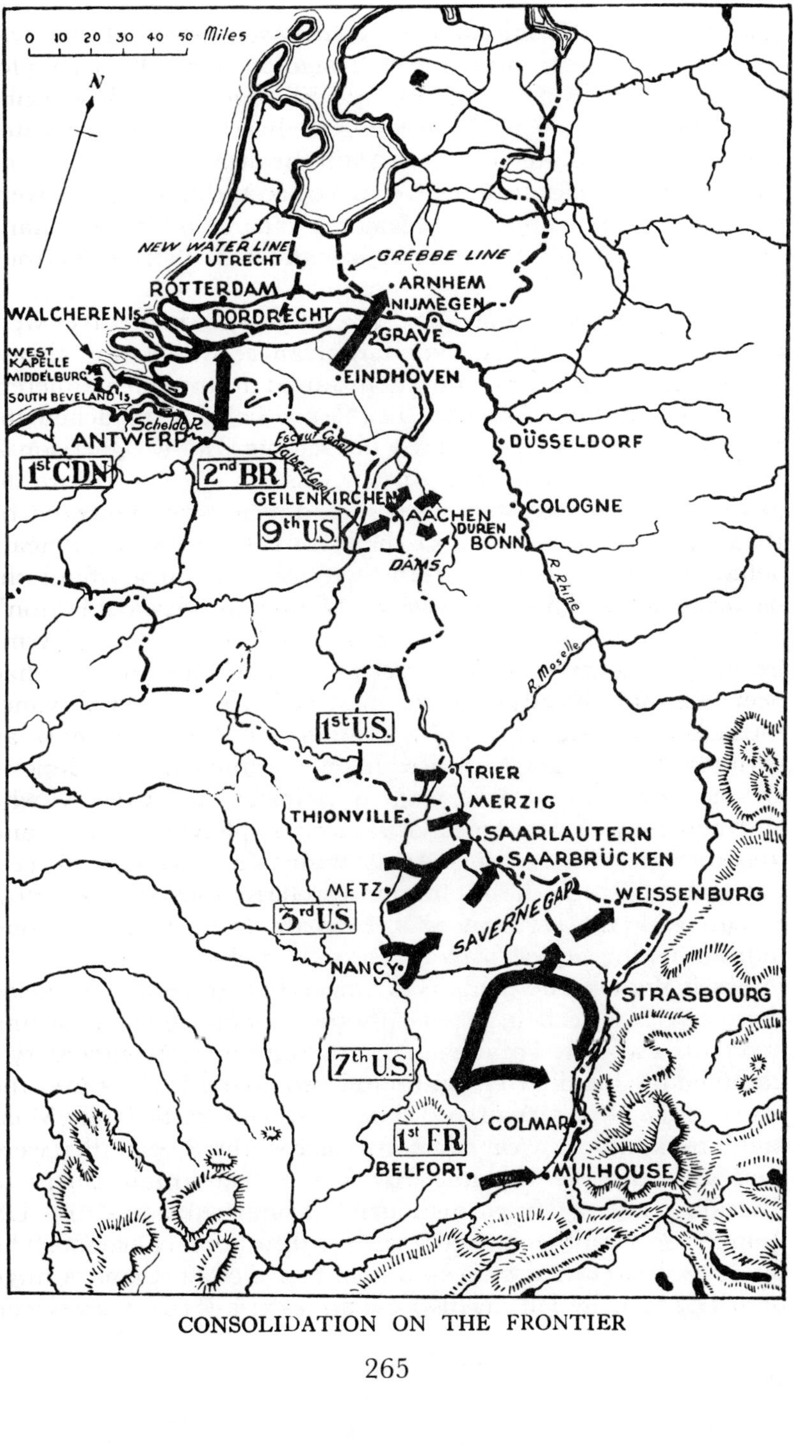

CONSOLIDATION ON THE FRONTIER

divisions from the 1st and 9th Armies were employed. It was the heaviest and most concentrated attack of the whole campaign, and the fighting was bitter and prolonged. Ultimately the 9th Army reached the River Roer, but the 1st Army was held up after a small advance. Again, they too were frustrated by the spirited defence of the Germans and the appalling weather — the worst November so it was said, for many, many years. Moreover, Bradley was rightly anxious that if the US forces crossed the Roer, the Germans might breach the Schmidt Dam and flood the Roer valley, and so engulf the American troops. He decided therefore that the dam must be captured first, and the attack was at its height when the Germans launched their offensive in the Ardennes on 16th December. This was directed at the weakest spot in Bradley's line-up, and wrecked the whole of his plan.

Things might not have been so bad if both Eisenhower and Bradley had been firmer in their control of Patton. After a conference at Brussels on 18th October between the Supreme Commander and Montgomery and Bradley to discuss the plans for the November offensive, giving priority to the thrust by US 1st and 9th Armies, a directive was issued that 3rd US Army was to resume its advance 'when logistics permit'. This was a totally inadequate curb on Patton, who had by various means, many of them devious, acquired to the detriment of US 1st Army as much ammunition as he wanted, so he was able to argue that, as far as he was concerned, logistics did permit. The proviso that the operations of 3rd Army were to be 'subsidiary' and timed to assist the main effort in the north was so vague that Patton could always argue that, by blasting away at the enemy in front of him, he was playing a subsidiary role which was timed to assist the 1st and 9th US Armies. There can be no doubt that Bradley, excellent general though he was, deferred far too much to Patton's flamboyancy and excessive optimism. He accepted the brash assertion that he could easily break through the German West Wall and reach the Saar in three days. In fact it took him six weeks. There was no excuse other than bad weather available to him. His 3rd Army consisted of ten divisions, four of them armoured, numbering in all over a quarter of a million troops; against him were ranged only a quarter of the strength in men and one-eighth of the strength in armour; he had at his disposal an almost unlimited amount of artillery support and devastating bombing from the air. Like all the Americans, except Lawton Collins of US VII Corps, he frittered away his overwhelming resources in a 'broad front' attack, enabling the Germans to fight, to withdraw, to fight again and then stand on their strongest defence line. Lawton Collins would have done what Montgomery or any intelligent general would have done, and that was to punch a hole on a narrow front with a concentration of all resources available. When 3rd Army ground to a halt before the main defences of the Saar, the planned resumption of Patton's offensive on 19th December had to be abandoned in order to meet the threat of the German advance far away beyond his left flank.

The most spectacular success in the Allied November offensive was achieved by the 1st French Army. Within a week they had arrived at the upper reaches of the River Rhine after breaking through at Belfort. Before the end of the month, in conjunction with 7th US Army, they had captured Strasbourg. Further north, the 7th Army had also reached the Rhine. Unfortunately for the Franco-American forces, they had bypassed to right and left a considerable enemy concentration in the area between Mulhouse and Colmar, and this 'Colmar Pocket' was a serious hindrance to 6th Army Group operations, and required a great effort before it was finally neutralized. The French Army was exhausted and lacked reinforcements, so that after a most promising start the original breakthrough could not be exploited.

Allied Intelligence was aware of considerable movement of German formations in early December, and Eisenhower and Bradley expected some sort of enemy action in the Ardennes forest area where the 12th Army Group was stretched out in a thinly-held line. Nevertheless, the size and weight of the attack took everybody by surprise. It was learnt after the war was over that Hitler personally devised the plan, which was basically a repeat of the Blitzkrieg of April and May 1940. The grandiose objective was to cross the Meuse, to bypass Liege, which was the US administrative base and stiff with troops, and to strike out for Antwerp through Namur and Dinant, in order to threaten Brussels. If it had succeeded in its entirety it would have been a major disaster for the Allies, totally disrupted the campaign and probably have prevented any crossings of the Rhine into the Ruhr, thereby prolonging the war indefinitely. Field Marshals von Runstedt and Model were most apprehensive that the whole of the rebuilt forces in the West were to be committed in a gamble, which if it did not come off would leave them with no reserves to meet an expected major offensive on the part of the Allies as soon as the severity of the winter weather began to abate. Montgomery expressed the opinion that a modified plan of limited objective might well have succeeded, but that there never was any hope of a breakthrough as far as Antwerp. The British would have been able to put a stop to that. Except for the over-ambitious objective, the great care and skill with which the operation was planned earned his admiration. The Germans were also lucky with the weather, for low cloud and mist covered the movements of the armoured formations and grounded the Allied aircraft.

On 16th December, the German offensive began with a heavy artillery barrage and the dropping of parties of parachute troops to secure key positions ahead of the advancing forces. Further afield groups of saboteurs rode in captured US jeeps, wearing American uniforms or civilian clothes; they caused considerable confusion and cut a large number of telephone wires. The breakdown of communications and the isolation of command headquarters made for a failure of appreciation and lack of control. When the first snippets of information came filtering through, Bradley was inclined to dismiss it all as a mere diversionary attack of limited significance, but Eisenhower, with a prescience which did him great credit, reacted more quickly. His first action was to initiate a move of US 10th Armored Division from the south and 7th Armored Division from the north to cover the flanks, and a commitment of the reserve formations under SHAEF control, of which the most significant was that of 101st Airborne Division, which was directed to Bastogne.

The Americans crumpled before the onslaught. Two infantry divisions were overwhelmed and brushed aside. By the end of the second day, the Germans had driven a salient into Belgium twenty miles deep. Elsewhere the enemy progress was slower, and on his right, where these were first of all four and then another four US divisions in the way, their resistance prevented a breakthrough. When confirmation of the seriousness of the situation reached him, Eisenhower ordered the cessation of all attacks along the whole front, and told his various commanders to be in readiness to move to join the battle. The so-called cautious slowcoach, Montgomery, who was in fact far quicker to read a situation than any American, had already made dispositions to move formations from British 2nd Army across to thwart any German advance upon Antwerp. The 19th of December was a black day for the Allies. Although the Germans were foiled in their initial attempts to capture the important road junction towns of St Vith and Bastogne, they had split the American front in two and driven a deep wedge into Allied-held territory. As Montgomery put it, there was 'little to prevent German armoured cars and reconnaissance elements bouncing the Meuse and advancing on Brussels'. To protect the city and the British supply areas, he posted detachments to block all roads and also, in order to deny a crossing over the Meuse, at various bridges over the river.

Through the 18th and 19th of December, rumours were flying round the city; those Belgians who had fled before the advancing Germans added to the fear which gripped the inhabitants. Emerging from the Headquarters of 21 Army Group in Avenue Louise, one was aware of an atmosphere of near-panic. Awareness is the proper way to describe the impact on the consciousness. One cannot hear an atmosphere of panic, one cannot see it, one cannot smell it, still less touch or taste it. Extra-sensory perception (ESP) is undoubtedly a fact of life. Although dogs are supposed to be able to smell fear in human beings, what is the explanation of a dog's hackles rising in a room where no-one is present, or the awareness in humans of another presence in a dark and silent room where nothing can be seen or heard? Even within our headquarters a feeling of anxiety abounded, although the administrative staff were working flat out to cope with Montgomery's wholesale movement of formations, and in each case an ever-changing axis of supply. In particular, the move of 30 Corps across the US axis and behind the right flank of US 1st Army was a most complicated and difficult manoeuvre. By the evening of the 19th, the full impact of the situation impressed itself on Lieutenant-General Bedell Smith, Eisenhower's Chief of Staff. Not only were there no American forces available to prevent an enemy advance well past Bastogne and the isolation of the gallant band holding out within the perimeter, but there were no forces to plug the huge gap between the 82nd and 101st US Airborne Divisions. The only defence between the Meuse and Brussels was British 30

Corps moving into position with its four divisions. Worse, the huge bulge which the Germans had created meant that Bradley's 12th Army Group headquarters was completely cut off from all communication with Hodges' 1st Army and Simpson's 9th Army. The only sensible course was to put these two Armies under Montgomery's command. Eisenhower agreed, but when he spoke on the telephone to Bradley during the night of the 19th to pass on his orders, the 12th Army Group Commander strenuously objected, not on logical grounds, but merely because it meant transferring his Armies to British command, and what was particularly galling, under the personal direction of Montgomery, whom he disliked so much. For operational reasons Eisenhower had no other choice, and even if he had appreciated at the time the violent criticism it was to produce from the United States press and people at home, he would still have had to reach the same decision.

Montgomery's manner and behaviour in furtherance of his new command was positively unhelpful and most unfortunate. It was probably when he was on his way to visit the two American commanding generals that he called in at HQ 21 Army Group. His terse, brashly self-confident words to us — 'I'm in overall command again; that means that everything is under control', was just what we wanted to hear, but this self-same attitude only made the staff at Hodges's and Simpson's headquarters extremely resentful. The implication in his attitude was plainly that the Americans had made a mess of things, and that he alone could put things right.

As Montgomery later recorded, the Germans made the fatal mistake of not pushing advance elements to 'bounce' a crossing over the Meuse; they wasted time and effort in trying to capture Bastogne, completely underestimating the gallantry and courage of the American defenders. The defence of Bastogne, which never yielded, was one of the greatest moments in American military history. For eight days, against overwhelming odds until relieved on 26th December by the 4th Armoured Division from Patton's 3rd Army, they contemptuously rejected all demands to surrender or face annihilation. St Vith had fallen on the 21st and the Germans, notwithstanding the dogged fighting of the American forces in contact with the enemy, had created a bulge forty-five miles wide and sixty miles in depth, and at one point penetrated to within four miles of the River Meuse.

The Battle of the Bulge, as it became known, showed up clearly the difference in tactical approach between Montgomery and the American top Commanders. He was the scientific professional; they were the emotional amateurs. Applying Montaigne's precept, *Il faut reculer pour mieux sauter*, he believed that there were times when it was advisable to 'shorten a line', even if it meant that at some points a slight withdrawal was necessary. The Americans had never been conditioned to anything which resembled a retreat, and if the enemy was too strong, it was better to be overcome where they stood, or to hang on in the hope of rescue. Whenever Montgomery suggested a slight withdrawal to a better position, Hodges of 1st Army and Ridgway of 18th Airborne Corps strongly objected. Montgomery has been most unfairly criticized for presuming to make such suggestions, but Eisenhower himself requested him to consider giving up some ground in order to shorten the line and collect a strong reserve. This was the true professional touch, and in this one suspects the hand of Bedell Smith, who had a better grasp of strategy and tactics than any of the other American 'top brass'. Montgomery was wise enough not to press his views, and Ridgway had to learn the lesson the hard way. Driving on to the rescue of Brigadier-General Hasbrouck's 7th Armoured Division holding a horseshoe defence at St Vith, the 82nd Airborne made contact with the 7th Armoured, only to leave the way open for a powerful German force to outflank him and drive deep. Far from being rescued, Hasbrouck was compelled to retreat in a brilliantly-executed withdrawal across the River Salm, and thus saved the remnants of his gallant division. The next day Ridgway ordered him to stand and fight, although Hasbrouck, whose courage could never be called in question, knew it was suicidal and said so. Fortunately Montgomery had learnt about this stupid order, and gave instructions for the 7th Armoured to withdraw into reserve. So they lived to fight another day, but no thanks to Ridgway. Divisional Commanders like Hasbrouck and Gavin, commanding 82nd Airborne Division who had earned such praise at Nijmegen, fully understood that, however much the troops might complain, there were times when a tactical withdrawal was essential, and that to stand and fight to the death was a pointless waste of good men.

For the next three days after the fall of St Vith, the Germans were held in the northern sector, but in spite of courageous resistance by American troops, continued to advance elsewhere. Montgomery was confident that there was no risk by now of the Germans achieving any of their objectives. He remained unmoved by the thought that the Americans were becoming increasingly restless at his refusal to commit the British 30 Corps to battle. As long as the Germans were moving further to the south west in their advance and away from their primary objective, he was content to wait for the most opportune moment to go over to the attack. This policy was quite contrary to American philosophy. As it happened, Hodges was able to disregard caution, and rather than keep Collins's VII Corps in reserve as Montgomery intended, he was able to jump the gun. Although apparently going along with the plan for these troops to swing back and get into position for a counter-attack at a later stage, he privately agreed with Collins that he could go over to the attack at his discretion. On Christmas Day, 'Lightnin' Joe' Collins, living up to his nickname, launched the 2nd Armoured Division against the northern flank of 2nd Panzer Division, which was waiting for gasoline and reinforcement. The reinforcements were headed off, and the forward troops were encircled. After two days of fighting the enemy resistance was overcome, and any further advance was prevented, and with the relief of Bastogne on 26th December it became obvious to Allies and Germans alike that Hitler's gamble had failed. There was no longer any danger that the Germans would cross the Meuse, let alone threaten Liege or Antwerp.

Nevertheless the Battle of the Bulge continued for another three weeks. Beginning on 3rd January with a planned massive counter-offensive in which British and US troops all took part, and in which Collins's VII Corps was yet once more in the forefront, the Germans were gradually forced back and finally routed. By 16th January, the gap in the American front was closed. US 1st Army reverted to 12 Army Group command, although 9th Army remained with 21 Army Group while the attack on the Rhineland was planned and carried out. The Allied Air Forces were able to join in once the weather cleared on 24th December, and at the end of this great battle they claimed not only the destruction of 1,620 enemy aircraft, but well over 13,000 vehicles destroyed or damaged along with a very large number of railway locomotives. The Allied Armies inflicted death or

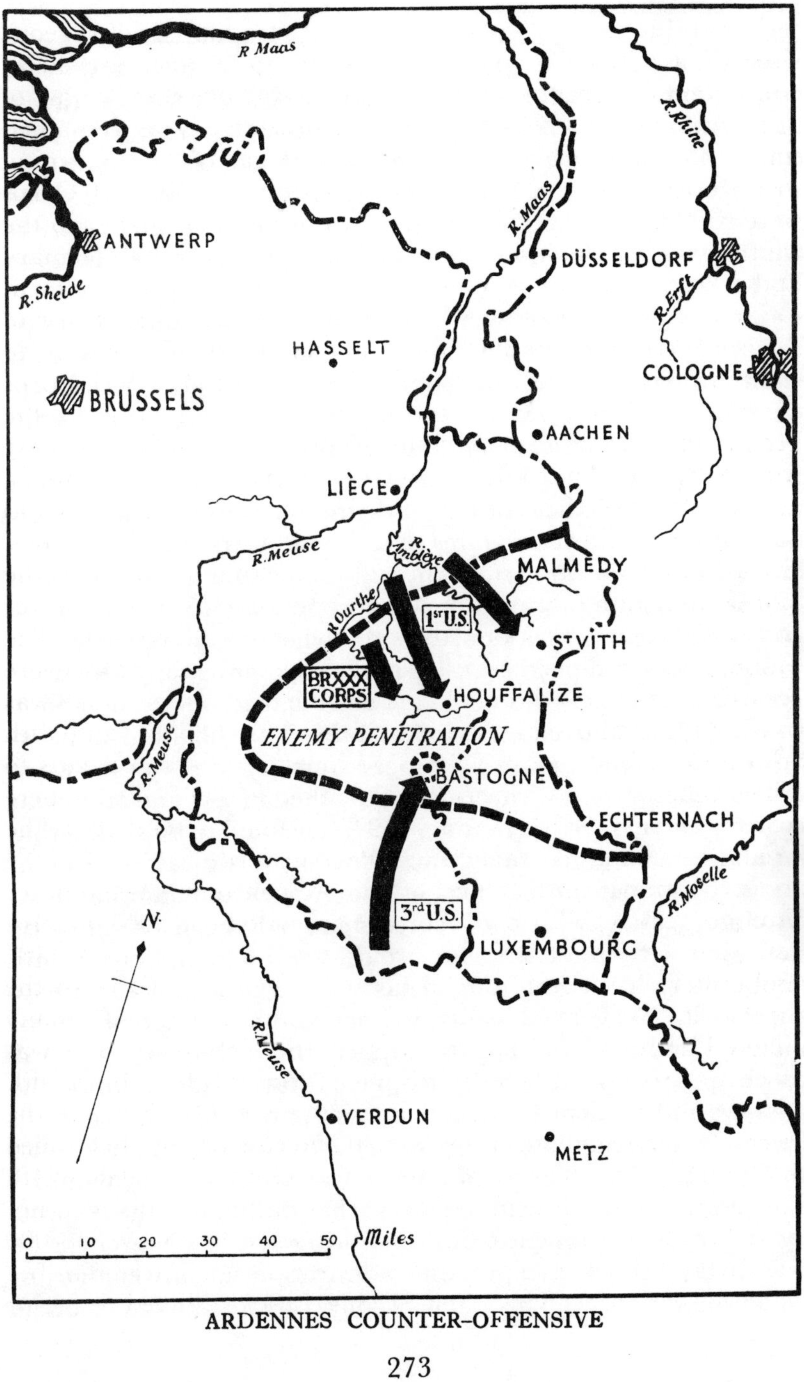

ARDENNES COUNTER-OFFENSIVE

serious injury on 120,000 men, took 110,000 prisoners and wiped out 600 tanks and a large number of guns and other equipment. The Allied Commanders now knew that the defeat of Germany was inevitable, and set about planning the final stages of the war, which, because it would take place on German soil, would involve a fanatical resistance by those troops who were still loyal to the Fuhrer, and those who believed that there was no future for them in an Allied occupation of their beloved Fatherland.

This battle was a great Allied victory, devised and controlled by Field Marshal Montgomery, but for which he, as was his wont, unlike the American Commanders, recognized that it was the soldiers of the United States armies who deserved the credit. What a pity that Patton could never bring himself to say to the British soldier what Montgomery said of the troops of the other nation — 'The battle of the Ardennes was won primarily by the staunch fighting qualities of the American soldier'. At our level of a headquarters staff, the saddest feature at this time was that the reaction of our opposite numbers at US Army Group and US Army headquarters to what they regarded as Montgomery's implied criticism of their Commanding Generals' performance largely destroyed the mutual trust and co-operation which we had enjoyed for many months. The Alliance was never quite the same again. Things were made worse when Montgomery, at a meeting with the Press and the war correspondents on 7th January, 1945, seemed to be saying that he and he alone had saved the Allies from a disaster brought about by the incompetence of the American Commanders. Montgomery was his own worst enemy. Even if privately he may have thought so, he would never consciously and deliberately have gone out of his way to proclaim his innate superiority. Nevertheless his manner and his choice of words, dictated by his single-minded application to the science of war as he understood it, made it appear that he alone knew the answers and he alone had found the solution. On the other hand, he could communicate easily and effectively with the troops on the ground. There probably never was any General, with the exception of Patton, who so earned the confidence, the respect, even almost the affection of the fighting soldier. Moreover he was always quick to express his admiration for any soldier, of whatever nation, who had done his duty and fought with courage and gallantry.

When the 'top brass' fell out with each other and only co-operated because they were ordered to, it was just as well that each Army Group became answerable only to the Supreme Commander at SHAEF, and the links between the staff of SHAEF became stronger as those with the US headquarters weakened. Each Army Group from now on had its own separate task. There was no opportunity for misunderstanding and suspicion to be generated at staff level. Each headquarters was separately kept busy without pause or rest in the planning and the execution of the Allied offensives deep into the heart of Germany which were to lead to ultimate victory. It was only at the very top level that the grand alliance was in evidence.

Bradley's dislike of, Patton's contempt for, and Hodges's disagreement with the British Commander-in-Chief must have rubbed off to some extent on their senior staff officers and from them down to middle level. Although whenever we had occasion to meet, the old friendliness and mutual enjoyment of each other's company was there, nevertheless at the back of our minds there was the sneaking feeling that something splendid had become tarnished. The cause of all this was a failure of the 'top brass', except Eisenhower and Bedell Smith, to appreciate that difference of temperament, difference of outlook, difference of military philosophy might cause misunderstanding, misunderstanding leading to suspicion, and suspicion sometimes to active dislike. Eisenhower realized this and, although not a great tactician or strategist, knew when to deal firmly with a display of temperament verging on rank disobedience. The measure of his greatness was that he was determined to make the Alliance work and, once he had decided on a course of action, just as determined to see that his subordinate commanders did what they were told.

It must have been towards the end of the first week in January 1945, when the Battle of the Bulge was at its height and Allied forces were engaged in bitter fighting trying to force the Germans back to where they had come from, that something happened which could have occurred in no country at war other than Britain. There arrived a signal at HQ 21 Army Group addressed 'From VIP to C-in-C'. That meant it was personal from Winston Churchill to Field Marshal Montgomery. It read something like this: 'Pray inform me why troops fighting in the

Ardennes have for days been without food, drink or winter clothing.' As had happened more than once before, a Churchillian intervention came to me for necessary action. We were astonished. It could not be true. One of my majors was sent off to the battle area to find out whether something indeed had gone horribly wrong. Back he came many hours later with the information that it was as we suspected, a complete fairy tale. So we set about some back tracking and unearthed a remarkable story.

The Prime Minister walked into a sitting of the House of Commons accompanied by his Parliamentary Private Secretary, Brigadier Harvie Watt, just at the moment when a Labour Member of Parliament was asking the Secretary of State for War if he had any information why troops fighting in the Ardennes had for days been without food, hot drink or winter clothing. Churchill heard this question and at once ordered his PPS to send the signal person to person. The Member of Parliament had in his hand a letter which had been sent to one of his constituents. It read, 'Dear Mum and Dad and all at home, You're lucky. Here I am in a slit trench a few yards away from the Gerries, perished with cold and could do with a hot cup of char and a bite of food I ain't had for a hell of a long time.' In truth, like many a young lad he was putting on an act, as any parent or Member of Parliament ought to have realized if he had stopped to ask how a letter could get from the front to a home in London within forty-eight hours if there had been any breakdown in the administrative system. The young soldier was nowhere near the front line; he had nothing to do; he decided to write home; his hands were warm enough to hold a pencil and write perfectly legibly. He handed the letter to the post orderly, and then continued to wait for his next meal and hot drink. We all had too much to do to bother with letting the Member of Parliament know that this young soldier had involved the Prime Minister, the Commander-in-Chief, the whole Parliamentary system, several officers, senior and junior, and taken up a lot of valuable time when nationally important issues were at stake in order to investigate a bit of 'bull shit', as the Army would have called it.

Having interrupted our routine by dealing with this *canard*, we then were able to resume our unending chores. As a matter of fact, the officers at HQ 21 Army Group were probably a lot

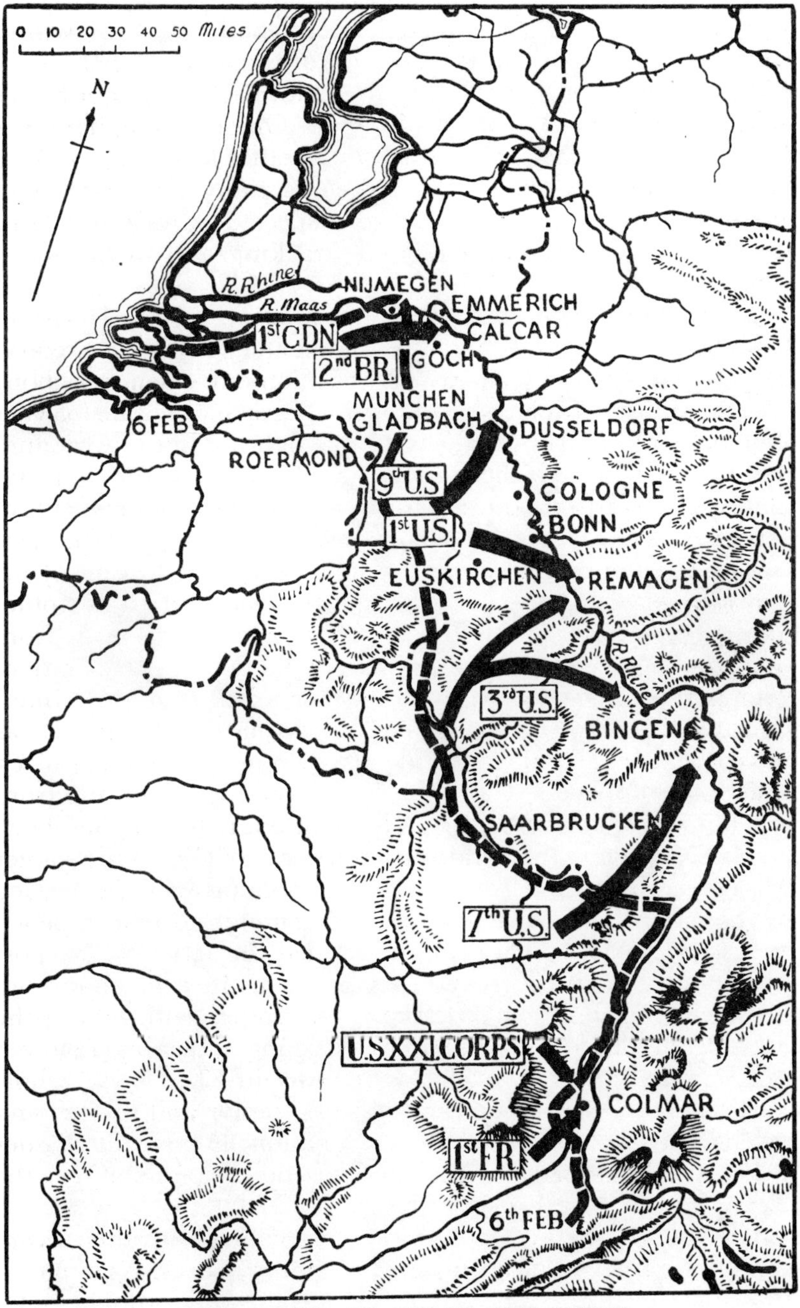

OPERATIONS TO REACH THE RHINE

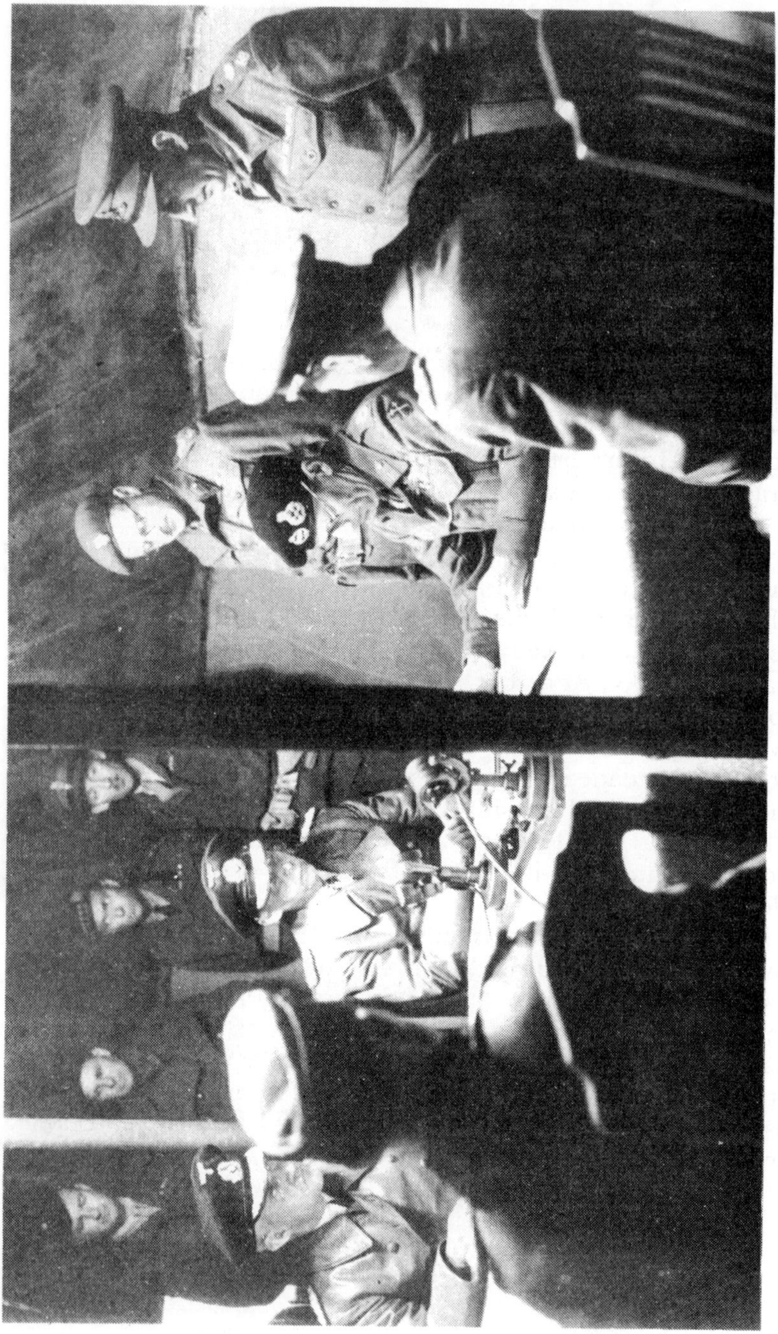

The Surrender at Luneberg

Imperial War Museum

colder than the young soldier. There was no fuel and no heating in the apartment block where we had our headquarters, and the temperature was well below zero. The Commander-in-Chief walked in one day and, seeing his staff officers working in greatcoats, scarves and mittens, at once personally ordered a large number of stoves and fuel to be flown out from England immediately, for as he said, his officers could not be expected to work at a high pitch of efficiency unless they were tolerably warm.

There were two stages in the final push for victory. First there was the battle of the Rhineland, and then there was the crossing of the Rhine itself. This was meticulously planned and prepared. Every conceivable operational and support assistance was provided, from artillery gunfire to aerial bombing, from paratroops to commandos, from boats to bridges, from pontoons to amphibious tanks and vehicles. It all paid off, but our preparations caused some wry amusement to a young Soviet Colonel and Hero of Stalingrad who was posted to me for liaison. When asked through the interpreter how the Russians crossed the River Dnieper, he replied that they just had to cross; some swam; some floated across with pieces of wood; many drowned; more were killed by enemy fire. 'How many were lost?' was my next question. 'Oh, maybe 10,000, maybe 100,000; but enough men made it to the other side.' There was the difference. The Russians had a complete disregard for human life, and millions could die. The British could involve the Prime Minister and the Commander-in-Chief in the welfare of one single solitary soldier. BOLLSHIT

Three months after this conversation the war was over. My Soviet Colonel had already left to join in the triumphal entry into the ruins of Berlin. Field Marshal Montgomery received the surrender of the German forces in the British sector on 4 May, and on 8 May, 1945, there followed the final and complete act of capitulation. Hitler was dead. Nazi Germany was utterly destroyed, but Stalin was poised to create a tyranny of another sort to take its place.

14

RETROSPECT

It is a moot point whether the United States or Britain and France contributed more to the rise of Mussolini and Hitler and therefore indirectly to the Second World War. Britain and France betrayed the League of Nations and the principle of collective security, and allowed each dictator to get away with naked aggression. The United States abandoned their own President Wilson's magnificent concept of a world organization united to keep the peace presenting a barrier to any country which was minded to go to war. The most powerful nation in the world failed in its duty to mankind, for great power brings with it great responsibility, and there can be no excuse for backing out. Nor can there be any excuse for a country like America to stand by and do nothing when the storm clouds are forming and war is imminent. Perhaps the fairest judgement is that both Britain and the United States bore an equal responsibility. The performance of both nations was something of which neither could be proud.

There can however be no doubt that the American leaders, both political and military, were more responsible than their counterparts in Britain for creating the conditions which led to Russian control of the greater part of Europe. It would be unfair to suggest that they ever foresaw the consequences of their actions, and on the credit side, once they realized what the Soviets had done and might intend further to do, they presented a resolute attitude to contain the threat of conquest and tyranny. Nonetheless the fact remains that for forty years the world lived under a state of armed neutrality between the two superpowers, fearful of some incident which might set in train a disaster of incomprehensible magnitude. Now at long last the two leaders of these great nations have come together to take steps jointly to lessen the threat of nuclear war. But none of this need have happened if President Roosevelt had been broader-minded, and General George Marshall and General Dwight Eisenhower had been less rigid in their strategic design. It was a real tragedy that all three were conditioned in their thinking by the fixed belief that Britain was more interested in keeping the British Empire than simply seeking the defeat of Hitler's Germany. Once Eisenhower was made Supreme Commander at Allied Force Headquarters for the North African campaign, he began to appreciate that the British leaders, whether Winston Churchill the Prime Minister, or the Chiefs of Staff or the top Commanders like Alexander and Montgomery, or the Admirals, were all imbued with only one desire, and that was to win the war. He was however guilty of appalling misjudgement when he concluded that Stalin and his generals were easier to come to terms with than the British, and that the Russians had no imperial designs. Perhaps he may be forgiven for this, having had to bear with Montgomery for so long, and having no opportunity to know anything of the extent of Stalin's tyrannical brutality.

Eisenhower cannot escape criticism for his failure to see the weakness of American strategic thinking, and for being too much dominated by his mentor and chief George Marshall. In his approach, Marshall was not only diverted by the mistaken belief that the real reason why the British were continuously pressing for priority to be given to the Mediterranean and Italian campaign was the preservation of the British Empire, but in any event he preferred the use of massive resources in a head-on clash — a sort of power politics in the realms of war. Marshall could never bring himself to give unbiased consideration to the British strategy of a peripheral approach. Moreover the withdrawal of troops and equipment from the Italian front in order to launch Operation 'Dragoon' on the French Riviera coast, a secondary and almost pointless exercise, was a monumental error. General Mark Clark, the senior US Commanding General in Italy and later the American High Commissioner in Austria, with the qualification of the man on the spot both in war and in peace, was forthright in his criticism. In June 1944 he noted that, with the Boche defeated, disorganized and demoralized, it just did not make sense to take from his command two corps headquarters and seven divisions and send them to France, and after the war was over he described the decision as one of the out-standing political mistakes of the war, and if the Allies had got into the Balkans before the Red Army it would have drastically reduced the influence of Soviet Russia. There one has an American who knew better than anyone else what was the right thing to do, firmly coming down on the side of Churchill and Alanbrooke against his own superiors in Washington.

As to Montgomery's proposal for a single powerful thrust into the Rhineland after the breakout from Normandy, the reason which Eisenhower later gave for its rejection was false. It was untrue to say, as he did, that the proposal was for a 'pencil' thrust; it was nothing of the kind; it was for a powerful thrust with the added resources behind it of a grounded 3rd US Army. It may have been true that the German forces were sufficiently reorganized as to be capable of resisting a 'pencil' thrust, but it was untrue to say that the enemy was strong enough to withstand the sort of push which Montgomery had in mind. In this the evidence of the German generals is to be preferred. They admitted after the war that they could not have contained a quick follow-up and breakthrough with a force of fifteen divisions or more such as Montgomery was urging upon the Supreme Commander, and they were mightily relieved to be granted a reprieve. The reasons which Eisenhower gave were not only false, but were an attempt to cover up and gloss over the real reason for his refusal to go along with Montgomery's proposal. It was a decision reached upon political grounds. He was afraid that the American public would not have accepted the restraint on Patton's 3rd Army in favour of a British Commander's advance.

As Supreme Allied Commander, Eisenhower should have been courageous enough to grasp the nettle and to make the correct strategic decision, even though it went against his own predetermined policy of a 'broad front'. It is unlikely that the war would have been over by Christmas if he had done what Montgomery had desired, for once inside German territory there were enough indoctrinated young soldiers to make it difficult to overcome the final fanatical resistance of a desperate enemy. It would however have got the Allies over the Rhine in enormous strength as a springboard for later exploitation and development, and there would have been no German counter-offensive in the Ardennes. In the event the war was probably unnecessarily prolonged by about three months or so, and the Allies may well have lost the chance of getting to Berlin before the Russians. What a difference to history that would have made!

The greatest misconception in the mind of the great American public and of course the Hollywood movie makers was and still is that 'Uncle Sam' had come to the rescue of the exhausted and defeated British, whose part in winning the war was minuscule compared with the overwhelming contribution from across the Atlantic. To begin with, this ignores the fantastic achievement of the British in facing alone for over a year the whole might of the Axis powers, and the courage of the people in withstanding the nightly bombing from the air, something which no American town or hamlet had to endure. It also ignores the fact that without British inventiveness and skill the armed forces of the United States would never have had half the technological aids on which they came to rely.

The first and one of the most important British inventions was that of radar. Although the United States, Germany and France had all developed elementary radar systems during the four or five years before war broke out, it was the British who led the field in the development of this invention. Whereas the first commercial production of radar systems for the use of the United States Armed Forces was not put in hand until 1939, the Air Ministry of Britain adopted the system devised by Sir Robert Watson Watt in 1935. The first warning stations were begun in 1936, and a complete chain of these in the south east of England operated by the Royal Air Force was established at the beginning of the war, well before the air battles in September 1940. Earlier in that year, British scientists and electronics engineers introduced a form of multicavity magnetron which made microwave radar a practical proposition, and revolutionized its use and the extent to which it could be used on land, at sea and in the air. The year 1940 marks the beginning of radar as we now know it. It was a British invention, but we were prepared to give to the United States full information about it, even before Pearl Harbor brought them into the war on Britain's side. Of course it was inevitable that in due course the Americans came to believe that it was they who invented radar. That did not matter so much as the tragic fact that once the British made available their knowledge, then, as happened over and over again, they failed to capitalize on and develop their initial head start. The Americans had the trained technologists and the laboratory and manufacturing facilities, and by 1943 Britain was left well behind.

The same thing happened over computers. The first ever computer was the one built to crack the German cipher codes — the very top secret operation known as Enigma. But of what avail is the boast that the British invented the computer? Our computer manufacturing capacity was and is pathetic, and all the so-called Western nations and Japan have long since taken over from us.

Then there is the jet engine. The jet engine used in aircraft today is based on the original design of Frank Whittle, an English Royal Air Force officer who is generally recognized by those who know about these things as the father of the jet airplane. In fact the first jet-propelled aircraft to take the air was the German Heinkel 178 which flew in August 1939, but the design was abandoned by all later developers. Whittle took out a patent for a jet engine as far back as 1931. In 1937 he successfully tried out a prototype engine, but because of the the exigencies of the threat of war and the priority given to mass production of combat aircraft, his first test flight of a jet-propelled aircraft was postponed until 1941. The Americans, no doubt to their surprise, were to begin with never in the hunt. But alas!, as so often was the case, the British failed to support their own innovator and to capitalize on his inventive genius, and allowed the Americans to take over Whittle's design and to become the pioneers in the mass production of the jet engine. Rolls Royce in England tried valiantly to catch up, and ultimately succeeded in joining in the manufacture of the jet engine as we know it today.

The real triumph of the British aircraft industry in the immediate pre-war years and the early years of the war was however the design and production of the Spitfire fighter aircraft. This by common consent of fighter pilots of all nations was the finest combat aircraft built by any country. It was designed by R.J. Mitchell, and took over as the main single-seater aircraft of the Royal Air Force from the Hawker Hurricane. The chief disadvantage from which the Spitfire suffered was that its limited fuel capacity gave it a shorter range than the German and

American fighters. This had quite an impact on the planning for the invasion of Normandy.

Much has already been said about the use of specialized armour in the assault stage of Operation 'Overlord'. The Duplex-Drive (DD) tank, an invention of an Hungarian immigrant domiciled in England, was recognized by all the Allied Generals as an important element in a seaborne assault. When properly handled and not launched too far out in rough sea, it proved to be of considerable moral support for attacking infantry and presented a fearsome and terrifying sight to the surprised defenders. The other specially-designed tanks such as the flail tank for beating mines, the mat-laying tank and several other of the so-called 'Funnies' were all designed by the British Major-General Hobart. They proved to be invaluable to the assaulting troops on the British beaches, and the more sensible US commanders bitterly regretted their failure to include them in their plans for the assault. On 'Omaha' beach in particular, hundreds of young Americans paid with their lives for this omission.

The thousands and thousands of United States soldiers and sailors who went ashore on the many islands in the Pacific and all those who landed on the beaches in Normandy would never have considered for one moment that the landing ships and the landing craft had anything to do with any country other than their own. Yet they were wrong in this assumption. In 1941, Captain T.A. Hussey of the Royal Navy went to America with designs for a Landing Ship Tank (LST), a Landing Ship Dock (LSD), and a smaller vessel, the Landing Craft Tank (LCT). The Navy wanted them, but as all dockyards and shipyards were fully occupied, the Americans were requested to build them for British use under the Lease Lend agreement. The US Navy Department refused. Ultimately Captain Hussey persuaded Harry Hopkins and General Marshall to take an interest in these craft. After Pearl Harbor, the designs were accepted and adopted together with an additional craft, the Landing Craft Infantry (LCI), and the US Navy Department began turning them out by the hundred, but precious few ever got into British hands. Every one was kept under Admiral King's tight-fisted control, almost entirely for use in the war in the Pacific. Indeed, so few got back to Europe that most of the Landing Craft in Operation 'Overlord' had to be built in Britain, and even the American troops had to manage without much help from Admiral King. Except for these British-built craft, this was yet another occasion when the product of British inventiveness and pioneering work in design was passed over to the Americans to produce, which they did without much, if any, acknowledgement.

Then there were the 10,000 ton prefabricated merchant ships, known as Liberty ships. These were produced by the score by Henry J. Kaiser. How could these be anything but American? The prototype was in fact designed and built and launched in the shipyards of Newcastle-upon-Tyne. The Liberty ship was no more American than the longboats of Alfred the Great.

It is a fact of life, which the British have learned to accept with a wry tolerance and an occasional outburst of indignation, that the vast majority of the American people assume that everything big and fine and modern has been made in the United States. The average citizen, and particularly the average country boy, is woefully ignorant of what goes on in the outside world. Three illustrations will suffice to make the point, all properly authenticated by persons who were present, two of whom are personally known to me. There was the young man from the Mid-West who, on learning that he was being posted to an air base in Norfolk, East Anglia, asked if they spoke English over there. There was the soldier, one of 15,000 being carried across the Atlantic in the SS *Queen Mary*, who said to one of the ship's officers 'Say, why can't you Limeys build ships like these?' — a somewhat incongruous question if he had stopped to ask himself what British officers were doing running an American ship. Thirdly, there was the serviceman on the first *Queen Elizabeth* who persisted in the assertion that it was an American ship and not a British one, who clinched his argument with the rhetorical question 'It's the biggest ship in the world, isn't it?' followed by the proposition in his opinion, 'That means it's got to be American'.

Moving from the Atlantic Ocean back to Germany in May 1945, the British Army of the Rhine, as it became called, faced an enormous task in trying to cope with the aftermath of a war which Hitler had allowed to go on for too long. Thousands of prisoners had to be collected, an equal number if not more of refugees and displaced persons had to be rounded up, cared for and fitted in somewhere. The shattered towns and villages had to be cleared of debris, and all the vast organization of military government imposed upon a defeated nation. This is not the place to record in detail or at all what was required and what had to be done. There was no contact with our Allies. Each nation had its own territory to look after; zones were created for the British to administer and for the Americans to administer, and so for the most part we led our separate lives and the Alliance of war became another kind of alliance in which senior officers of different nations met in committee, not on the battlefield or in Army Headquarters.

There was much to be done and no let-up for staff officers at Army Group Headquarters. Our tasks were variegated — some almost trivial, some overwhelming in complexity. One which came my way gave me great personal satisfaction, and that not merely because it was the ostensible sign of the victor proclaiming his triumph over the vanquished, but for reasons private to myself in the context of heredity. The Commander-in-Chief ordered that the pipes and drums of the Scottish Regiments should be assembled and where necessary brought out of store from home depots in the United Kingdom, and a massed band in full get-up would put on a show in the large square of one of the towns we occupied. They were a magnificent sight, marching and counter marching in their khaki jackets, kilts and sporrans, glengarries and tam o'shanters and for a short while my thoughts were with my great-great-grandfather, who during the Napoleonic Wars had been wickedly press-ganged in his native Scotland by the dastardly English and put on board a man o'war, but who jumped overboard in the Bristol Channel, swam ashore at Porlock in Somerset and there founded a new tribe, half Scots, half West Country English. I thought too how privileged I had been to have been given command for a short time of a company in the Gordon Highlanders, where incidentally I found that some other officers had credentials far slighter than mine to wear the kilt. The war created a curiously motley crowd of those who, though fiercely and narrowly nationalistic on the football field, joined together to be proud to call themselves British.

Finally, months after the war had ended, there was the occasion in Berlin about which Colonel Val Duncan, himself a railway man in peacetime, rejoiced to tell. The Russians had challenged the other Allied representatives at a social gathering to a toast-drinking contest. The contest was limited to those of the rank of Major-General or equivalent or above. Lined up facing each other were twelve Russians and a motley dozen from the Allies. There was one odd man out. Unable to field a full team of Army or Air Force rank, the British came up with a suggestion that the head of the Railway Section of Civil Affairs ranked at least as the equivalent of a Major-General. He was dressed in a black jacket and striped trousers, or pants as the Americans would have it, which was the typical uniform of the British Civil Service, but despite his unimpressive appearance there flowed through his veins the blood of generations of hard whisky-drinking forbears from his native Scotland.

Each representative had to nominate a toast — whether Stalin, or Roosevelt's memory, or Winston Churchill, or Eisenhower, or Montgomery, or whoever and whatever. Toast after toast was drunk, and innumerable glasses of vodka tossed down in one gulp. The Americans, quite unused to this sort of thing, failed early on. Gradually the remainder of the contestants collapsed, leaving finally two apparently indestructible Russians and the sole surviving representative of the Allied team. The civilian contender raised his glass and, so it is believed, inspired his failing senses with the toast of 'The Flying Scotsman', not, as might be imagined, the 51st (Highland) Division, but what was much closer to his heart, the daily passenger train from London to Scotland hauled by 'Pacific' class steam locomotives, probably the most beautiful, certainly the fastest railway engine in all the world. The two Russian Generals buckled at the knees and slid gracefully to the floor. Britain had triumphed yet again.

EPILOGUE

The special relationship between Britain and the United States, first forged in terms of Allied effort in the Great War some seventy odd years ago, always was, still is and probably always will be of vital importance to both countries, and to the peace and prosperity of the whole world. This relationship lies at the heart of the much wider concept of the North Atlantic Treaty Organization, better known by its initials as NATO, which would have collapsed and still would if either Britain or the United States were to pull out. Although in the economic context and in the field of social welfare the Western European nations form an integrated community, this does not apply to questions of defence and military philosophy where different nations have different views. Even though there is no longer a threat from the Warsaw Pact nations of Eastern Europe, the need for NATO still exists, if only to maintain stability throughout Europe and the Middle East and to that end American involvement is vital.

At NATO the United States has not only borne by far the greater burden in its degree of contribution, but its representatives have from the beginning introduced and then handed on a tradition of complete co-operation. If one takes a highly-qualified and competent American and puts him down to work in Brussels where he rubs shoulders with others from a dozen different countries, he becomes a totally different creature from those who function in the Pentagon. NATO has proved to be the most successful practical alliance of a number of nations that there has ever been, and the American members are conditioned to participate, to listen and to exchange opinions. In Washington it seems impossible for the admirals and generals to realize that they need not always 'go it alone'; nor do they seem to concede that Britain and other nations may be able to help with advice based on experience; nor do they appear to have learnt from their mistakes.

The history of the last forty years reveals a number of occasions when the United States, to put it mildly, have not exactly covered themselves with glory. In the Korean War they showed to begin with that they had forgotten much that they had learnt from the alliance in the Second World War. In Vietnam they would not listen to Field Marshal Sir Gerald Templer, who openly admitted that it took eleven years to defeat the communist guerillas in jungle warfare and whose advice, if it had been taken, might have saved the United States from ignominious withdrawal. In the more recent invasion of the tiny island of Grenada, the whole operation was a shambles and the field communications so chaotic that one officer had to use a pay card in a public call box to get in touch with his own unit headquarters. The miserable failure of the desert mission to rescue the hostages in Iran was the result of an operation which was badly planned, far too complicated, and confused in conception and execution. Unhappily the catalogue is endless, and little is to be gained by a full recital. These examples are sufficient to show how much the United States has got to learn, and how much it is incumbent to be humble and not aggressively self-confident.

For their part the British must not be smug and complacent. The Falklands War demonstrated that, when aroused, the nation responds and has leaders on whom they can depend. The careful planning, the co-operation between the Navy, the Army and the Air Force and Government agencies led to an operation the like of which has never been seen before, and which in terms of logistics was a stupendous performance. The least successful part of the whole business was the heavy casualties in men and warships from the use of the Exocet weapons. As soon as the campaign was over, the three Arms of the Services got down to the study of counter-measures. The British, in spite of criticisms that as a nation they are slow and often too late, are capable of achievement which can be matched by no other country in the world. The American people would be well to acknowledge this. A true Alliance is a genuine partnership in which each party contributes much and receives much, and which succeeds when ignorance is banished and misconception is overcome.

The need for a special relationship between Britain and the USA was starkly demonstrated in the immediate aftermath of the invasion of Kuwait by Iraqi forces. President Bush responded to Saddam Hussein's outrageous conduct with a recognition, which was new for an American, that an aggressor cannot be appeased and must be faced with force if necessary. By sheer coincidence and good fortune Prime Minister Margaret Thatcher was present to stand, literally, shoulder to shoulder and whole-heartedly to pledge British support and assistance. It was an attitude which was approved by almost every Briton. By contrast, the degree of support from France and Germany and the rest of Europe was very low key. As it turned out, the alliance between Britain and the United States was the lynchpin of the coalition forces in the Gulf War and the way the two nations performed together was the clearest proof that neither country should attempt to go it alone in times of crisis.

INDEX

F

G

H

N